# A SOCIETY OF SIGNS?

*A Society of Signs?* is an introduction to current debates around the themes of culture, identity and lifestyle. Such debates often begin with the assertion that we live in a 'society of signs', as opposed to a 'real' society: a society where buildings, clothes, cars, consumer goods and, above all, films, videos and television programmes swamp us in a sea of communication. In this saturated environment, it is no longer easy to tell the true from the fake, or the past from the present. Topics covered in this volume include early debates in the study of popular culture, the difficulties that sociological approaches face in dealing with hyperreal aspects of culture, discourse theory, the 'society as text' metaphor and postmodernism.

*A Society of Signs*? will help students of sociology, media and cultural studies to make sense of these often complicated arguments by:

- summarising and critically discussing some basic approaches in social theory and cultural analysis;
- offering specific readings of some of the work of writers including Barthes and Giddens;
- reviewing work in more traditional areas, for example, the sociology of identity and the embedding process found in social life;
- giving advice on further reading.

**David Harris** is Senior Lecturer in Social Sciences at the College of St Mark and St John, Plymouth.

# A SOCIETY OF SIGNS?

*David Harris*

London and New York

First published 1996
by Routledge
11 New Fetter Lane, London EC4P 4EE

Simultaneously published in the USA and Canada
by Routledge
29 West 35th Street, New York, NY 10001

Typeset in Palatino by
Ponting–Green Publishing Services, Chesham, Bucks
Printed and bound in Great Britain by
Clays Ltd, St Ives plc

*British Library Cataloguing in Publication Data*
A catalogue record for this book is available from
the British Library

*Library of Congress Cataloguing in Publication Data*
Harris, David, 1947–
A society of signs? / David Harris.
p. cm.
Includes bibliographical references and index.
1. Culture. 2. Popular culture. 3. Identity (Psychology).
4. Life style. I. Title.
HM101.H289 1996
306–dc20          95–31320
CIP

ISBN 0–415–11128–5 (hbk)
ISBN 0–415–11129–3 (pbk)

# Contents

# Acknowledgements

I should like to acknowledge the patience and skills of my family; the librarians, 'support staff' and students at the College of St Mark and St John; and Chris Rojek and Mari Shullaw for their encouragement and perseverance. Special thanks are due to T.G. Lowman who miraculously reappeared at the right moment to help me focus this material.

# Introduction

It is almost a commonplace to suggest that societies all over the world, but especially in 'the West', have undergone substantial social and cultural changes in the last decade or so, and that this has produced a huge debate among academics and other commentators about how to understand these changes. The title of this book points to one popular way to begin to consider these changes: we live in a 'society of signs' as opposed to a 'real' society, a society where buildings, clothes, cars, consumer goods and, above all perhaps, films, videos and television programmes swamp us in a sea of communication, try to tell us something about themselves and ourselves. In this saturated environment, it is no longer easy to tell the true from the fake, or the past from the present: films grip us with enough realism to move us to tears or to convince us that we really know the truth about historical events like the assassination of Kennedy, while a visit to any nearby 'heritage site' will reveal the skill and accessibility with which the past is recaptured and displayed. Images and signs seep into our consciousness, so that even those of us old enough to remember actual historical events (such as life in Britain during World War Two, or, in my case, Britain in the 1950s) tend to get their memories inextricably mixed up with films depicting the period, and come to think that life really was lived in black and white.

Parochial interests are not typical, though. Inevitably, it is the American cultural landscape that for the European attracts most attention. Umberto Eco, for example, travelled from one tourist spectacle to another, spanning advanced holographic technology in New York, museums, stately homes, Disneyland and San Diego zoo, to experience both excess and 'insane abundance', and

'Universal Taming . . . the oscillation between a promise of un-contaminated nature and a guarantee of negotiated tranquillity' (Eco 1987: 51).

Eco describes the effect of visiting William Hearst's castle in California as being overwhelmed by fixtures, fittings and furnishings that do nothing else but try to communicate with the visitor, to signify, 'the obsessive determination not to leave a single space that doesn't suggest something' (ibid.: 23). The mixture of antiques, genuine and reconstructed, 'is like making love in a confessional with a prostitute dressed in a prelate's liturgical robes reciting Baudelaire while ten electronic organs reproduce the *Well-tempered Clavier* played by Scriabin' (ibid.: 23–4).

Eco describes this excess, this fusion of real, fake, obviously fake and hidden fake, past, present, fantasy and naturalism as hyper-reality. He is aware of the difficulty of simply denouncing hyper-reality as 'bad'. There is clearly a 'good' liberating fantastic side, experienced joyfully by tourists. But more importantly, experiencing hyperreality raises fundamental questions for our usual established senses of reality and the ways in which we analyse it. Eco is not just mocking American tastes, for example: 'Can we be sure that the European tourist's pilgrimage to . . . St Peter's is less fetishistic?' (ibid.: 39). Baudrillard, after an equally fascinated visit to a Disney theme park, made a similar observation, pushed still further: Disney sites are 'presented as imaginary in order to make us believe that the rest is real' (Baudrillard 1983: 25).

In other words, hyperreality is not a limited experience for us, confined to specially built tourist sites, but is a contagious or 'explosive' one. We are not far from a suspicion that arises daily in our experiences with others, I suggest, although we might use different terms to express it: that other people are trying to 'create a false impression' of themselves and their companies or products, by trying to communicate with us in a particular way. Others (and it is always easier to begin with others) dress in a particular way to try to communicate 'trust', 'intelligence', 'efficiency', 'street credibility' or whatever. Promotional videos for universities always show busy, happy students, dynamic night life in adjacent cities, nice clean buildings on sunlit sites, the best equipment in laboratories, and employers rushing to snap up graduates; and anyone who has been involved in one knows how contrived and carefully constructed that image can be.

Again the suspicion soon dawns that those others are not alone, and those cases of 'inauthenticity' not unique, however. We all create impressions, play roles and present our best selves when we go to interviews, write assignments or try to impress our partners. The notion that buildings, clothes or most other objects are designed and used primarily as signs to communicate something becomes a way of understanding most aspects of life. Following this argument, hyperreality becomes the major condition of life in modern, or postmodern, societies.

A growing number of communications experts search for new materials to be brought into this system of signs: advertisers plunder the past for 'images', or borrow from artistic or creative films, for example. These images are lifted from their original contexts and detached from the things they once referred to ('referents'), 'purified' into signs, and combined into new messages attached to new objects (see Williamson 1978 for a classic analysis). To cite an example from British TV, an advertisement for Rolo (a chocolate confectionery) borrows the look of a famous scene from a French 'New Wave' film of the 1960s, stripping the scene away from its original context and intention (to use 'jump cuts' to experiment with the conventions of cinema), and running it together with themes from earlier Rolo advertisements to create a fashionably ironic statement that both promotes Rolo as a sweet of great value and reminds us that this is only an advertisement and that we are far too British to take ourselves that seriously.

But to a large extent, perhaps, we all do this, less consciously and less expertly, but in the same spirit. Punks deliberately and consciously blended and mixed items from everyday life (men's leggings, safety-pins) and from pornographic underground magazines (rubber wear and bondage paraphernalia) to 'make a statement', according to Hebdige (1979), as did many youth cultures before them. But 'normal' people do the same, albeit in less spectacular ways, as 'the sociology of everyday life' indicates (for example, Goffman 1963; Truzzi 1968; Turner 1975): even respectable professionals are well aware of the need to present a front while 'on stage', and they manipulate the usual props of clothing, special equipment like stethoscopes, and carefully managed speech and interaction. Again, the idea of personal interaction as a performance is contagious: reflecting on it leads you to wonder about your own performances and, eventually, perhaps to begin to doubt whether there ever is an 'authentic' way to deal with people, with no performance just 'natural' behaviour.

With this implication, a dark side arises to complement the 'playfulness' of some of the earlier work.

The stress on performance has led to a whole new interest in the personal and the subjective, and, again, this has led to writers describing the characteristics of everyday life in (post)modernity in terms of a restlessness and rootlessness, of flexible identities, accompanied by either a sense of playfulness or of deep anxiety, with both a capacity and a need to escape the pressure accompanying the constant need to express oneself. We shall be debating the issues raised by personal identities and lifestyles in more depth in Chapter 7.

The saturation of social life by endless streams of signs might well be a topic that both academic writers and 'normal people' experience, and at times we shall be considering everyday experience (including mine, as an inducement for you to reflect on yours) in the midst of some high-powered theory. To shift perspectives is the task now, however, and we need to examine some of the theoretical controversies behind the sorts of descriptions of modern life with which I began.

A shift to theory is usually one that raises apprehensions in the minds of both readers and writers, but it is still necessary to clarify some important theoretical and political issues, even if this might run the risk of excesses of a different kind. I am aware of my own feelings, for example, while reading some of the pieces for this book, of being dragged on to an alien terrain of Continental philosophy where innocent attempts to clarify the problems of identity as most participants understand it lead to a long and difficult detour into the philosophy of identity as Fichte, Schelling or Husserl might have understood it (which is quite a different thing). A strange belief in philosophy as the most important discipline, as offering some privileged insight used as a source of clarification, able to referee disputes between the social sciences, lingers in the works of Derrida, Lyotard, Baudrillard and even Habermas, and is hard to dispel, even when, at the end of a long and hard argument, those same writers often admit that important sociological or empirical questions have been implicit in what they have been discussing and require urgent analysis. This book insists instead on the continuing importance of sociological analysis and on the right of sociologists to interrogate and read philosophical analysis critically, not just as a matter of disciplinary rivalry, but in order to foreground the interests of 'normal' participants as well, amidst the excesses of what can look like lofty intellectual games. At the same time, no sociologist can proceed naively, as if the status of sociology were clear and accepted, with no agendas of its own, or with some simple automatic connection with the interests of 'normal participants': those issues have been raised acutely (if not uniquely) in 'postmodernism' and deserve a response. Let us accept the challenge as a way into some of the theoretical issues.

There is one additional issue. To a large extent, the disciplines I am discussing here are fundamentally incompatible: the concepts used by sociology, Marxism and postmodernism do not easily translate into each other, and it is also a question of privilege or priorities in analysis. Sociology and Marxism tend to persist in the view that the social or economic 'levels' of social life are fundamental in various senses, and need to be used to explain the cultural or philosophical level. Postmodernist writers and other deployers of the textual metaphor insist on the independence of the cultural level and, indeed, insist, in a phrase which will become familiar, that there is 'nothing (worth analysing) outside this level'. Nevertheless, struggles go on to replace one sort of analysis with the other, to develop a Marxist analysis of postmodernism (as Jameson and others attempt – see Chapter 5), or a sociology of postmodernism (quite often involving the work of Bourdieu).

This cannot be done satisfactorily, in my view, although it is always possible to opt for one approach (on the grounds of personal political allegiances, perhaps, or a more mundane self-interest in keeping a research tradition going). Instead, my purpose here is a prior one – to demonstrate, if I can, that none of the approaches is self-sufficient. I should confess that I hope to demonstrate this above all for advocates of textuality, who seem to have been particularly successful in persuading many of my students and many other commentators that it is sufficient to insist that social life is a text, and that sociology and Marxism are dead.  My counterarguments will take the form of 'immanent critique' (showing that the work accomplished under the sway of this  metaphor does not meet its own tests of adequacy), and the demonstration that the forbidden alternatives might be just as useful (but by no means beyond critique themselves). I do not have any 'prime knowledge' to offer the reader at the end (which will persuade them that, after all the discussion, Habermas is the best analyst, for example), nor do I have an embryonic master synthesis of my own waiting in the wings, alas.

We do discuss some attempted syntheses, though, especially that developed by Giddens after his own masterly review of the options (and, specifically, of many of the writers in the traditions we are discussing here). Syntheses of any kind are not the main interest of this book, though: there is a more modest interest in setting out agendas and keeping open options – and in asking basic questions which can sometimes get lost in the heady delights of general theorising.

Let us begin with some classic conventionally sociological questions, for example, and use them to explore some issues. How widespread are the phenomena I began with? How much of everyday life is devoted to communications and the exchange of signs? To place this question in the specific debates of later chapters, how many people actually do plan their lives around the notion of a pursuit of the politics of identity, how many would see themselves as likely to follow the advice of lifestyle counsellors or to find consumerism as the major form of expression of their lives? Are there definite social patterns to the phenomena described as 'seriality' in modern identities: does everyone feel free to experience different identities one after another, or do you need to be financially secure, independent of the power of institutions, or a member of some privileged group? Quite a lot seems to turn on answers to questions like these, I argue in Chapter 7: briefly, if you see widespread participation in the new lifestyles, you are more likely to use terms like 'postmodernity' or 'postculture' to describe them, implying a pretty radical departure from both old ways of living and old approaches to understanding those ways of life, as we shall see shortly. The alternative – which sees such new lifestyles as confined to some elite or leading group of metropolitan stylists with identifiable locations in terms of social class, say – makes things more familiar and predictable, preserves the old sociological techniques of analysis (class in this case), and also preserves some of the old political stances while we are there (if social class is not dead, neither is socialism).

Despite the importance of these questions, though, it is hard to find any answers to them, even in the writings of social theorists like Giddens. There is instead a feeling that sociological questions such as these are no longer appropriate. As we shall see, especially in Chapters 2, 4 and 5, sociology and Marxism are redundant according to 'postmodern' writers like Baudrillard and Lyotard, and their work has been contagious in this respect too. At one level we find straightforward dismissals of these disciplines.

Yet there are also sophisticated arguments directed at the founding assumptions of both theory and methods of sociology and Marxism. We can already begin to trace them, perhaps, in what I have been describing as a shift towards hyperreality: briefly, if our sense of reality is determined by the flux of purified signs, we need to grasp this, using methods based on linguistics and not on sociology or Marxism; there is no need to go 'outside' of the signs themselves to look at economic structures or social institutions (which is what social science classically does). Social science still struggles to try and persuade an audience that it has found 'real' explanations for the construction of advertisements or theme parks or personal styles by referring to the alleged determinations of these phenomena in structures of stratification and struggle (of class, 'race', gender, say) – but these are at best a gloss, a traditional mode of analysis. The methods and perspectives used to 'uncover' these structures simply construct the characteristic data of social science (empirical patterns of class ownership of automobiles, say), which must take their place as one option alongside scores of alternative ways of considering the problem (using other variables like age, perhaps, as Pahl (1993) suggests in his contribution to the controversy over whether 'class' still exists, which I review in Chapter 5).

The classic concepts of social science are rooted not in 'science' but in metaphor. Social and cultural life is conceived as a 'commodity' in Marxism, for example, with its connotations of commercial exploitation and class domination stripping goods away from their traditional uses and making them into abstract and alienating forces. In Durkheimian sociology cultural 'symbols' are metaphors for social structures and 'social facts'. These sorts of traditional analyses can no longer capture the free-floating autonomous nature of cultural life, it is argued, where people cross the old barriers, reject the old constraints, and construct their own identities with signs purified by long periods of use and via substantial cultural transformations well away from their origins (as we argue in detail in Chapter 5).

The abandonment of social science also makes redundant the kind of quantitative questions which I posed earlier. They belong to another paradigm, so to speak. The sorts of 'data' which are now relevant cannot be captured by the techniques of social science with any sort of credibility any more, and new forms of 'evidence' are as important, including those produced by a new kind of 'poetic sensibility' to the spirit of the times.

We can now see another issue arising. If classic social science is redundant, after a coruscating critique of its very foundations, what sort of analysis is adequate? We have already signalled a turn towards a kind of linguistics. This will serve to introduce another major theme of this book – the notion that social life is best considered as a form of textual activity, as the construction of narratives or other sequences and manipulations of signs. This metaphor seems to offer a full acknowledgement of the trends we discussed at the beginning, and it has been a powerful one in the arguments for shifting perspective. A number of writers deploy it, although I have chosen to explore it most specifically through a reading of some of the central and often-cited essays by Roland Barthes (in Chapter 4), and via the stalwarts of 'postmodernism' (largely Lyotard and Baudrillard, in Chapter 5). As will become clear in those chapters, the notion of social life as a text has a number of implications: all social and cultural life is becoming text-like, texts can only be analysed within themselves, for example, via new concepts which fully acknowledge the interwoven nature of textuality, and the playful habits (proper) texts have of citing each other and of opening out readings for new and fascinating kinds of cultural pleasures. The short pieces in Barthes's (1977) collection have enjoyed a very wide currency in the field of cultural studies in particular and have spawned work on the pleasures and functions of 'texts' as diverse as the motor scooter or the James Bond movie. The 'postmodernist' case and its predecessors in 'poststructuralism' have had a similar impact in social theory, and will be more familiar, perhaps, to sociologists or students of media studies.

I have said that I intend a critical reading of this work in order to guide reflection upon the usefulness of the whole metaphor of social life as text, and I find a number of problems with Barthes's essays, which helps me to trace similar ones in 'postmodernism'. A central problem concerns the tendency of the metaphor to offer a mirror image of the limitations and constraints of the metaphors of conventional social science: an excessive autonomy to match the excessive determinism of Marxism, perhaps, as contexts of power and domination surrounding texts are played down. There is also a strange ambivalence and doubt over the issue of relativism. Textual metaphors lead you into relativism as 'external' criteria to judge texts are denied: strictly speaking, it becomes impossible to categorise texts as 'ideological' or 'liberating', for example, independently of the ways in which readers interact with them, but this is too strict for most writers, who still want to comment upon and evaluate cultural trends and intervene in the politics of the day. As we shall see, this sort of problem leads to another: the radical critique of 'foundationalism' in the social sciences can also return to haunt those who unleashed it.

Again, this is an example of an excessive critique, one which goes further than it needs, so to speak, in the pursuit of some philosophical idealist final resolution of problems, and which has arisen in many philosophical works before, leading to sterility and self-cancellation, 'pathos'. Yet before we can afford to feel smug, as non-philosophers, we must consider our own positions, and once more it is impossible to come out with naive sociological assumptions intact. There is much in the view, for example, which says that sociology retains its integrity only by allowing someone else to suggest limits to its enquiries, some tradition, some residual 'common sense', or some outside groups demanding 'simplicity' or 'relevance', for example.

And the textual metaphor refuses to be obediently dismissed and to stay outside this issue as well. It is impossible to avoid a guilty recognition of the points made by Barthes and Lyotard (or Derrida for that matter, which I cite briefly in Chapter 5) that the apparent lucidity and simplicity (compared to European philosophy) of sociological or Marxist analyses of popular culture are largely a trick of pedagogic writing, which often turns upon unrecognised connections between 'everyday' and academic discourse: such analyses either simply rephrase 'everyday' insights in fancier language, or hide their differences and complexities behind the resonances between sociological terms like 'class' and everyday conceptions.

Finally, there is the issue of synthesis, again. Is there no way forwards between the excesses of the textual metaphor and the old determinism in Marx or Durkheim? In the struggles between 'action' and structure in sociological theory, which we review in Chapters 1 and 7 (at different levels), both sides tried to account adequately for the phenomena highlighted by the other, of course; but, with work like Giddens's, a third option appeared: to focus, in effect, on intermediate social practices that were shaped both by the actions of individuals and social structures. Although Giddens's solutions have been much discussed and criticised (in Craib 1992a, for example) and are not adopted wholesale in this account, the option has a habit of recurring – in the necessity for concrete contexts or practices of reading or viewing, for example (Chapters 4 and 5), or in the need for an examination of concrete practices of 'reification' or 'embedding' in questions of identity (Chapters 6 and 7), or in a need for suitably detailed and complex practices of social reproduction (Chapter 1). The Conclusion speculates a little about what such an account of actual social practices might be able to do for Habermas as well.

This account is structured by personal and pedagogical concerns. Readers will not necessarily share these concerns, and will have some of their own. I am especially aware of the rather constrained context in which students (the audience I have in mind) could be reading this book. You may well be concerned to dip into the book, perhaps driven by an 'instrumental' interest in stripping out enough material to help you assemble an assignment that will score well. I have tried to make the chapters and the sections inside them suitably discrete in order to permit this, although it can produce a little repetition and redundancy. I have tried to include links with other chapters to show how arguments progress and develop there, for those with more time. I have suggested additional reading and tried to indicate where my book fits into conventional debates (the better to help you organise some debates in your own work), in order to encourage deeper perusal.

Here, however, it is necessary to remind anyone who has not yet tried that the original writings of Foucault, Derrida or Lacan, say, are 'difficult', certainly compared to the more familiar textbooks of conventional sociology. As indicated above, this is deliberate. If one holds the view that discourses, texts, languages are endlessly free-floating, open and constructive, it follows that it becomes impossible to do any simple summary of one's points, for fear of contradicting this view and lapsing into an unwarranted 'literalism', or a naiveté about language and its privileged function as representation. As Young (1981: 7) puts it: 'Looking (mistakenly) for a completed system, the reader finds it impossible to pin down and systematise a series of texts . . . Once this aspect is recognised, however, the reader can feel less bewildered, and reassured that at least this being at sea is to the point.' Naturally, this sort of effect cannot be encouraged too far in a textbook, though.

Having outlined the concrete issues that led to my own reflections on these issues, let me turn finally to the structure of the book in more detail. Chapter 1 begins with some early debates in an attempt to study popular culture, and I try to outline some of the basic issues that have arisen, primarily for sociologists, via a consideration of various models, dilemmas or choices. In Chapter 2, I raise some of the difficulties that sociological approaches face in coming to grips with the kind of hyperreal aspects of culture with which we began. These chapters are basic and are designed to cover some ground which will be familiar to sociology students, perhaps with a 'twist' towards the debates which are to follow. For those students who have never done any sociology, it might be worth starting here: I mean no offence, but it is common to have to convince such students of the point of trying to trace any social dimensions to cultural activity, which often seems to be simply the 'expression' of some writer's or film director's personal insights, or the spontaneously collective decision among individuals to adopt the same clothing, sporting interests or whatever. For both sorts of student, it is worth trying to see what it is in Marxism or Durkheimian sociology and their theories of 'social reproduction' that have been so abruptly dismissed as redundant by some of the 'postmodern' writers.

Chapter 3 considers some of the work in 'discourse theory' which attempted to develop a Marxist analysis of culture using certain resources in linguistics to do so. Foucault appears in that chapter as representative of 'poststructuralism' as well as in his own right. Chapter 4 offers commentary on the 'society as text' metaphor via an extended discussion of several small essays by Barthes; as I have said, Barthes's reasons for going beyond Marxist analysis are reviewed in particular. In Chapter 5, I open out into a broader account of 'postmodernism', by considering the issues raised by the notion that social science derives its legitimation from its 'textual' qualities as a series of narratives. Again, I have angled this discussion towards a consideration of some of the philosophical debates triggered by poststructuralism, and directed at (and often cited in) major approaches to the study of popular culture. As I have indicated above, I intend no easy dismissal of these works, and I can offer no decisive rejection or alternative (although I consider those of other writers). My intention is simply to enable some sort of initial student participation in what can seem an arcane and remote dispute that invites a side-step followed by business as usual.

Chapters 6 and 7 return to more substantive issues as a kind of test for the theoretical frameworks we have considered. Chapter 6 tries out Marxism and postmodernism in particular by examining some recent accounts of developments in film and television or video. Recent debates on identity and consumerism, and their connections, if any, with the familiar sociological variables like class, 'race' and gender occupy the bulk of Chapter 7, which also features a debate between two different sorts of analysis of modern lifestyles, both widely cited, in Lasch and Giddens. These topics are taken as indicative of wider aspects of 'modernity', and I try to develop a subtext addressing the issue of the relevance of sociology to these debates.

# 1

# Sociological perspectives and the complexities of modern life

There has been considerable social and cultural change in our societies, and many people have lost faith in the old ways of explaining those events. Sociologists have not been immune. To begin to shape this towards a debate about sociology, the anxiety is that culture might have broken free from the normal social constraints into some floating hyperreality, making the old ways of understanding redundant. Traditional societies were different, perhaps, and their cultural activity remained constrained by social structures or organisations of various kinds, to such an extent that it could be 'read off' from a knowledge of such structures. In modern or postmodern societies, that possibility no longer applies.

Several authors (for example, Giddens 1991b) are aware that there is a danger in this view of misreading even traditional societies and seeing them as changeless, fully socially determined with little individual autonomy or creativity. If we are not careful, we are not far from the popular stereotypes of pre-industrial societies as dominated by mysterious religious allegiances or by common, rather primitive social values of punishment and retribution. These stereotypes can appear in contemporary commentaries on Islamic societies or ethnic minorities in Britain (see Sivanandan 1990).

There is a danger too of reading the classical works of sociology in this rather simple way, especially if you want to make them 'disappear' (we shall consider disappearance in Chapters 4 and 5). In the interests of arguing for a clear break with the past traditions of the subject, it is sometimes easy to label the classical analyses of Durkheim or Marx, or of other systems such as structuralism, as 'determinist', and to argue that the fully floating 'postculture' of modernity makes them redundant.

Before this redundancy is celebrated, though, it is necessary to examine the sociological traditions in more detail, especially if they are not very familiar (as is often the case with students of popular culture or media). This chapter will attempt to take seriously the question: where does culture come from, and what social factors 'embed' (produce or constrain) it? We shall be asking whether sociological analysis can still offer anything to this debate, or whether we need to break with the old traditions and pursue more of what I have called literary or poetic analysis.

## SOCIAL REPRODUCTION

If we begin with some of the issues raised earlier about culture, it is apparent that the classical analyses of functionalism or Marxism did operate with some kind of 'reproduction' model whereby cultural ideas and practices were determined ultimately by a need to preserve key elements of social structure (like a type of solidarity based on commitment and belief, or a particular mode of production). What follows must be a very simplified discussion, and much has been written on these topics, as you will see from more advanced texts and courses. Craib's (1992b) introduction or Collins (1994) could be useful additions at this stage. Recent commentaries on Durkheim include Alexander (1990) and Austin-Broos (1987), while Marxism (with asides on Weber) is ably summarised in Sayer (1991). I see my task here as trying to provide enough in a simple summary at least to persuade readers that the argument is not over, that sociological theory is still worth reading.

In certain of the writings of Durkheim and Marx, to take those writers as representative for a moment, the form of reproduction was indeed a rather simple one, but there are also what might be called local or concrete variants.

### Durkheim and social solidarities

For Durkheim, Lukes (1975) tells us, the symbols at the heart of belief systems were derived from some *conscience collective* or, later, from the main set of 'collective representations' provided by social life itself. They operated as codes to represent social life, and these codes were reinforced in a tight way by the patterns, organisations and rituals of everyday life. Social life and symbolic systems overlapped and reinforced each other in a pattern of considerable 'moral density'. The case study here, which can stand for all cultural activities, is the analysis of religion.

Lukes's reading of Durkheim on the sociology of religion raises the possibility of three sorts of connections between religious belief and social systems (having dismissed both psychological and religious explanations). First, there is a causal mechanism whereby religious beliefs 'stated and expressed in a non-objective, symbolic or metaphorical form truths about the "reality" underlying them and giving them their "true" meaning. The "reality" Durkheim discovered was, of course, "society"' (Lukes 1975: 460–1). More specifically, the connections between actual social rituals and the depth of religious feeling are causal ones, and Durkheim even experimented, Lukes tells us, with attempts to causally link specific beliefs with specific social arrangements, such as 'the development of religious universalism to the growth of interchanges between tribes' (ibid.: 465).

The second most obviously sociological connection is a functionalist one: religion 'strengthens the bonds attaching the individual to the society of which he is a member' (ibid.: 471, quoting Durkheim). It is easy to see mourning rituals or festivals of remembrance in this functional sense, but Durkheim also pointed to the unifying powers of various emblems or religious symbols. At such moments, ordinary life is idealised, our 'better nature' comes through, and we experience feelings of confidence, strength and social purpose.

The third relation – what Lukes calls the 'interpretative' one – sees religion as having a more cognitive function, enabling the expression or representation of what are basic social dilemmas about relationships between individuals and society, about obligations and responsibilities. All the dilemmas arising in social life are found in a religious form: the overwhelming nature of the collective appears as the sacred or divine; rituals offer a chance to become aware of social obligations; the common idea of the soul stands for the 'continuity of the collective life' (Lukes 1975: 467, quoting Durkheim), and so on. Similar themes of seeing religion as a mythologised social science are found in Marx too (and in Lévi-Strauss as we shall see), and, of course, are supposed to give way to a real social science.

The implications for contemporary life leap out of such work, and it is not surprising to find Durkheimians thinking of apparently secular rituals in the same way – such as those surrounding national sporting activities, political inaugurations or even the ceremonies of modern academic life. Graduation ceremonies represent the idealised version of academic life, with everyone in their best dress and on their best behaviour, and with ceremonial speech as a kind of idealised academic discourse. Given all the old props of power, symbolised in dress, music and ceremony, it is hardly surprising that even the most cynical students are often moved to feel the power of the collective.

But this sort of reading can be overdone, and may indeed have reached excessive prominence in Durkheim's work (arising in part from his methodological concerns to pursue a scientific sociology where social life was caused by social facts – see Gardner's helpful essay in Austin-Broos 1987). Even Durkheim was aware of the tendency of cultural practices and social organisations to emerge from social embedding, though, Gardner argues; but whatever autonomy was generated, whatever innovations were produced, there was always a constraint derived from the need for belief systems to relate to the perceived realities of social life (for them to be functional, for individuals as well as more generally). In concrete terms, social rituals would reinforce the functional patterns that developed.

However, religious symbolism does permit reflection of some kind to take place (especially the rational forms that developed in industrial societies). Even the most immediate and orgiastic rituals liberate actors from mundane routines and permit them the freedom to think about society, and then re-embed them in an immediate network of social and moral obligations.

The crisis of industrial societies, for Durkheim, lay rooted in the pressure on the *conscience collective* arising from the increase in both the size and the complexity of industrial societies (differentiation) which no longer permit the regulating mechanisms of social life to be experienced directly by the participants (to put a rather contemporary gloss on the argument). This might look rather liberating to us, but excessive detachment from the social tends to be treated rather pessimistically by Durkheim (although he also held no illusions about the oppressive nature of social life in traditional communities). Successful socialisation liberates individuals as well as reproducing the collective. After all, we must live in a collective, with an existing cultural tradition, and thus 'Liberty is the daughter of authority properly understood . . . to be free is to . . . act with reason and to do one's duty' (Durkheim 1956: 89–90).

Excessive individualism, by contrast, leads to *anomie* (being without guiding norms) or other variants of egoism (not being able to constrain one's appetites or realise one's limits, for example). Even here, though, Durkheim argued that a kind of naturalistic 'realism' would tend to prevail, in that cultural constructs still had to make sense, to correspond to some extent with the perceived realities of life.

Clearly, this has a strong echo in some of our debates on the excesses of individualistic lifestyles, for example. One difference from modern commentaries, though, is that Durkheim clearly felt that new social constraints would emerge to control excesses and re-regulate or re-embed these activities. This is the famous new kind of 'organic solidarity', a way of living together that permitted the maximum amount of individuality, autonomy in the 'profane' sphere of everyday life (such as in leisure or political preferences or economic activity), yet which still operated with a set of core 'sacred' values such as belief in the nation. Here, though, it was necessary to devise specific policies and interventions, to do the integrating work of society explicitly and with the guidance of social science. Durkheim's recommendations ranged from considerable and radical reforms of the economic system to the establishment or revival of definite solidarity-producing organisations and practices – 'moral education' to be pursued via belief and social ritual in schools or work-based guilds, for example ('rational substitutes for religious notions', in the words of Lukes 1975: 112). Now we have an adequate social science, Durkheim thought, with what would be called in some quarters 'modernist arrogance', we could intervene.

## Structuralism

In later writers, such as the French 'structuralists', it is possible to see these ideas developing (not without rethinking – see Giddens 1979 for one account). Instead of notions like 'collective representations' (with their unavoidable hints of 'group minds'), it might be possible to ground the notion of a social unconscious. We need such a notion, it might be argued, to explain the unknown (except to sociologists) mechanisms that influence us in the necessary functional directions, or that quietly 'cause' us to develop particular forms of solidarity and the cultural representations with which we think them.

There is a clear trail from Durkheim (and Mauss) to the work of Lévi-Strauss on the unconscious as a cognitive structure, consisting of sets of binary divisions underpinning actual cultural arrangements such as kinship systems, cultural taboos or rituals and myths. Another possibility sees the work of structural linguists like Saussure (see Culler 1976a) as belonging to the same tradition: the language system itself, with its distinctions, differences and rules of combination, makes up the collective unconscious. Of course, both thinkers criticised aspects of Durkheim's approach too (see Giddens 1979 for one account).

Both cognitive and linguistic structures can be seen as originating in the same mythical past of a simple community, perhaps even one based on some version of 'human nature', gradually developing more and more shared understandings. Social change occurs via the development of this system of shared understandings. At the end of a long process of social development, classically an evolutionary one, present members of the community are left with a cultural legacy with which they construct their 'own' concrete cultural practices and phenomena. Underneath the complexity of these practices can still be found the basic types of solidarity or the basic binaries or codes, and much influential cultural analysis can take the form of excavating these underlying structures.

As quick examples: Lévi-Strauss's structural anthropology was based on the powerful and economical logical models found in structural linguistics (you might try his famous essay *Structural Analysis in Linguistics and Anthropology,* in Lévi-Strauss 1977 – still one of the best introductions to structuralism). In his later work on kinship systems, as Leach (1970) explains, Lévi-Strauss shows how the apparent complexity of a range of kinship systems across different societies and across time spans (patriarchal, matrilocal, polygamous, polyandrous and the rest) can all be explained as basic variants of a fairly simple structure: four terms (brother, sister, father, son); three types of relations (consanguinity, affinity, descent); and two pairs of oppositions (warm and cool).

On a more obviously popular cultural note, a piece by Eco (1979) provides an initial example of more recent 'structuralist' analysis.

Eco's concern is the narrative structures of Ian Fleming's James Bond novels, and he offers an account which deliberately refuses to explain events in those novels in terms of either the individual character and 'personality' of Ian Fleming or of the 'psychology' of James Bond. Instead, we are offered an analysis of the 'formulae' of the novels, and the underlying codes (in the form of moves in a game, for example). The specific contents that differentiate the novels are derived from the 'common opinions shared by the majority of the readers' (Eco 1979: 161). Of course, it is possible to argue that a Bond novel is not art, but commercially produced trivia: nevertheless, we can begin to see the appeal of structuralist analysis, perhaps. The well-known anti-individualist stance of the approach is also clear, I hope, and we shall expand it later.

## Modern functionalism

Again, we can only be brief, and more extensive discussions are available. Let us confine ourselves here to the theme of attempting to understand some of the complexities of modern social life using functionalist analysis. For the American 'founding fathers' of sociology, it became essential to recognise more complex strata in cultural legacies, especially when studying the USA in the first half of this century.

To summarise a long discussion, Parsons (for example) came to see differentiation and specialisation as common and essential qualities of modern societies like that of the USA, which he modelled as an adaptive machine. His own work went on to develop an exhaustive model to describe the ways in which societies implemented the necessary 'functions' of adaptation, goal-attainment, integration and latency (see Craib 1992b: 43). These functions are expressed in more and more complex ways as societies change and adapt both internally and in response to changes in their environments as they compete with others. Crook *et al.* (1992: 5) offer a useful discussion of the two types of changes: 'a continuous and incremental elaboration and separation of subsystems', on the one hand, and 'fundamental differentiation leaps or evolutionary breakthroughs', on the other. They point out the cultural implications of this analysis: increased differentiation leads to cultural fragmentation *and* the development of new kinds of cultural and political integration mechanisms.

## Subcultures

The tensions between social constraint, individual lifestyles and cultural change are also explored in the discussion of modern subcultures. These can be thought of as alternative ways of life, although still with some values shared with the 'mainstream' culture (this is not without its problems as a definition; but then, so are definitions of culture, as we know). Sociological analysis tries to uncover the hidden social or structural constraints at work even here, where cultural alternatives seem to be developing.

The most famous version of subcultural formation, perhaps, involves the idea of 'social strain'. In Merton's (1968) work, strain arises between the officially endorsed values of an open society, where individual achievement is possible and desirable, and an elitist economic system that increasingly tends to close off real opportunities and chances to outsiders. Deviant cultures, including those of the professional criminal and the drop-out, arise as (limited) subcultural 'solutions' to these strains (as does 'ritualism', the tendency to 'go through the motions', a feature of modern life for Lasch 1982, to which we shall return). Again, at the concrete level of analysis, these theories are still common in everyday attempts to explain the social context of deviance (broadly defined to include not just criminals, but alternative lifestyles, the peculiar domestic habits of the socially mobile, or the nonconformist in modern organisations).

Marxist versions of the notion of subculture are perhaps better known, especially via the famous studies of youth subcultures in Hall and Jefferson (1976), Willis (1978, 1990) and Hebdige (1979). We shall come to them below, but the work displays classic problems in trying to close with social complexity using general theory. Briefly, subcultural styles can be seen as 'solutions' to social problems (in Marxist terms, problems produced by the class system as experienced especially by youth), but there is within the work a growing tendency to find this restrictive, requiring to be supplemented with more specific analysis of the contents of those subcultures: of the precise significance of clothing or music in punk, say. The tensions between social constraint and cultural autonomy take on a methodological note too, as we shall see: can concepts like *bricolage* or homology really manage these tensions, or do we need additional concepts from other disciplines grafted on, so to speak?

## Solidarities

We have been discussing complexity above, and have noticed that even subcultures feature some kind of solidarity, in the form of a capacity to unite members locally and, less obviously perhaps, in the form of a structural connection to, or origin in, the wider culture. However, these insights are not confined to analysts of deviant cultures, but are noticeable in current political debate in Britain, and can be found behind a number of reforming political interventions in British social policy, particularly those launched by social democratic socialists.

However, as these examples suggest, it is perhaps more difficult these days to appeal to new senses of community. The social democratic state is in crisis, split between the need to promote ever-deeper penetrations of market rationality on the one hand, and to promote these kinds of solidarities among people on the other (see Habermas 1976). Further, politicians in the earlier Thatcherite era tended to favour liberal theory (which Durkheim had criticised) instead. Solidarity was addressed via the more superficial kinds of appeals to public opinion and some measures to increase the state's power to dominate, without much real social reform at the base, so to speak. One consequence of these alterations of policy has been outlined by Baudrillard in his famous pronouncements about the masses as indifferent, sceptical 'black holes' into which exhortations, party political broadcasts, public relations statements and advertisements all pour without result (see Rojek's essay on Baudrillard's politics, in Rojek and Turner 1993).

If the picture at the level of national politics is one of disillusion and loss of faith, the Durkheimian tradition can still be found carried on in work on current local solidarities, whether those of church congregations or of football crowds. Collins (in Alexander 1990) reminds us that the notion of social experiences coding patterns of belief and underpinning solidarities has been developed in analyses of the education system by writers like Bernstein and Bourdieu. With these writers, beliefs and categories of judgement are still deeply embedded (as in the notion of 'habitus' in Bourdieu or, less formally, in definite ways of life, including speech patterns and child-rearing practices, in Bernstein).

It is difficult, if not logically impossible, to think of social life without any solidarities or embeddings, with total and widespread *anomie* or egoism. Local attachments to social life must persist, Durkheim was to argue, and their absence led only to suicide. Thinking of that prediction puts the current debates about freedom and disembedding into question once more, as Warde (1994), writing on modern consumption patterns, reminds us: to borrow his rhetoric, can we really see shopping as being as radically unconstrained as the social conditions that produce suicide?

'If people were making choices every time they confronted a situation of consumption, social life would become insupportable' (Warde 1994: 891). Instead, Warde argues, consumer behaviour is still constrained, regulated or indeed activated by a number of social mechanisms including social networks, the old divisions of labour between the genders, the persistence of conventions ('the ... residues of class cultures'), and even socio-psychological defence mechanisms like 'complacency'. These coexist with the much 'newer' devices allegedly specific to modernity, like life-style guides, personal counselling manuals, lifeplans and the rest (which we discuss in Chapter 7).

## Nomic processes

One legacy of functionalist analysis is a need to restore to current discussions some awareness of the locally embedding solidaristic or reproductory practices found in everyday life, to avoid an unnecessarily one-sided treatment. Switching slightly from Durkheimian terms, we need an account of the *nomic* processes of everyday life, in Garfinkel's phrase, that continue to operate even in modernity. We hear a lot about divorce, for example in Giddens's (1991b) work, but not about (re)marriage; we have a rather abstract discussion of 'pure relationships', but no acknowledgement of the classic work on establishing practical 'other-directed' relationships (discussed briefly below).

To take another popular area, to which we shall return, there is much discussion of the amiable *flâneur* wandering through the cultural arcades of cities, but we need to balance this with analysis of the social conditions of the city resident trying to find housing and encountering the stratifying and familiar effects of markets and housing classes (see Savage *et al.* 1990). Moreover, residents are likely to 'read' city life quite differently from visitors. For example, I have visited Melbourne on two occasions, and much enjoyed playing the *flâneur*, wandering round and enjoying the tremendous cultural diversity of the city while coping pretty well with the language and local customs (including the peculiar method while driving of turning right at junctions where there are trams).

Wandering round your home town (mine is Portsmouth) is quite different, of course. Locals can read the architecture in terms of local politics and insider knowledge: which developments attracted rumours of local corruption; how disappointed (some) local residents felt when they saw the grotesque concrete development called The Tricorn (which, apparently, received an architectural prize); the mixture of despair and amused disbelief that greeted the redevelopment of the city centre; and the derision at the pompous heritage-industry-type names of the new streets ('King Henry the First Street').

If we move beyond abstract discussions of 'the consumer' or the city wanderer, we shall also encounter the familiar effects of gender 'normalising' these activities: Pahl (1990) points to the impact of gender and marital status on consumption patterns, for example, while Wolff notes that there is no such thing as a *flâneuse* – 'Women could not stroll alone in the city' (Wolff 1985: 41).

There is also a tendency to miss the texture of everyday life in accounts of modernity, to focus on the exotic rather than the mundane, and, classically, to focus on just those areas of cultural adventure and experiment which are then held to be somehow characteristic or expressive of life itself. In contrast, much classic sociological work stresses the nomic character of everyday life, the search for and the very production of order. Giddens himself refers to Garfinkel's work on the accomplishment of stable gender identities, and the considerable amounts of negotiation, interpretation and response to the interpretations of significant others that such accomplishments require. Other ethnomethodological analyses have pursued the theme of the construction of social order in a variety of everyday activities such as telling stories, holding telephone conversations, even walking together (see a general commentary, such as Heritage 1984).

Most sociology students will also think of the symbolic interactionist material (which we shall review below). It is relatively easy to illustrate these processes by mundane examples of social encounters as part of university life – learning how to operate in particular social settings like 'seminars' for example, including learning the social and linguistic competencies required to offer an adequate response, take a turn, add to the discussion in an acceptable way, disagree with previous speakers in a suitable manner, and so on. Indeed, substantial research has been undertaken on these matters in educational settings (see, for example, the section on studying classroom language in Hammersley 1989).

The educational example also helps in understanding a point that was made earlier, about the need for cultural innovations to correspond at some level to some 'naturalistic attitude'. The geography of the naturalistic attitude has been well sketched by Schutz (1971a) in a famous essay in which he argues that we operate with a set of typifications organised, basically, around a set of perceptions and motives with the actor at the centre based, as it were, on a starting point of 'here and now'. As he suggests, this causes difficulties in encounters with a 'scientific attitude', apparently written from an abstract, disinterested and de-centred perspective, with quite a different set of typifications and relevance systems. Any teacher or student can recognise this sort of cognitive problem which is very clear when encountering social sciences in particular: for example, shortly before writing this section I was teaching a media studies class, where it was clear that an academic reading of a *Jaws* movie (seeing the shark as a representation of 'nature' and sexuality, for example) simply starts in a different place and works in a different way compared to the 'normal' type of engagement and interpretation offered by relatively inexperienced students (who wanted to discuss the special effects and their personal impact, or to imagine what they would have done with certain scenes had they been the director).

Any teacher will know how difficult it can be to persuade new students to consider arguments like some of those we are to discuss in later chapters – on the disappearance of texts or the death of the subject, say. Any participant will detect sheer scepticism advanced towards such arguments by newcomers to academic life, who simply see them as absurdly unrealistic or fanciful, the result of a silly game or an affectation, having nothing to do with 'the real world'.

Pedagogic institutions are designed to disembed ideas and beliefs, and sometimes they do so very effectively, as I know from my own case; but there are substantial conservative (or *nomic*) forces to overcome even in these purpose-built organisations. Is it really credible to suppose that much more fleeting and limited

12

contacts with disembedding forces while strolling in cities, shopping for clothes, going on holiday in exotic locations, or watching MTV will have overcome the resistance of the natural attitude?

## Structures or series?

We have noticed a number of specific embedding mechanisms, or local solidarities, so to speak: organisations, belief systems, everyday practices ranging from other-orientated relationships to naturalistic attitudes which govern perceptions. However, it can be misleading to infer from these patterns a continuity with the classic functionalist accounts. The question now is whether or not these specific mechanisms operate in a particular direction, whether they overlap to produce a deeply or densely embedded structure, steered by some functional integrating mechanism, or whether they offer individuals merely a series of habituses, in Bauman's (1992a) words, a series, network or labyrinth rather than a structure in the old sense.

Certainly it can no longer simply be assumed that there are underlying functional mechanisms of adjustment in the sense of a social evolutionary drive to regain social equilibrium or some 'underspecified goal' whereby all human beings strive to maintain a social existence, working away beneath or behind the surface complexities of social life. Everyone feels sceptical towards these metanarratives these days. It is certainly very difficult to imagine a totally fragmented society as a permanent way of life for the majority of people, and it is not surprising to find some drawing back from this scenario, possibly even for Baudrillard, as we shall see.

Social life beyond the small scale and immediate could persist as a mere simulacrum, or it could be reduced to a functional public core of impersonal bureaucratic relations or economic exchange relations. It is possible to predict the rise of fully postcultural communities, perhaps – 'imagined communities' or large-scale 'new social movements'. Whether any of these can generate sustained social systems is much more debatable, however: in the slightly obscure words of Durkheim: 'Either the *conscience collective* floats in a void . . . or else it is connected to the rest of the world by [some material] substratum upon which, consequently, it is dependent' (Gardner in Austin-Broos 1987: 85).

We shall discuss in the next section similar dilemmas facing Marxism. Perhaps the safest option for now is an agnostic stance of waiting to see if things get more fragmented or whether they will reintegrate into larger patterns of solidarity, as Crook *et al.* (1992) suggest.

## MARXISM

The whole project to tease out the mechanisms of the social transmission of culture can be revitalised, made concrete or 'material' with an injection of Marxist theory. The processes of differentiation and development of culture can be read as a struggle over the production of culture, and this enables the analyst to connect the cultural sphere (or 'level') to the economic and political. In this reading, 'mainstream' culture should best be seen as a set of values and practices which somehow favour the dominant social class, allowing for certain complications, as in the famous term 'ideology'. Sometimes the connections are clear and obvious, and 'vulgar' interests (in Marx's phrase) are detectable behind the promotional efforts of big business which wishes to conceal the undesirable aspects of its activities, stresses the good that it does for the community as a whole, and pleads for even more exemption from taxation or restrictive health and safety regulations or whatever. One of the great pleasures of Marxist analysis lies in the ability to undertake this sort of unmasking of specific interests that lie behind the bland claims to be offering some universal good. As with Durkheim, we have a large amount of material to discuss here, and there is a need to be schematic (and occasionally dogmatic).

There are a number of problems immediately; for example, in the way Marx uses the term 'ideology' to refer to a number of things: the false beliefs of political opponents deriving directly from their class position (what we might call 'vulgar' or 'practical ideology'); and the better-developed, rational, more autonomous but still flawed theories of rival social scientists ('scientific' or 'theoretical ideology').

The former practical or vulgar ideologies tend to be embedded in social life, to use our terms, in fairly simple and direct ways. They are the 'ideas of the ruling class', according to one formulation, and as such simply enjoy greater currency and political power than those of the oppressed classes. Or they emerge rather like Durkheimian codings from the ways of life of industrial society: feudal society provides us with particular models of the

14

political system, while industrial societies produce the need for new social roles and political forms (to paraphrase another formulation). These practical ideologies need only be locally shared, and sometimes they clash and find specific expression in the open political struggles of the day – over the 'natural' length of the working day, over the rights of workers and work conditions. More generally, traditional cultural and social institutions – work patterns, family life, rural communities and solidarities and sentiments based on them – were ruthlessly and unsubtly destroyed.

The institutions which replaced them emerged in the shadow of industrial capitalism – private property, the 'free' labourer, market forces, and Parliament (merely a committee of the bourgeoisie as a whole in the formulation of Marx and Engels's *Communist Manifesto*). These were invariably more abstract institutions offering more abstract cultural possibilities, such as the 'commodification' of culture, or an isolated individualism (see Sayer 1991).

With theoretical ideologies, and with the political ideologies of more sophisticated regimes, there are different sorts of less-direct embedding mechanisms, however. Marx also refers, after writing the *Manifesto*, to political ideas having a reasonable autonomy, not so closely tied to the immediate vulgar interests of the ruling class nor to the existing technological needs of producers. Political ideas of the past can have effects, and they can be wielded to produce specific cultural or political support, for example, for the rather curious regime of Louis Bonaparte in France in the 1850s and 1860s.

For the more developed theoretical ideologies, like Ricardo's political economy or Hegel's philosophy, there are different analyses again, devoted to the concepts themselves, so to speak, rather than attempting to reduce their effects immediately to the class position of those who advocate them. Briefly, those concepts incorporate the wrong kind of abstractions, insufficiently disentangled from the specific practices observed by the analysts.

As an easy example, consider Marx's brief and brutal critique of Bentham, whom he dismissed as 'with the driest naiveté ... [taking] ... the modern shopkeeper, especially the English shopkeeper, as the normal man' (Marx 1977: 571). It is easy to see how, for Marx, the notion of a minutely calculating, profit-seeking human nature became incorporated into the heart of Bentham's philosophy. We are on very controversial ground in even suggesting that Marx had a constant critical method or theme throughout his work, but similar-sounding critiques can be found in many other places: Hegel's political philosophy offers too easy an accommodation between his concept of a universal state and the actual State of Prussia; while the political economists operated with a 'common-sense' definition of the commodity which failed to penetrate its real nature as a peculiar combination of two kinds of value. Other analysts (liberals like James Mill, for example) stressed the flexible and even democratic nature of the distribution system in advanced capitalism but failed to grasp the connection with the highly exploitative production system; socialist politicians hoped to reform certain specific aspects of the system (for example, via 'fairer wages') while leaving the mechanisms that generated them intact; and so on.

Here we have the deployment of the famous 'deep/surface' (or possibly 'generalities') approach in Marx. The forms in which commodities or political institutions actually appear (the 'phenomenal forms') are misleadingly simple and abstract and must be grasped by a particular method which refuses altogether to employ them, and generates correct scientific knowledge instead.

This sort of argument is really similar to ones that we shall discuss which claim to have replaced their rivals and thus made them and the objects they study 'disappear'. Marx (and Marx and Engels) claim, for example, to have solved the mystery of Christian religion by exposing its basis in material conditions, or to have 'put an end' to (Hegelian) philosophy or to the 'German ideology'. Later Marxists have tried to claim an equally decisive dismissal of sociology, by accusing it of operating with phenomenal forms 'on the surface' (such as 'socio-economic group' or 'community').

Let us pursue in more depth the most famous example in Marxism: the mystery of the origins of profits, or rather, of economic growth (a growth in value, rather than a mere excess amount of cash left over). People actually running small businesses need not worry about the source of wealth – if they manage things properly, they can pay all the bills and there is a surplus left which they can dispose of. It is tempting (especially for small-business proprietors) to see the source of this surplus in the dynamic management practices of the entrepreneur, or in some quality of the system of economic organisation itself, or in the special qualities of money or trade – but Marxist analysis suggests that labour is the source of the surplus.

Labour appears, on the surface, as a simple commodity, a mere 'factor of production' like land or capital goods (tools, factories, machinery and the like), and it is purchased at the fair market rate, just like any other commodity. Once it is put to use, however, it is unique in that it produces additional value – it adds value to the other raw materials to produce finished goods of a higher value. Thus, a misleading combination of 'fair' prices for labour with an unacknowledged exploitation of its unique properties is what provides the puzzle, especially if you are pursuing the kind of enquiry that likes nice unambiguous concepts and terms, one where things obediently fit simple analyses. Sayer (1991) has an excellent and more extensive discussion.

The social institutions of capitalism ensure that this unique quality is deployed to the benefit of the owners of capital and not the owners of labour. The idea of 'private property', for example, means that capitalists can do with labour what they will once they have hired it for the day, and that they own the goods that are produced in the labour process. 'Custom', the law and, if necessary, religious sanction support the idea of a rather long working day (in the early stages of capitalism); long enough, if all goes well, for labour to produce enough goods to pay for its hire before the end of the day and then go on to produce surpluses. Later, political and cultural pressures, and social scientific theory in 'management studies' for that matter, combined to focus attention on the productivity of the labour force: hard-working, well-trained, adequately motivated, committed or easily threatened workers can be persuaded to work hard enough to pay for their own pay rises or cuts in hours, while still generating surpluses for others to dispose of. To anticipate the terms of later discussion (Chapter 7), this is how social practices and ideas become 'embedded' in an economic system.

In this way, we can relocate and refocus analysis on to the real if hidden determinants of social life. We can understand apparently isolated cultural developments as embedded in and as reproducing the social relations of capitalism. There are many examples: the causes of crime lie not with individuals but with the 'criminogenic' state apparatuses in capitalism (to cite the project of 'critical criminology'); or, more specifically, 'moral panics' about street crime should be traced back to political action designed to resolve some underlying crisis affecting welfare capitalism (to cite Hall *et al.* 1978 and their analysis of 'mugging').

The examples cited above should also help us to expose some of the problems in such a claimed 'break' with sociology, which we discuss below.

## Embedding mechanisms in Marxism

*Harris's preference for Durkheimian formulations —*

To return to our main theme, and avoiding some obviously massive theoretical labour to summarise discussions of what Marxist knowledge might be and how to produce it, we have a number of embedding mechanisms at work in Marxism (and serious problems in trying to grasp exactly what is at work in a process like 'economic determinism' as a consequence). To borrow from a discussion in Mepham and Ruben (1979), embedding takes place:

- in 'real relations' (for example, the actual relations between bosses and workers in production);
- via the 'phenomenal forms' we discussed above, which can scarcely depart from the system that produces them and thus appear 'natural';
- in 'ideological categories' (more developed and 'scientific-looking' but still rooted in the phenomenal forms at crucial moments; and, Lecourt tells us, ultimately nested within practical ideologies (see Macdonell 1986).

Whether these processes are ranked in some sort of order of importance is another large area of debate, and one which is at the heart of the controversy about determinism in Marxism. Ultimately, we have implied so far, all the categories (at least) of belief systems can be traced back to a mode of production that limits, constrains, embeds or determines them in some final sense, despite their apparent or even their real autonomy in some respects.

To return to the issue of modern culture, there are many examples around us these days that Marx did not address directly. Above all, there are problems with those which seem to have emerged from distinct and separate cultural practices, or to have been so worked upon and developed, so transformed by the activities of autonomous specialists, that they have escaped any conclusively determining traces of their ultimate origins.

One response is to add to lists like Mepham's what he calls 'discourse practice' in order to try to come to grips with these

e.g.

modern examples and, no doubt, to respond specifically to emerging work on the 'society as text' metaphor. It was thought possible to further extend Marxist analysis into a wide range of familiar modern cultural practices, granting a certain amount of autonomy to them, but preserving a link to overall systems of domination (as Thompson 1984 puts it). We shall consider a number of alternative positions in Marxist linguistics and in 'post-Marxism' in what follows, but in general the problem is obvious: how much can continue to be added to Marxism while insisting that it is still Marxism?

From a different tradition within Marxism, accounts which borrow from the works of the Italian Marxist Antonio Gramsci have been very influential in analysing some aspects of popular culture in Britain, for example. Gramscians use concepts like hegemony (a kind of political leadership exercised through cultural initiatives) and Gramsci's work on different types of intellectuals to argue that 'mainstream culture' will contain combinations of different elements: not just the worldviews of the ruling class, but some neutral or 'traditional' elements, some tentative or emerging ones, still in the process of being worked out and developed, whose implications are not yet clear. Some elements will even be designed deliberately to represent the views of subordinate groups, attempting to 'win consent' to the general operations of the state.

A key text here is one produced by Marx himself to comment on the political culture of the new Empire in France in the 1850s and 1860s (*The Eighteenth Brumaire of Louis Bonaparte*, in Marx and Engels 1956). Marx refers to this culture as being a combination of 'borrowed languages' (echoes of earlier examples) and a mixture of ideas belonging to different politically active groups (including class fractions), welded together (or 'articulated', in the modern term) to produce an overall perspective that does not simply represent the views of a capitalist class but which preserves the system overall). Gramscian work went through a number of evolutions (Harris 1992) but used the same basic ideas to try to grasp the ways in which the spectacular Conservative political interlude in Britain throughout the 1980s managed to gain popular support, or to argue for new socialist 'articulations' to respond to the social changes introduced by new technologies.

There are a number of implications here. Culture now has a certain kind of partial autonomy (which we shall explore in the next chapter), and certain cultural specialists appear to have an important place as articulators. To prevent these implications from leading us to abandon Marxism altogether (as many analysts have done), it is necessary to try to continue to preserve some connection with the basics of capitalist society, the class struggle and its institutions. Briefly, culture can only be granted a 'relative autonomy' (a contradictory term for some critics), and specialist articulators must still be implicated in the deliberate or unnoticed distortions of ideology (if they are bourgeois). Socialist articulators and strugglers generally still need to be able to claim some genuinely universal audience to be Marxists.

The dilemmas about articulators of different kinds can be seen best, perhaps, in Gramscian analyses of the mass media, where well-intentioned journalists still 'code' an insufficiently criticised reality in ideological ways (Hall *et al.* 1978). The superiority of the analytic 'codings' of the Gramscians themselves is argued for, but it is not all that easy to separate the two, especially where Gramscian analysis uses journalistic evidence itself. All of these conditions gave a good deal of trouble, as we shall see, when 'post' writers of various kinds (including post-Marxists) began to interrogate these claims to superiority in Marxism.

Again, there are also dangers that political enthusiasm will overwhelm analysis. The best brief example, perhaps, concerns the attempt in some writers' work to represent any kind of unusual or unpredictable reactions to mass cultural phenomena as 'resistance'. In this spirit 'resistance' can mean anything from thoroughgoing critical analysis of a cultural object using Marxist categories, to the rather less spectacular ability to view *Jurassic Park* and remain unmoved by the special effects.

Although there is no time to review it in depth here, the ambiguities are well displayed in material that attempts to describe the school cultures of black youths or of young women as exhibiting 'resistance within accommodation', to incorporate both the apparently rebellious and the apparently conformist observed behaviour of those groups within the one all-embracing account of 'hegemonic domination' (see, for example, Mac an Ghaill, in Woods and Hammersley 1993). The snag is, to be brief, that 'quietness' among such girls, for example, can be seen equally as accommodation or as resistance, and there is also a danger of seeing everything as political (there can be no 'ordinary' quietness).

## INTERACTIONISM

At this point, many sociology students will be able to anticipate what is coming next. For the less experienced, we shall introduce this section by considering an obvious alternative to the Durkheimian or Marxist approaches we have outlined. In 'common sense', individuals construct cultural and social practices, and, as we have already suggested, the main nomic or embedding mechanisms are experienced at the individual or at least the very local level too. What approaches are available to develop this common experience?

The usual main alternative to functionalist or 'structuralist' accounts consists of a (rather constructed) interactionism, usually based on the work of the American symbolic interactionists like Mead or Blumer, with Goffman or Hughes or Strauss as later advocates. Sometimes, in Britain, Weber is bundled up with these writers as a theorist of action, although, as Collins (1994) argues, there was in fact little real influence from Weber. The main encounter for British sociology students is likely to be with the famous and highly readable 'applied' materials via ethnographic studies of education (such as those in Hammersley and Woods 1976) or of deviancy (as in Becker 1973). As Collins argues, though, this sort of application was a fairly recent and specific one and, as a result perhaps, the distinctively American theoretical or philosophical context of what he calls 'microinteractionism' is not always clear. As usual, we shall find time for only a rather quick and basic summary, starting with a quick overall sketch.

The enabling myth here is that social life grows out of interaction between individuals, in dyads or in larger but still primary groups. A process of mutual orientation takes place as individuals strive to interpret the meanings of the other's actions or utterances. The process is facilitated by the immediate face-to-face context in the enabling myth – utterances and actions become symbols in a fairly direct sense of referencing some common experience. It becomes possible to anticipate the actions of the other, to 'take the role of the other', in Mead's classic phrase, to generalise, and to become aware of one's own appearance(s) to the other, as in the famous distinction between the 'I' and the 'me'. These developments enable further reflection upon action, further orientation to the (various) others, until we end with the establishment of a working social relationship. In this way, participants socialise each other, so to speak (and, of course, the support for ethnographic research from this perspective is also easy to trace – here, groups socialise the researcher in this interactive manner, leading to more sympathetic understandings).

From this primary sort of interaction, it is possible to generalise to less intimate groupings and encounters. To switch theorists for a moment, others may be more distant from us, less available immediately, Schutz (1972 – especially section 4) tells us, but the principles of understanding these distant others are the same: we perceive their actions, typify them, and place them in an interpretative context as if they were more accessible. Naturally, our interest in more distant others is not so intense, perhaps – to paraphrase Schutz, we are happy if we understand the postman's actions sufficiently well to help us establish that he is delivering mail, and we don't need to know if we have entirely understood his personal philosophy. Schutz (specifically) does propose to use Weber's sociology of action here.

It is relatively easy to project this kind of approach to interpersonal understanding on to the broader canvas of social life and social institutions more concretely and sociologically if we follow, say Berger and Luckmann (1971), on the 'social construction of reality'. Their particular enabling myth is in a location familiar to nineteenth-century British economics (and much criticised by Marx in that field): the desert island. Imagine a desert island occupied not just by Robinson Crusoe and Friday, but by a larger primary group. The interactions among them would soon establish patterns, conventions and, eventually, institutions, Berger and Luckmann suggest – the group would have to establish some sort of division of labour among itself; some ways to regulate sexual activity and child-rearing, perhaps, some social rituals to maintain morale and a sense of integration, and so on.

Once again, it is easy to think of the notion of functional prerequisites. The desert island would be an interesting thought experiment to pursue when we consider our later questions about the extent of cultural creativity and its autonomy from social embeddings of various kinds. Would life be very different from what the survivors had known from their earlier societies? Could they generate a completely new set of cultural or social arrangements, and, if so, what would be needed to generate such novelty, and what constraints would remain? Berger and Luckmann themselves are rather Durkheimian in their approach.

As time passes new generations are produced on the island. The newcomers understand their social surroundings differently, though, and are born into a relatively fixed set of arrangements. Eventually, these arrangements become reified (in the general and controversial sense in which Berger and Luckmann use the term), and become 'social facts', external constraints. The sense of authorship of these arrangements is lost, the myth suggests, except on unusual occasions. Those who benefit from the existing patterns have a vested interest in keeping things that way – a way in which Berger and Luckmann try to incorporate Marxist themes as well as Durkheimian ones. When advocates of change do attempt to re-author social life, they find themselves with fixed agendas, existing patterns, a tradition to deal with, quite unlike their fortunate forebears who had broken (potentially at least) with their pasts as soon as they landed on the beach.

The approach has been much discussed (see Collins 1994 again, for example). As any experienced sociology student knows, any interactionist accounts can be successfully critiqued by reversing the objections to structuralist ones. Here, social structure, conflict and power are undertheorised: they are explained, but in insufficient depth and detail. The picture of social structure that emerges is a rather voluntaristic one, for example, with an optimistic belief that all that holds it together is ignorance of history or political laziness. The same sort of voluntarism at a more local level leads to optimism that crime or underachievement could be solved by getting policemen or teachers to rethink their labelling behaviour: to explain the particular shape of institutions in our society, for Marxists, we should need to know exactly how *capitalist* institutions emerged, of all possible reified forms. Without grasping the peculiar history of capitalism, we are left with a rather weak and apologetic functionalism again: private property and all it implies emerged from some early agreement to regularise interaction (instead of being implicated from the beginning in manipulation, exploitation, armed conflict and struggle, as in Marx's own account).

Interactionist work is good at pointing to the mechanisms of social order at the interpersonal level, and at allowing for a certain reflexivity or creativity among social actors. Even here, though, classic interactionism might not have gone far enough, and the approach has been accused of limiting reflexivity and interaction to the kind of strategic action or 'making out' that is permitted to some groups in advanced capitalist societies (see Collins 1994). A far richer and more extensive kind of interpersonal interaction is proposed by Habermas (see Habermas 1987), as we shall see: negotiation and mutual orientation are not limited to immediate demands of getting by in everyday life within norms, but are to extend much more broadly across the whole range of social action and the validity claims implied by them.

After this brief summary, let us isolate some issues of particular importance for the arguments in the rest of this book: what problems and dilemmas arise when we consider interactionism as a theory of popular culture? At first glance, interactionism looks very promising, and in its general approach and above all in the detailed material that it generates, it seems to describe very well everyday life in modern societies. Indeed, with Goffman especially, it is quite easy to reconcile interactionist work on the self and on identity with many of the asides and provocations of 'postmodernism'.

Thus Goffman (1975) offers us a richly detailed account of the mechanisms and processes whereby people negotiate their identities, or 'present' their various selves. It is one of the best accounts of what later writers were to describe as the quintessentially 'self-referential' characteristics of experimental film or theatre, and does more than most cultural commentators to chart possible audience transformations of the cultural materials they receive. It is a fascinating read, based on Goffman's own work and on little snippets garnered from the press and from other commentaries; we shall be illustrating the points made in due course.

Goffman manages to generate all this material without referring to anything like 'floating signifiers' or 'crises of representation', and in a way which has led some to see him as a major bulwark against linguistic imperialism (as in Collins's reading of him as a Durkheimian, for example). Other writers (such as Tseëlon 1992 or Bovone 1993) want to claim him as more innovative, as breaking with conventional sociology and anticipating postmodern work on the self: here, Goffman's denials of an orthodox morality of 'authentic' self or his insistence on the emergence of the self in interaction are the key moments. It will come as no surprise to find that both readings can be supported by Goffman's actual commentary, partly because of his particular interest in description (and in creating his own terms to catalogue what he has found) rather than in explicit sociological theorising.

In the interests of championing sociology against postmodernism (which is what we are doing in this chapter), let us take on and critique the readings of Goffman as early postmodernist. (The chapter on postmodernism restores some balance.) Not only is Goffman's terminology quite different, as is the intention, in my view (no grounded attack on metanarratives), but the examples he chooses are from everyday mundane life. This technique not only helps the readability of the pieces, but also leads to an exploration of some of the important social constraints on everyday life which can be lost in the more enthusiastic celebrations of 'nomadic subjectivity' or 'self-monitored lifestyles'. Many examples are to follow in later chapters, but one small one will suffice here.

In the middle of a lengthy discussion about the fabrication of the frameworks people use to organise their understandings and interactions, Goffman (1975: 180) cites a case of 'serial containment', where 'the plotter . . . [is] . . . taken in by parties other than those who he plotted against: . . . two pickpockets kneeling in a church robbed Andres Quinonez . . . while he was praying, and were arrested by a policeman kneeling behind them'. Not only does the whole discussion of fabrication suggest a decided division between authentic and false (in this case criminally false) selves, but the issue of the power to impose frames is also clearly implied: it is unlikely that victim, pickpockets and policeman engaged in much debate about who had the right to contain whom. Of course, it is possible to argue that Goffman never fully develops these issues of ethics or power.

We shall never settle these debates about Goffman here, but they do point us to others which will again echo throughout this book. Briefly, immediate problems arise over matters such as cultural or personal autonomy and constraint, and, on a parallel track, matters such as cultural relativism and the political, aesthetic or ethical implications that arise. The concrete examples we study will reveal complex intertwinings and possibilities, just as Goffman's do. On a different level, there are recurrent technical or 'philosophical' issues too. I have focused, in this chapter and throughout, on one I call 'the production of the concrete', and I discuss it initially in the Introduction. It also appears in Collins's account of the philosophical strands in interactionism. From one end, the issue concerns the ability to generate a concrete sociology out of more general philosophies of mind, whether these be derived from American pragmatism or European phenomeno-logy. The options here are as unattractive as they are with other more linguistic general philosophies: social life has to 'express' or be 'recognised' by some philosophy of mind (inevitably with a residue or via some procedure of privileging particular aspects of social life). From the other end, the rich descriptions of social life engendered by interactionism have to be grounded somehow if they are not to seem personal or trivial, and it is this that leads to ambiguities in Goffman of the kind we have seen, or to more organised disputes about whether social or linguistic practices are better groundings (as in Goffman's debates with ethno-methodology – again summarised in Collins 1994, or extended in Goffman 1975, esp. ch. 13).

## THE COMPLEXITY OF SOCIAL LIFE

The examples we have seen in this chapter indicate that classical sociological perspectives have a common problem in that they tend to the over-general, to the neglect of specifics or concrete application. It is this problem that leads to a tendency to reduction-ism when it comes to analysing cultural matters – at its worst, culture is seen as a mere derivative of structure (variously de-fined). Less dramatic consequences include the cluster of tend-encies to overpredict chosen aspects of cultural events: function-alist accounts overpredict conformity and regularity, Marxist accounts overpredict class politics, while interactionist accounts overpredict personal awareness and creativity.

These are well-known problems, and there are attempts to minimise this tendency to overgeneralise, to simplify and reduce, in most examples of 'applied' work. However, a turn towards the concrete in 'applied' analyses is not always that easy to accom-plish. Common strategies include the simple addition of com-plexity, so to speak, when analysis turns from theoretical to empirical levels. I feel happier illustrating this tendency with Marxist approaches, although functionalist or interactionist ones are just as suitable.

One classic study in leisure studies – Clarke and Critcher (1985) – can be selected as an example that comes to hand. Clarke and Critcher ground their analytical frameworks in both a comment-ary on contemporary events and in a history of leisure provision at two levels. The first, general or 'theoretical' level consists of a model derived from Gramscian Marxism which features a story of continued oscillation between two moments in the continuing struggles for hegemony. The two moments are represented by the terms 'settlement' and 'crisis', depending on whether things are going well or badly for the ruling class (or its fractions). The model is then 'applied' to actual history in the form of an account of concrete developments in leisure provision in Britain. This actual history is suitably complex and concrete – but it is less clear that it has been *generated* by Gramscian analysis itself in anything but the broadest outline. The actual source of the concrete historical account often seems to arise from classic bourgeois history, for example.

Adding bourgeois (that is, strictly speaking unreliable and ideological) empirical contents like this is common in Gramscian analysis, as I have tried to argue elsewhere (Harris 1992). In some cases, it might be contents added from journalistic histories (see Hall *et al.* 1978), or from ethnographic data (see Willis 1978, 1990). Although these data are managed within Gramscian frameworks in the form of general commentaries and reservations about their inadequacies, there seems to be never enough time to address the issue of interpretation adequately, to winnow out thoroughly what can and cannot be trusted, so to speak. A sceptic might suggest that this leads to a rather pragmatic attitude towards such data, where examples that seem to fit are simply cited, and those that do not are exposed as inadequate.

Theoretical complexity can be added to functionalism too, as we have seen already. Parsons (see Craib 1992b) and Merton (1968) clearly tried to synthesise other approaches in their systems and frameworks, for example. Parsons adopts a technique that Craib (1992b) calls a 'filing cabinet' approach, where (briefly) social action or conflict is added as a separate level or as a special subcategory in an overall system of some complexity. Craib (1992a) hints at similar criticisms in Giddens's synthesis, to which we shall move below.

Merton's approach is different, perhaps, in that he tries to move towards empirical complexity by adding concepts like 'dysfunction' or 'latent function', or by addressing issues of inbuilt contradictions (as in 'social strain') or, for that matter, unintended consequences as in 'self-fulfilling prophecies' (Stzompka 1986 offers a sympathetic commentary). The famous work on deviancy (in Merton 1968) summarises these developments, and incidentally serves to remind new students that Mertonian functionalism is not at all naively conservative – the classic middle-class form of deviancy is ritualism (as we have suggested), and while this is not illegal, it is as socially damaging as professional crime, Merton suggests. While these analyses remove some of the obvious value-judgements of classic functionalism (what we have called its tendency to overpredict conformity and stability), however, they have the effect of reintroducing a suspiciously pragmatic or tauto-logical note, as Merton was only too well aware (such as in his discussion of *anomie*, for example): now, for example, functionalism can explain everything using one or other of the opposed terms 'function' or 'dysfunction', and we may have no really clear rules to help us decide which term fits particular practices best.

Turning back again to Gramscian analysis, Clarke and Critcher (1985) also want to 'add in' feminism to account for gender as a complicating factor in their analysis of struggles over leisure policy, without any real explanation of how and whether gender and class do just add together; this is common in that sort of writing at the time. 'Race' too can be included in this way, although, again, it is not at all easy to accomplish this smoothly, as the extended discussions of this issue reveal (some of which we explore in later chapters).

Substantial problems arise with the project to 'add' some sort of linguistics to Marxism too, to try and close with the specifics of ideological significations (which we illustrated here with Mepham's work). Subsequent chapters explore the unfortunate consequences of liaisons of this kind. Whether it is Barthes or Foucault who is bolted on, it proves hard to keep at bay the tendencies towards linguistic imperialism, where we come to see the central concepts of Marxism not as privileged devices to keep linguistic analysis on the track of exposing ideology, but as linguistic practices themselves, as equally open to deconstruction.

Bourgeois sociology or psychology can be added to Marxism openly or implicitly too, a number of commentators suggest. Turner (1981) has argued that much of the effort to explain concrete patterns apparent in the development of social classes – in Poulantzas, say – owes a great deal to Weber. Downes and Rock (1988) refer to Gramscian analysis of deviancy as 'left-wing functionalism', pointing to the legacy of 'social strain' theories.

Now, slightly derogatory terms like 'bolting on' imply some sort of naive or tactical rapprochement, and this is really rather unjust. To balance my discussion, it is necessary to remember that this is rather a purist's critique, and that it might be unjust to insist that 'applied' pieces constantly foreground the theoretical issues involved in attempting such mergers. There is a danger here, and elsewhere, of attacking sociology on the grounds that it is not a particularly specialist kind of philosophy.

## Social poetics

If the kinds of alternative commentaries recommended were evidently superior to the ways in which sociologists have proceeded, we could simply switch to them. However, I find the alternatives based on the 'textual' metaphor to be extremely variable and often to exhibit the same kinds of problems we have just discussed.

Postmodernists, for example, suggests Jameson (1992), simply turn their backs on the problems of 'applying' theories to actual concrete events. Not for them the problems of relating general theories of economic bases to accounts of cultural superstructures, for example, as in Marxism. They want to take the temperature of the times without any kind of thermometer, in Jameson's phrase. How is this done in practice? Culture and the economy are just 'fused' by the use of the same general term (postmodernism) to describe their alleged central characteristics.

Foucault will do as an example to demonstrate another common stylistic characteristic: he writes deliberately so as to let language play, at the expense of conventional 'clarity', to encourage ambiguity and open up poetic meanings, to 'frustrate summary, paraphrase, economical quotation . . . or translation into traditional critical terminology' (White, in Sturrock 1979: 81).

Such poetics have their place, of course, but we are far from any attempts rigorously to discuss concrete complexities as some kind of test for theory. If you read Foucault, Baudrillard (or even recent Bauman or Giddens) from any sort of background in sociology, you will find in them a seemingly arbitrary or frankly tactical use of empirical examples, massive generalisations based on these slender resources, and the cheerful interweaving of all sorts of theoretical resources, from psychology, sociology, history and ethics, for example. This can make for a good read if you enjoy poetics, but of course it makes such work distinctive and unassailable.

Without the usual conventions of arguments or evidence, we are very much in the hands of the poets and their skill in evoking for us their own sensibilities and in involving us in their readings; this has an obvious academic and social consequence: 'discourse . . . [of this kind] . . . becomes impenetrable to any critique based on ideological principles different from [the writer's]' (ibid.).

That doesn't stop such writers making criticisms of their own, of course. To cite (and reverse) Bennett's (1990: 271) discussion of the procedures of literary criticism, poetic endeavours might well allow no readings to be 'validated as finally true', but that doesn't stop them 'allowing that some [approaches] may be disqualified as false, partial, inadequate or incomplete'. Whether this can be done on agreed principles, or whether it all depends on the tastes and judgements of the critic, is open to debate.

## Giddens and structuration

It is possible to find sociological writers who *have* quite explicitly foregrounded these issues. We cannot pursue the details here, but a sketch is offered in passing of some aspects of some of the better-known synthetic moments in social theory – such as Lacan's 'linguistic' re-reading and incorporation of Freud, or Baudrillard's of Marx (both in Chapter 5). Other work can only be noted here, including the marvellously interdisciplinary works of the classical 'critical theorists' (see Held 1980 for a particularly useful account, or Crook 1991), or the much-admired complexities of Simmel (see Frisby 1984, or in a more concrete application Rojek, in Rojek (ed.) 1989). Habermas's own exhaustively synthetic project is well described in McCarthy (1984), among other commentaries, and some implications appear in the Conclusion.

I want to end this chapter with a sketch of one approach which will be well known to sociology students – the 'structuration theory' of Anthony Giddens. Again, this is a huge project, extending over decades, and we can do no more than provide a quick overview here – Craib (1992a) offers a readable discussion (and a list of critical discussions of Giddens's work), and the best single piece by Giddens himself is probably still the chapter in Giddens (1982), or the later essay in Bryant and Jary (1991). The applications of this work in terms of Giddens's analysis of lifestyles in modernity will be pursued later, but the theoretical labour is of primary interest here.

Massive labours to read, comment upon and incorporate a huge range of theoretical literature, including all the French theorists associated with structuralism and poststructuralism, produced classic pieces on each of the main sociological approaches we have discussed here (for example, Giddens 1976, 1979, 1981). A powerful synthetic approach was also developing (or, some would argue, already implicit).

What is interesting about Giddens's approach is that there is no attempt to produce a simple unitary synthesis of the many different pieces in the scheme. To anticipate a term developed in Crook's (1991) critique of postmodernism discussed in Chapter 5, Giddens operates not with a 'monism', a simple single world-producing process (language, or a mode of production), nor even a set of dualisms (the classic oscillations between 'structure' and 'action' beloved of textbook sociology) but with a duality, a structured bifurcation, producing a two-level model of the social.

There is the structural level, which is far more abstract in Giddens than is the case with conventional sociologists (like functionalists). In Giddens (1979: 66), for example, we are talking of a 'set of generative rules and resources' which exists 'virtually', as a kind of set of potentials, rather than being concretely manifested in space and time, a kind of sociological variant of a linguistic system, a *langue*. Such structures are not produced by social subjects of any kind but can be inferred or presupposed from actions and practices, as the enabling 'rules and resources' for such actions and practices.

What is often called 'structure' in sociology, the actual patterns of institutions, is seen as existing at a separate concrete level, and Giddens uses the term 'system' for this level. Social systems are crystallised out of the enabling rules and resources of structures by a particular general type of action – 'structuration'. Because structuration involves a dynamic of its own, the links between (virtual) structures and (concrete) systems are never simple or direct.

Structuration involves a central characteristic of human activity derived from interactionism – a capacity to monitor actions reflexively – permitting a degree of creativity or autonomy in the construction of systems. Structuration also simply presupposes power (in both positive and negative senses, the power to create as well as to prevent or limit), so we can avoid a major criticism of interactionism and begin to incorporate aspects of Marxism or other theories of power. Finally, concreteness, specificity and a certain externality of social life are presupposed in that structuration produces unintended consequences at the systemic level which get reified into 'social facts'.

It is possible even after this very brief account to see the importance of Giddens's work. He offers a glimpse of a solution for sociologists to the endless oscillation between functionalism, Marxism and interactionism for sociologists, a way out of the endless banal calling forth of one to critique and modify the other (a variant of which, in the form of an endless circling between 'oppression' and 'resistance' or cultural passivity and activity, affects British cultural studies too, in a famous critique by Morris 1988).

More importantly for our immediate purposes, Giddens offers a way to generate the concrete complexities of social systems and institutions from general social theories which spell out the 'rules and resources'. This offer is located (in Giddens 1979) in a particularly relevant context – those very theories that want to explain social life as 'linguistic', as textual. In this setting, Giddens offers a general critique which appears in a number of specific ways when we proceed to consider textuality as a metaphor later: that 'linguistic' accounts cannot explain the systemic level of social life without some concrete agent (a reader, a viewer) operating in a concrete context. Unfortunately, as we shall see (in Chapter 4, for example, when we look at the work of Roland Barthes), such an agent is often forbidden in advance by the textual metaphor.

Of course, Giddens has his critics in turn (including Craib 1992a, Dallmayr in Giddens 1982, Gane 1983 and McLennan 1988). We shall not pursue them at the general level, although we shall consider more critically Giddens's 'applied' work on modernity and identity. However, we might fairly easily anticipate a common 'technical' theme in these critiques: can a synthesis of this kind really proceed without doing violence to some of the specificity of the positions being synthesised (Gane) or perhaps even just being collected (Craib), or without managing some rather strained categorisations (lumping together 'rules' and 'resources', for example – see Dallmayr)?

The latter point is also taken up very effectively by Thompson (1984) in a sympathetic critique (in Chapter 3 we examine Thompson's own developments from Giddens's position). The notion of a 'rule' is far too general in even the later work (after some sophistications which bring their own problems), and this produces difficulty precisely in the area which we examine here (the generation of the concrete and the complex). One direct consequence is a matter we discuss in Chapter 7 – a very abstract discussion of individual choice at the expense of an analysis of actual social constraints (which is forbidden by the excessively general focus, as we shall see).

Nevertheless, any position can be criticised on these technical, and possibly purist, grounds, and at least Giddens's work serves to offer a rebuke to those who seem to think that sociologists are simply unable to reply to criticisms of their general theories, and that this naively warrants the wholesale abandonment of sociology and the adoption of a new 'root metaphor'. As we implied, Thompson wants to develop these arguments still further.

Finally, Giddens's work points to, even if it does not solve to everyone's satisfaction, the major problem with alternative theories and metaphors too, we shall suggest: their own inability to produce or account for concrete social practices from general theories, except by glosses, 'bolt-ons' or literary tropes.

# 2

# The politics of cultural autonomy

The issue of the extent of cultural autonomy can now be approached as a topic in its own right, so to speak. For many of us, cultural activities do seem to be relatively free of social constraint. Much cultural analysis focuses on the creative or autonomous aspects of cultural production – the ideas that film directors had and their struggles to realise them in the studio system, say. However, there may well be hidden constraints too, and we need more than a simple voluntarism or idealism to tease them out, as most of the analysts I review in this book would argue. The debate arises when we discuss the best way to do this. In this chapter, I shall be reviewing some 'materialist' or sociological work again, with a particular interest in the politics of cultural autonomy, before turning to later writers in subsequent chapters.

## CREATIVITY AND SOCIAL CONTEXTS

This debate has already arisen when we were discussing the social or economic or political dimensions of culture in the last chapter, or when we raised the issue of subcultural resistance. We noticed a pattern of innovation and continuity in terms of the 'parent' or 'mainstream' culture, for example. Although we did not explore it in Chapter 1, there is some famous work on seeing youth subcultures as inversions of mainstream values: rebellious youth simply reverses the official values of homes or schools and stresses untidiness, lack of punctuality, impoliteness, minor lawbreaking, long hair (if parents wear it short), cannabis (if parents use alcohol), and so on.

Other youthful possibilities include parodying official conventions, as in the provocatively excessive neatness of British mods (see Hebdige 1979). It is possible to conform to official values ironically, of course, or even to push them to absurdity in satire.

On a more individualistic level, there are terms like *bricolage*, used to explain cultural change in Lévi-Strauss's work. Briefly, the *bricoleur* is a kind of cultural odd-job man who manages to stitch together cultural fragments in a novel way. New myths are created in this way, from pieces of older mythical material, old themes and stories, and various cultural legacies. The talent of the *bricoleur* consists in working contemporary references into this material, and occasionally perceiving that material that lies to hand can be pressed into service – that honey can be made to stand for important bodily fluids, for example, or that cooking can become a symbolic activity, in Lévi-Strauss's examples.

These cultural possibilities – bricolage, parody and irony – are sometimes taken to be the characteristic forms of a 'postmodern sensibility' (Newman, in Appignanesi 1989, wants to add allegory and simulation). They certainly display very interesting ambiguities. On the one hand, they represent a form of cultural innovation that breaks down the barriers between separated spheres (especially high and low culture, as we shall see), and they do seem to display a fashionable disinterest in authorship (the author or director as odd-job man). On the other hand, many sociological analysts find them rather conservative, involving the rearrangement of existing cultural fragments, their mere inversion, rather than any sort of decisive break, critique or departure. There is a deep dependency on mainstream cultures to provide the fragments or the lifestyles about which youth can become ironic, so to speak.

This seems to restore some kind of sociological analysis again, of course – postmodern sensibility becomes a kind of cultural deviance, different from mainstream culture, but still explicable. Cultural events and phenomena can still be analysed usefully as representing some social, economic or political practices or forces. The rest of the chapter pursues this debate: how important is it still to know something of the social context or origins of a film or novel, for example, or to try and trace some coded political interests in the ways in which characters are depicted or narratives developed? Can the social origins of an idea or practice still be traced through processes like inversion or parody or inter-textual reference that we have mentioned, and, even if so, are those origins still active, so to speak, in the determination of meaning?

## THE SHIFT FROM REPRESENTATION TO SIGNIFICATION

In this section, we can begin to explore some possibilities via a discussion of some concrete examples. One theme which emerges is the role of the specialist in moving cultural forms towards a greater level of autonomy from the social contexts in which they might have originated. Again, it is important to resist too easy an account – specialists themselves have ties with social contexts, possibly even unconscious ones, and, of course, sometimes they work in the interests of dominant groups precisely to limit politically or commercially dangerous forms of autonomy.

### Media studies

The peculiar hold which Marxist traditions have tended to exert in modern British media studies has led to much work operating on the basis that the main task for critical analysis is to expose ideological representations of various aspects of social reality. These representations are crucial in an underlying and continuing hegemonic struggle, it has been argued.

Many students will have become familiar with work which draws attention to the ways in which women or black people are (mis)represented in popular TV programmes (classically in soap operas or television advertisements, but also in sports coverage, news and current affairs, comedy programmes, and so on), and will have considered how these representations arise from the sexist and racist values of dominant groups. These values, and the underlying struggles to maintain a dominant place for them, *can* still be detected, it is claimed, behind all the specific artistic, commercial and technical values and processes at work at the more specific levels of the television and film industries. Ideologies have an unconscious effect, in other words, in the very practices of film-making, in the 'spontaneous' decisions to represent criminal characters as black males, or 'natural feelings' by females, or, indeed, in the very (male bourgeois) logic of narrative.

Another important collection of work (for example, Hall, Connell and Curti, in Bennett *et al.* 1981) discusses the ways in which ideological abstractions like 'the nation' are represented in TV programmes or films – as a mystical community of equals 'underneath' all the petty conflicts of everyday life, as a family, as an abstract combination of odd social groups (any groups except classes).

The discussion of 'realism' in film or television (and novels) also tends to centre on the politics of representation, and analysts have focused upon how the concrete ambiguities and contradictions of historical events (strikes or battles, classically) have been smoothed out into simpler representations of heroic individuals, 'good' versus 'evil' forces, and so on.

However, it has become apparent that this interest in what films claim to be representing or depicting or illustrating is no longer sufficient, either to explain the production values of the pieces, or to account for the complex pleasures of the audience watching them. Many recent films, even popular ones, tend not to be 'about' anything specific (at the time of writing, the Coen Brothers' films seem to be particularly mentioned in newspaper critics' versions of this lament). Avant-garde films and TV or video have never been interested in realism, of course, but now many TV advertisements, music videos and cult films have also drifted 'from representation to signification', from a 'documentary' look to a free-wheeling 'artistic', playfully 'experimental' style that exploits the specific technical possibilities raised by film or video, that often refers to other attempts at experiment, and which offers 'personal vision' or 'unfinished' visuals which the audiences can use to find their own meanings.

We are going to explore some examples from both film and television in greater depth in later chapters. As a quick example, Fiske (1989a) suggests that even 'serious' television such as news programmes offers a signifying bonus or excess, on top of the solid representations of reality that are underway. We find even straight anchorpersons offering a form of commentary on the processes of news construction in ways which audiences enjoy: playful interjections by the hosts of lengthy programmes about local election results offer perhaps the most recognisable examples for British viewers.

Of course, generalisations must be avoided. This shift to playful signifying is attracting attention in academic media studies as a current phenomenon, but its novelty is probably a little contrived. However, all cultural phenomena seem to display the potential for internal development, in principle at least. There is often a tendency for practitioners to experiment, to liberate themselves from the burden of realistic representation, a burden imposed in different ways and at different times. Sometimes these experiments are successful, but they usually involve a struggle with 'external' factors (commercial or institutional pressures for example), as we shall see.

## Games and sports

To take another substantive example, games like (British) football or cricket might have had their social origins in early folk festivals or religious ceremonies, and might still represent social functions (or even symbolic class struggle) in the rituals they display – but the rules have long since been codified and developed subsequently in a rational way by bodies of specialists; and it is highly debatable if a knowledge of their social origins helps us to understand play on the field.

Some changes take place in a familiar social context. Sports like American football or modern athletics have undergone change under the influence of rational calculations of how to increase crowd appeal or maximise sponsorship and TV coverage (Whannel 1986). Here, then, the developmental impulse comes from the intervention of specialist professionals operating in a commercial environment and aiming at a mass market.

As a final example, a recent British controversy has arisen over plans to develop a new 'superleague' for Rugby League clubs. In exchange for large amounts of money, and considerable television exposure, those clubs which have been selected to take part will have to meet the needs of televised sport. The fans are worried that this will tear Rugby League away from the very context which gave it its success to date – especially the ties of the clubs to specific localities, towns and working-class traditions. Rugby League clubs have even been asked to merge with local rivals. The game seems set to follow soccer into a commercialised mode (see Critcher's piece, in Waites *et al.* 1982), with highly paid 'stars', a lucrative transfer market, an attempt to ignore local audiences in favour of a mass international televised audience, and so on.

## Culture 'high' and 'low'

'High' culture (or at least its 'progressive' or avant-garde wings) also refuses merely to represent, and instead displays a specialist interest in commenting on, or developing the conventions of, the particular art form, whether this be painting, drama, poetry or architecture. It is still possible to view a painting as a 'documentary', or a building as a simple machine to live in, but a reaction against realism has long been underway. Here the dynamic does not necessarily come from commercial interests, which may even oppose these developments, but from some specialised interest in aesthetics held by practitioners or critics (sometimes combined with a radical politics, as we have seen with surrealism above, but in nearly every case contaminated by suspicions of elitism). For Newman (in Appignanesi 1989) this very elitism, this claim to possess a theory which explains and generates experimental and unpopular forms (of painting or architecture), is at the forefront of populist rebellions against modernism.

As popular culture develops, the same kind of aesthetic impulse, even if not codified so formally, is detectable, some writers have argued, via processes like 'disembedding', as we shall see. People develop tastes in clothing, music or leisure which are no longer tied to the old collective standards and constraints and which go far beyond the simple functional needs to keep warm and well shod. As they become experienced and knowledgeable, practitioners of popular culture can develop their own aesthetic interests and become connoisseurs in their own right (see Tomlinson 1990). Again, though, there is a price to pay for connoisseurship, this time in terms of a vulnerability to the infernal arts of the 'culture industry'. We explore the issue in more depth in later chapters.

## Academic culture

The role of a specialised intellectual interest is perhaps seen best, and certainly closest to home, in the very development of academic subjects (which are branches of culture worthy of study in their own right, as I have been suggesting throughout). No participant or commentator can fail to notice some sort of split between those demanding that academics focus on topics that are 'relevant' or 'vocational', that relate to 'reality', and those voices arguing for some form of autonomy for academic life, for 'pure' science or maths which operate with non-empirical 'objects' and consider non-technological problems, for a theology that roams beyond the immediate exigencies of current doctrine, for a nonfunctional study of English literature, or for studies that have no immediate apparent usefulness (like 'dead languages'), or whatever.

Social sciences can offer the most heated debates, with constant demands to limit sociological theory to immediate policy concerns, to represent those concerns exclusively, as it were, in its concepts. Sociological theory has specialists, a momentum and an agenda of its own, however; indeed, it is possible to see postmodernism itself as the triumph of this specialist interest, a playful pursuit of implications regardless of whether the resulting concepts actually represent any particular empirical 'problem': social theory does not always have to be 'about' something either!

Many British politicians would be very unhappy about this insouciance, of course. The existence of a noticeable conflict over these matters serves to remind us to beware of a simple claim of a unidirectional movement towards autonomy and signification – autonomous cultural activities can also be re-embedded, brought back under the control of various institutional frameworks. Bennett (1990) offers a particularly promising account of the intertwining of critical impulses and disciplinary apparatuses in the modern university, and we shall return to this issue in the Conclusion.

## Weber and the role of intellectuals

Whereas the first chapter discussed Durkheim and Marx, Weber probably offers the clearest emphasis on the role of specialist intellectuals (good summaries are found in, for example, Schroeder 1992). The model here is the analysis of world religions. Briefly, religious systems clearly do have social causes and functions in the senses mentioned by both Marx and Durkheim (that is, they function as ideology to universalise the interests of particular groups, and they offer opportunities to worship society itself in collective rituals), but these functions alone do not fully explain the development of Christianity, to take the most obvious example. That development, especially the crucial one into Protestantism, was produced by a complex combination of factors, including the effects of theologians who pursued rationally some implications of Christian doctrine wherever they led, and however bizarre, stark and uncompromising the consequences. In the course of this pursuit, specific social groups were able, occasionally and variously, to identify their interests with those of the theologians, and this identification played a major part in the social success and diffusion of Protestantism. But this social function alone was never adequate to account fully for its social impact.

Indeed, in a famous irony, stern Puritan disdain for the pleasures and efforts of this world led to the development of an accommodating morality of work and probity as a personal duty (the famous 'work ethic') which played a crucial part in the development of the very worldly and amoral system of capitalism. Here, the congregation plays a major part in softening, compromising or operationalising the stern doctrines of predestination held by the theologians into a more popular version that says, in effect, that hard work on earth gains its reward in heaven.

More generally, the very separation of an autonomous moral sphere is a good example of a much wider process of 'differentiation', as writers like Lash (1988) argue. In Weber, there are ironic consequences again, since such differentiation plays a major part as a kind of escalator or catalyst in the public secularisation of society as the old dominant religious world-view becomes weakened.

Now this is a very quick account of an influential analysis, but it is designed to illustrate the complex possibilities once cultural processes become abstracted from social contexts and 'worked upon' by the sort of specialist intellectuals who have emerged in modern societies.

It is worth pointing out that these abstractions can return, as it were, to be 'applied' in social life: abstraction is never complete in religious thinking, and new, emerging events have to be interpreted to fulfil the main purpose of providing a theodicy (a theory of suffering). Further, religion does not belong only to intellectuals and there can be waves of populist theology which can wrest the initiative away from rational theology. There are also political or administrative factors, since organised churches have to maintain some secular presence, as well as a spiritual one, and this sort of agenda can have an effect. As a result, rather complex combinations and oscillations can occur in the actual content and form of religious belief: here it becomes dominated by charismatic celebrations of the spirit, cults and 'fundamentalism', there the organised churches settle down to an accommodation with the government

41

and become a state religion (see Turner 1991 for an extended discussion).

Studies of leisure and popular culture drawing on the work of Elias have offered a similar sort of account of emergence and complexity via the notion of a 'figuration' as the unit of social life (roughly, a flexible group of people held together by 'mutual orientation'). The approach has produced complex analyses of a range of phenomena, from the emergence of football hooliganism (for example, Dunning *et al.* 1986) to a highly detailed account of the development of modern tastes in cuisine (see Mennell 1985). A similar story of the concrete effects of combinations of social groups (sometimes temporary alliances), individuals and specialist innovators is apparent in these studies too. For a general outline of Elias's work, see Mennell (1992).

There is, of course, more of a debate about these writers than I have had time here to mention. Briefly, in both Weber and Elias, there are hints of a general theory as well as an empirical complexity. This is almost inevitable, given the need to select moments or trends from that complexity, or to 'typify', in Weber's terms. For that reason, Weber could be read as a theorist who uses terms like 'rationalisation' or 'disenchantment' to describe the long-term directions detectable in 'Western' societies, while Elias develops a notion of the long-term trend towards the 'civilisation' of appetites via a growing awareness of the needs and rights of others. Both writers are used as models to exemplify the attempt not to reduce too easily empirical complexity and emergent qualities to those long-term trends.

## STRATEGIC COMMUNICATION

This section follows the story of emergence and autonomy into a subsequent stage. We also shift the focus towards more local contexts. If cultural processes become abstracted and autonomous this does not mean that their social functions are ended (which is an impression you can get from some voluntarists). However, their new attachments to social groups might not be the same as their original ones. Cultural processes and phenomena ('signs' in the broadest sense) find themselves involved in all sorts of 'strategic communication'; for example, in what has been called 'sign wars' (Goldman and Papson 1994). As we have been implying, images, words, music and special objects are connected to strategic interests, by advertisers, salesmen, public relations experts, spokespersons for companies, pressure groups or governments, spin doctors, politicians and pedagogues.

It is not just elites who do this: Goffman, especially, has pointed to the widespread nature of strategic interaction, as we shall see, in discussions of the 'presentation' of the self, but it is convenient to remain with elites for a moment. Elites might be able to practise strategic interaction more effectively and systematically, for one thing. Certain elites might also tend to develop special kinds of strategic communication, such as 'distorted communication', where specific interests are rendered as universal ones (the terms are found and discussed in Habermas 1976). Clearly, religious leaders have to do this, as we have seen; so, classically, do modern politicians who attempt to represent the modern nation state as a community of all citizens while privileging the interests of certain dominant groups. It would be most unreflexive of me not to point to the many criticisms of organised academic life which attempt to enshrine a particular structure of 'judgement', in Bourdieu's phrase, a particular aesthetic as that universal interest which defines a university (Bourdieu 1988).

As has previously been the case, thinking of academic life leads to more concrete possibilities and complications. Strategic action is not always 'wrong', for example. Defenders of academic work might want to argue that strategic communication can be defended as a means to a liberating end, as when pedagogues insist that newcomers subject themselves to power in order to master a new discipline which will eventually empower them in turn. There are those who would also defend their peculiar structures of judgement on the grounds that they are genuinely 'better', in some sense, than popular alternatives, despite their partisan origins in the *haute bourgeoisie*.

Once academic work becomes abstracted and rationalised, there is a sense in which the better argument wins the day. There develops a convention that theories be chosen rationally, regardless of the social origins or functions of the advocate (which is more or less the grounds on which Karl Popper once defended the autonomy and specificity of science). Against this, however, we should set the view that the convention of rational theory choice is a part of the very structure of judgement that we began with, and it still represents an aesthetic, a 'perspective', posing as a universal, but in reality closely tied still to the interests, competencies and skills of one powerful group. Of course, there are also many other 'practical' determinants of theory or topic choice to be negotiated too.

With these complexities in mind, let us explore one radical option – that all communication is strategic communication – and develop our suspicions that an appeal to some apparently universal set of rules or interests, or an apparent tolerance for diversity, might be the most devious kind of strategy of all.

Modern advertising, according to Goldman and Papson (1994), can offer a form of this 'meta' level of communication, as it draws attention to the attempts to manipulate people while offering a product which nevertheless is supposed to appeal somehow: admitting to the power agenda while pushing the commercial agenda, to borrow their terms.

McLaren and Smith (in Giroux *et al.* 1989) have identified a similar two-level strategy in televangelism, where homely identification with the genuine puzzlement and reservations of the viewers, usually about moral concerns, is followed with a claim to 'prime knowledge', nevertheless. This is also the technique in classical (and academic) realism, where conflicting accounts or stories are offered to the reader or viewer in such a way as to deliver him or her, suitably confused or convinced of the academic credibility of the piece, into the interpretative schema of the narrator.

This, then, is the final irony in the movement towards autonomy, at least for postmodernists. There always was a danger of having one's cultural phenomena abstracted and turned into signs in someone else's discourse. To give a fairly trivial personal example, there was the shock for me in seeing a heritage-industry-type simulation of life in Portsmouth Dockyard where my father used to work. An animatronic dummy performed a parody of a skilled trade, and the intention was clearly to domesticate those images and bend them somehow to a congenial public front for the Dockyard, its history and its current redevelopment.

A suspicion of narrow strategic intent now affects all cultures, all claims to speak in a universal interest, however. Baudrillard gives several examples from the bewildering world of political action, where a bomb outrage at a train station, say, can be read as a terrorist act or as a government attempt to implicate rivals in a terrorist act. British readers may be more familiar with the long-running saga of conflict between Prince Charles and the Princess of Wales and the press releases this conflict has generated: is the prince really as eccentric as he seems, or is this image the result of a disinformation campaign waged by the princess? Or is that last possibility an attempt at a cunning smear introduced into public life by the prince trying to show how manipulative his wife is? Or is that in turn really a smear by the princess? We end in a state of 'vertigo' as endless explanations unfold in a circle of mutual incorporation. Any fans of Georges Perec will also note this effect, induced in his novel *53 Days* by countless reinterpretations as cunning strategies of the events related in the first few pages, and Goffman's (1975) Preface demonstrates the possibilities of 'framing', as he offers a series of comments on what he has just written, then comments on those comments – and so on.

## The end of culture?

This sort of vertigo may result in the 'end of culture' or in some form of 'postculture', where people no longer bother, no longer have the confidence or the naiveté to express themselves or be able to suspend scepticism long enough to immerse themselves in a cultural tradition. Sloterdijk's (1984) account of cynicism points out the implications for critique: cynicism or 'enlightened false consciousness', which sets in with any reasonable salary, he reminds us, as the only way to express oneself in a society 'ill with Enlightenment'. A kind of cultural consumerism may be the only option.

Opinions about the worth of such consumerism vary, as we shall see. And there is still some comfort for social critics of the older type, as long as people apply scepticism selectively, to elite spokespersons and their utterances: no one really believes those sincere advertisements, party political broadcasts or PR handouts. Instead a kind of sceptical apathy develops, a 'black hole' in Baudrillard's memorable phrase, into which disappear the most carefully crafted strategic communications.

There might be some sort of continuing dynamic, even here. Scepticism of this deep kind cannot support social life and it has to be brought into some sort of compromise with the commitments and relative certainties required to proceed. We have already seen how religious or political cultures possess the tendency to offer some sort of oscillation between the unresolved tensions of the populist and intellectualised elements they contain. Gellner (1992) uses this kind of argument to explain the persistence of (Islamic) 'fundamentalism' as some kind of alternative to postmodernism. Lane (1985) once identified a similar potential in Bolshevism in 'state socialist societies' in the then Eastern bloc, with the ruling party trying to harness and subdue the revolutionary legacy in the name of some kind of state religion in effect, but having to listen to mass memberships who also had access to a powerful source of critique in that same legacy. Whether even that oscillation is finally ended is by no means clear.

Again close to home, even conventional social theory seems to have failed to disappear. Despite the acute attacks upon its very basis, by postmodernists most recently, but before then by a number of other iconoclasts, sociology seems to persist as an academic subject and to survive in some form or another in institutions which were supposed to be about to enter terminal decline. Obviously, mundane interests have intervened to limit the abstracted, more autonomous theoretical ones. The kind of social theory that persists might be criticised from a 'philosophical' viewpoint as reproducing a number of erroneous claims, or persisting at the expense of an attempted strategic concealment of its flaws, yet it is an instructive example of the power of the mundane elements in cultural activity, close to home. No one lives in an abstracted autonomous cultural sphere: a purely theoretical position offers only a temporary identity.

It is possible that culture more generally might preserve the same kind of oscillations, with swings between commitment and scepticism, melting and solidifying, wandering and settlement (to use some popular metaphors). This is what produces an argument for the more concrete explorations of identity, consumerism and popular culture that feature below. However, whether these oscillations and concrete complexities can be seen as following some general trend is more doubtful.

A consensus seems to have merged among many commentators (for example, Crook *et al.* 1992) that there is a long-term trend towards social differentiation, that an escalation is underway that will tip us over the edge into postmodernism (and postcultures), held back only temporarily by a residual traditionalism. As a counter, there is a hint in some of the views I have just been advancing that implies that social and cultural life *must* oscillate, perhaps even in a law-like way. Such views might depend on some general view of human nature (a 'philosophical anthropo-

46

logy') like the ones we've discussed before, stressing the ultimately untameable, 'excessive' or 'rebellious' nature of human subjectivity, the 'functional needs' of societies, or the fundamentally non-strategic, non-distorted nature of the 'lifeworld' or the 'ideal speech act' in Habermas's work (discussed below).

Less 'philosophical' accounts might wish to connect oscillations with trade cycles (periods of affluence that alternate with periods of depression and bring with them periods of social change) or other economic trends: the move towards 'late capitalism', for example, in Jameson's (1992) hands. There are even attempts to connect cultural developments with chronological cycles (as in the idea of *fin-de-siècle* or a cultural variant of millenarianism). The intention in what follows is to remain agnostic about all of these for now, for reasons which will become clear when we discuss in more detail the current doubts about general theories.

## CULTURE AS TEXT

This metaphor engages our interest in particular, as the Introduction explained. It has become a power in recent debates about culture, both 'high' and 'low', and the implications need to be spelled out initially here. The debate crystallises several of the issues we have been discussing so far in this chapter.

When discussing 'sign wars', for example, the text-like nature of popular culture was apparent: advertisers and the other specialists were immersing fragments of cultures, abstracted signs, in new texts, new narratives or stories (including quite fragmented and unfinished ones). Cultural objects and practices become valued for their ability to yield signs of this kind, as Baudrillard argues (see Chapter 5), and the bases of former evaluations disappear. Baudrillard's discussion of simulation takes this further and argues that those texts are now so widespread in our society that they have become attached to all objects: so firmly attached, indeed, as to be fused with them inseparably. It is no longer possible to view, say, the Taj Mahal or the Grand Canyon without thinking of those objects and one's response in terms of the texts about them that one has read or viewed – tourist brochures, films, novels, other people's photographs, press stories, television advertisements, popular histories of the British Empire, and so on. The gap between any 'spontaneous', 'authentic', 'naive' or 'shocked' reactions and the intrusion of those texts with their comforting glosses is rapidly vanishing if it has not disappeared already. In this sense, we have a society of signs, a culture of texts.

You might be thinking at this point that it is always possible to resist these pre-supplied meanings and manage your own 'authentic' ones, but this is not so easy to establish. One tradition in media studies, known as 'positioning theory', suggests that the audience is powerless in the face of a compelling narrative, a simple victim of the text, so to speak. At its deepest, this approach posits that texts actually constitute subjects in the first place, provide them with the very ideas, taste and opinions they think of as unique to them, as we have hinted.

Some unpredictable, even bizarre, readings of individual films or tourist venues do arise. But what is the source of this unpredictable reading? The apparently individual subjectivity of the readers which helps them to resist the attempted positioning of specific texts and subvert them may itself be produced by the effects of other texts (other films or TV programmes, media studies textbooks, critics' reviews, and so on). In other words, audience unpredictability, novelty or resistance is best grasped as an effect of other texts, interacting in unpredictable ways, producing *intertextuality*, rather than as arising from some pure stream of unmediated experience somehow uncontaminated by any popular ideological texts.

This argument applies as a particularly useful corrective, perhaps, to those activist analysts who want to enshrine the cultural experience of oppressed groups as somehow pure and unmediated. There is sometimes a connected argument or assumption that this pure stream of unmediated consciousness is some sort of living legacy from the past, a continuing subterranean source of experience and 'common sense'. Yet this is open to debate. Did the black girls in Mac an Ghaill's study (in Woods and Hammersley 1993) get their critique of the ethnocentricity of English schooling from an unmediated cultural legacy or from the social science texts we know they were reading at their college? Did English 'skinheads' in the 1970s wish to preserve working-class community 'magically' in their cultural rituals because they somehow intuited or experienced directly those threatening social changes going on in London's East End, or did they come across the idea of decline and resistance first in the running themes of the British soap opera *Coronation Street* (to borrow Hebdige's critique)?

This argument, that it is impossible to avoid or 'get outside of' the effects of texts, travels, in much more elegant clothes, in French theory. We shall examine the work of Roland Barthes in much more detail in Chapter 4. To be brief, 'textual activity' is inseparable from thinking, writing, speaking and communicating, and therefore it constitutes culture, the argument goes. It does this not only in general, in principle, but in very concrete and practical terms: as we argued above, the processes of developing culture are seen best not as the unmediated expression of a pure subjective thought, but as the effects of certain textual operations, rules and conventions which emerge in the act of expression, in writing (in a general sense) itself. Leaving aside the specific flavour of Derrida, this kind of argument is common to all of the linguistics-based approaches, dating, in my career, back to Winch's attempt to render social science as a Wittgensteinian 'language game', through ethnomethodology's insistence that concepts like 'social structure' be replaced by a close study of the communicative practices of participants, and thence to the 'linguistic turn' in social theory and the eventual triumph of 'structuralism', 'post-structuralism' and, finally, French postmodernism in cultural studies.

## Hermeneutics

One tradition which we ought to mention here, however briefly, can be summarised by the general name hermeneutics. Very good general accounts of the relevant founding persons, and of contemporary debates, are provided by Palmer (1969) and Thompson (1983, 1984), and we explore the arguments in more depth in Chapter 3.

To be brief, hermeneutics can be defined as beginning as an attempt to recover the subjective meanings of authors of texts (classically, the Bible). Ricoeur was to argue in a famous article (1971) that all human action could be considered as a text, in that all action bore traces of subjective meaning of the actor. In this way, hermeneutics could claim to be some sort of universal social or human science, the model for sociology itself.

This can look similar to the model of textuality in Barthes, which we shall come to shortly, but in classical hermeneutics we are still working with a referential model of the text, as Thompson (1984) explains. Here, there are definitely events outside of the text, a context in which texts are produced (hence the term 'works' for texts, one which is explicitly rejected by Barthes, as we shall see in Chapter 4). Thompson (1984: ch. 5) goes on to explain how texts take on a 'distanciated' or objective existence of their own and thus enter new contexts in the act of reinterpretation, take on new references. These 'external' references are just as important as the purely internal relations between signs in a text.

Barthes comes to see these internal relations as the only ones, as we shall see. He, and other advocates of the textual metaphor, want to make that shift into texts as signification, as having effects of their own. No subject, either individual or collective, is there to be represented. The subject in hermeneutics changes but it never disappears in quite the same way.

It is worth anticipating some other aspects of the debate by mentioning two famous problems associated with hermeneutics. The first might be considered to be the methodological difficulties in analysing cultural events and products while one is still a participant in those cultural events: a number of attempts to try to find an objective way to analyse subjective meaning (including the use of Weberian ideal types) led only to the realisation that there can be no abstract truth or abstract method. Human analysts are inextricably a part of the very phenomena they are trying to analyse. This is one sense which is captured by the phrase 'hermeneutic circle': briefly, you approach a text with some subjective interests to help you decode or read it but find, in the very process of reading, more meanings in the text, and this permits a rethinking of those initial interests. A trip back to the text with the new expanded decoding system finds only that the new apparatus has disclosed (or perhaps constructed or permitted) still more meaning – and so on *ad infinitum*. This interpretative problem remains to haunt all attempts that claim to find a philosophical position which closes interpretation. This alerts us to a scepticism towards foundational concepts developed before postmodernists became fashionable, and we might be able to apply it to their writing too.

Secondly, the mere (!) recovery of subjective meaning in existing texts as the sole goal of a social science sounds very conservative and backward-looking. Thompson likes Ricoeur because he did have a theory of ideology, seeing one major role for actual texts as creating solidarities among social groups via an attempt to close off certain meanings and readings. Habermas was able to suggest that other human interests also existed – in social critique aimed at emancipation, for example. This has led to a whole debate about whether hermeneutics (or similar obsessions with existing texts) can be critical, and whether it remains politically marginal. These problems reappear too, you may notice, in later discussion (not really surprisingly, since I intend to use Habermas's work as one basis of my critique).

## Linguistic imperialism?

'Textual' approaches tend to be iconoclastic towards social science, aiming to criticise them as passé and to rebuke 'scientistic' or empiricist trends, as much as to grasp the cultural phenomena themselves. Critical techniques have included those designed to lay bare the effects of writing strategies in the great works of sociology or anthropology: briefly, the plausibility of social science accounts derives from the same sort of techniques, ultimately, as those deployed by novelists to deliver a sense of understanding and discovery (see Clough 1992 for an excellent demonstration of the critique aimed at ethnography). Since social science accounts must use language, and since many of the 'founding fathers' did not have the same kind of rather purist or specialist stance towards methods and logic, it is not surprising that this sort of criticism has found a target in just about every classic social science.

This iconoclasm, or imperialism as it seemed at times, has been resisted by those wishing to preserve the specifics of their disciplines, and this, of course, is the classic counter to very general theoretical arguments, as we shall see shortly.

There is also a more general strategy to distinguish between two types of formulations of the 'textual' approach. To use different terms (Hall's, in his Introduction to Hall *et al.* 1980), there is widespread acceptance of 'semiology 1', an approach that insists on the importance of linguistic activity in cultural terms, that agrees that the processes of coding social events and practices are very important in grasping modern cultural activity. Yet the fully fledged version ('semiology 2') – the version that says that there is nothing outside of the text, that the coding is all there is – must be resisted.

In Hall's words (based on Barthes's example), it is still necessary to distinguish between real dogs and pictures of dogs in films, since the latter do not actually bite. Strictly speaking, this is a ruse to avoid philosophical critique by invoking 'common sense' at a crucial stage, of course, but it is quite compatible with the argument throughout this book that there are legitimate differences between social participants' perspectives and interests and those of philosophers: one could almost define (and marginalise) a philosopher as someone who is indifferent to the biting qualities of real and filmic dogs. Participants should be allowed to tell their story, though, as Benhabib (1984) argues, specifically against Lyotard.

We shall return to the specifics later, but note for now that the boundary in practice between the two types of semiology proved very unstable, especially for the Gramscians like Hall and his associates. Chapter 5 pursues the issue.

## A retreat from the concrete?

For those who wish to continue with their non-semiological approaches, the common, general, textual nature of cultural phenomena is granted, but there is also a need to preserve specifics: it is still legitimate to ask questions such as: What *kind* of text is the object in question, and what sort of (social) context does it operate in? This kind of response is found, for example, in the attack on the implied relativism of structural approaches to literature that insists that, although both *Hamlet* and an advertising slogan are equally texts in the general sense, there are important qualitative differences and social functions implied in the two pieces which it would be foolish to ignore.

Then there are the differences between texts in another sense: some texts are deliberately constructed to be about other lesser texts, to help us to read these other texts, to fix the meanings of works of literature, TV programmes or even common pursuits like purchasing a new pair of shoes (as in 'lifestyle guides'). These differences too are lost if we are not careful.

Sociological commentary is just such a 'meta-text', and this has been criticised as an attempt to transform everyday life into its special 'deeper' categories, with an often implicit claim that these categories are privileged in some sense. Yet this same process is also apparent in any text that sets out to provide specialised comments on another, including 'philosophical' or 'postmodernist' commentaries. The commentator seems to be left with either accepting that the specialised text is merely another text, a simple offering from an enthusiast, perhaps, the product of a harmless hobby, or trying to reintroduce the issue of justification. The rather strange nature of some postmodernist texts might result from new solutions to these dilemmas, new forms of nonfoundational justification perhaps. Sceptics might be forgiven for suspecting that quite a bit of evasion, gloss, assertion, hyperbole and smuggling (see below) is also apparent.

Of course, philosophers want to participate in social life too, and do so, and can thus be accused of abandoning their own abstracted position on these matters. Baudrillard and Lyotard have been forced to discuss questions of value as their own arguments have led to a seeming support for the commercially inspired 'eclecticism' of modern popular culture (for example, see Lyotard's *Answering the Question: What is postmodernism?*, in Docherty 1993).

It is also always and inevitably paradoxical to assert, in a carefully constructed philosophical text, the relativistic nature of textual activity itself: is Derrida's work to be seen as some kind of text that escapes the features that he finds in others ('metaphysics'), or is it merely another text produced in the same kind of way but claiming to offer a different and better kind of metaphysics? Can we, and should we be invited to, deconstruct deconstructionist texts?

In France, a seminar on the politics of deconstruction apparently led to the development of a whole new Centre for Philosophical Research on the Political (Fraser 1984), and a flurry of papers set out to establish the best Derridean stance on politics (briefly, they ranged from whether deconstruction could be 'applied' to classic Marxist projects of ideology critique and, if so, how, to a later stage of using deconstructionist reflection on the whole process of 'the political' as such).

In both cases, some attempts at running with both hare and hounds were evident. Lofty retreat and reflection upon all political discourses as texts lead to anxiety about being left as a mere spectator of political activity, of navel-gazing while wars rage, social divisions deepen and neo-conservatism triumphs. On the other hand, active political engagement and endorsement raise problems for intellectuals of how to do the 'empirical and normative validation' of politics, in Fraser's terms, how to generate 'good reasons' for choosing political options. Here, advocates of various 'posts' face problems, since they have already argued that no 'foundational' or emancipatory claims for various political projects are coherent – which leaves dogmatism and irrational commitment, or purely local and tactical advantage.

Both would be unthinkable for intellectuals who have spent their lives trying to rise above these mundanities: such intellectuals have the impossible task ahead of them of finding good enough reasons for action that would pass their own specialist and razor-sharp scrutiny. As a result, French intellectuals found themselves in a number of contradictory positions, as commentators like Dews and Merquior (both in Appignanesi 1989) have pointed out. Perhaps this explains a postmodernist version of a 'retreat into art', the 'invasion of philosophy by aesthetic concepts', in Merquior's phrase, which has been noticed in the work of Lyotard in particular.

Geras (1988) points to a quiet smuggling-in of commitments. Fraser echoes Geras in commenting on another strategy, more in evidence at the French Centre, perhaps: endlessly to defer the issue of concrete analysis by replying to specific questions with analysis of discourses as such (offering in reply to criticism a 'discourse of discourses', as Geras puts it). Both critics suggest that these manoeuvrings are best seen as 'temporary waystation[s] on the exodus from Marxism now being travelled by the ... intelligentsia' (Fraser 1984: 154).

## The textual and the figural

Finally, there is one more debate on the textual nature of social life to examine: whether or not texts themselves are being replaced by images or 'figures'. This theme occurs in the work of both Baudrillard and Lyotard (and less explicitly in Eco – see his piece on Disneyland in Docherty 1993) and it has emerged in attempts to describe 'postmodernist sensibility' in Lash (1988). To generalise and simplify, Lash's argument suggests that social life is now presented and received as a series of images or figures which have particular immediate effects on viewers or participants.

The image models itself so closely on the reality it describes that it becomes fused with it (as a re-run of the debates about simulation). There is no room for any interpretation, or, in more elegant language, no distance between the image and reality, and thus no evidence of any signifying or textual work. Even signification collapses as a practice. The signifier becomes fused with its referent, leaving no room for any signifieds, to paraphrase Lash ('the signified', it will be recalled, is the thought or concept that the signifier used to refer to). With 'figurality' (if there is such a word), we have reached rock bottom (or point zero) for any interpretative social science.

Lash uses these arguments to account for developments such as 'mainstream postmodern cinema' (where spectacular effects experiment with the real – horror movies and action/adventure pieces like *Rambo* movies) – and 'transgressive postmodernist cinema' (which can feature non-narrative forms or invite the viewer to adopt a number of viewing positions).

With such examples, we can go on to consider the supposed effects on the audience. Immediate identification with the image seems assumed in the accounts by Baudrillard and Eco. Both stress the detailed reconstruction of reality in such images, the perfection of reconstructions of 1950s America in *The Last Picture Show*, or the clever ways in which Disneyland is so landscaped as to arrange a perfect illusion of being in Tahiti (or whichever pavilion you are visiting), even when you look out of the window. Lash allows slightly more ambiguity and disorientation, especially in 'transgressive postmodern' films. *Blue Velvet* is his example here, with its playful scenes (like the one with the clockwork robin) and its ambiguous positioning of the viewer in the sex and violence scenes (or even more with the problem of seeing Sandy as some kind of sympathetic person). Lash says that these are parts of the effect and are not aimed at making the viewer critically aware of the signifying process itself (unlike, say, French political cinema of the 1960s).

The whole account illustrates nicely the emphasis on surface rather than depth in postmodernist culture for many writers. Yet a number of reservations arose for me while reading these pieces, and I found myself, paradoxically, wanting to defend the 'society as text' metaphor against the 'society as image' one. I kept hearing echoes of an old debate about working-class culture in Britain, for example, that used to suggest that children in that culture thought in terms of pictures rather than words, that they reacted in some immediate emotional way to images without standing back and reflecting or considering implications in depth. One advocate of this approach (Bantock – see his piece in Golby *et al.* 1975) suggested that such children should receive a nonliterate, largely visual education. The postmodernists might be faithfully reproducing, in suitably modernised form, this old bourgeois aesthetic.

There were 'progressive' points to be made about the neglect of the visual and the immediate in this debate, however. Literary forms of analysis are themselves saturated with sets of bourgeois categories and judgements designed to differentiate and exclude. Lash cites Sontag's plea for an end to the dominance of intellectualised academicist analysis as the only way to understand culture, and it is easy to see the strength of this, especially when teaching film studies: an often-reported effect is a loss of spontaneous enjoyment of film. However, Baudrillard, Lyotard, Eco and Lash themselves continue to offer us not figures but discourses, sometimes of a very 'deep' kind requiring considerable mediation and interpretation.

It also seems unimaginable that any reader of a film or visitor to a Disney site could operate exclusively 'on the surface'. The material we reviewed above on the active reader would seem to contradict this possibility, for example. Inter-textuality resists the immediate identification of the sign with the real. The designer or director might try to control this inter-textuality, as Eco and Baudrillard imply, by a very careful attention to detail, for example – but it is uncontrollable as soon as an actual audience enters. They recognise actors they have seen in other movies, they think of other places they have visited and make comparisons, they think of commentaries they have read in the popular press on Disney or the production costs of the latest Spielberg.

Baudrillard, at least, knows the power of this form of inter-textuality when he suggests that the masses have become cynical and weary of political communications directed at them: the infernal arts of the simulators bring their own demise, and the retreat from text to image, if it exists, is a kind of politics of refusal. Yet we do not need to accept either alternative of an audience fascinated by signs or one which totally refuses them. These are abstractions again, and they are no substitute for concrete investigations.

Finally, no one can doubt the pleasures of being able to escape occasionally from the need to interpret and analyse. Many commentators have noticed the growth of leisure activities based on the pleasures of the body, for example, and any participant in an absorbing activity can testify to the delights of just being able to switch off and take part. The suspension of analysis or disbelief is crucial to any viewer of film or opera, for that matter, and so it can hardly be unknown to the highest of the bourgeoisie. Yet as Rojek's (1993) analysis shows, escape activities are heavily surrounded by the texts of the tourist industry, and, indeed, depend on them to a considerable extent.

## Textual metaphors and the politics of everyday life

Although we may not be among those privileged to have access to debates about the soul and future direction of socialism in Europe, it is possible to empathise with some of these debates, I hope, when considering the routine activities in which we are engaged as participants. In routine everyday life, as we move around the university, outside the seminar, we normally encounter strong boundaries between different sorts of texts, and strong contextual elements affecting the interpretation of these texts. In the heavily abstracted and idealised world of the philosophical debate, everyday concerns are suspended temporarily. When one leaves that debate, one can find oneself dealing with issues such as disciplinary hearings involving alleged plagiarism, to take an actual example that consumed a considerable amount of my time recently.

Detecting student plagiarism is, in one sense, a textual activity, involving the interpretation of a written piece and the extent to which it represents the thinking of its author. In the abstract, plagiarised texts might find themselves being discussed in seminars or staff rooms in playful debates about authorship or professionalism, or even in accounts of modern cultural politics (via the activities of the Situationists, as suggested above). I find colleagues are often amused by these debates, and they can display an ironic, self-deprecating or openly critical stance towards their own activities as assessors and writers and towards the ludicrous contradictions of their institutions.

If a student essay becomes the subject of a formal complaint, however, quite a different stance can ensue, as many readers will know: the student is held to be in breach of an important convention, which is apparently so serious a matter that it warrants a careful, semi-judicial inquiry involving some sort of quasi-legalistic framework (instead of an ironic or philosophical one). Consequences for the guilty are severe: they have far more to lose than an argument, and I have seen students denied a degree, forbidden to resit, and even having their records endorsed, which will effectively damn them, should they ever feel like returning to academic life.

If you are ever involved in such inquiries, I suppose you might consider turning to your tutor for help. If he or she had been reading postmodernist writing, one option offered to you might be to pursue an abstract analysis, a deconstruction, of the various conventions involved and how they claim to be universal and plausible while quietly suppressing or glossing particular concepts and interests. If this seems unforgivably marginal and indulgent, as well it might to a desperately worried student, any decision to intervene in some other way would raise for our imaginary postmodernist tutor all those problems of empirical and normative validation we discussed earlier – how could we establish any 'facts' about the essay and its authorship and style, and do these 'facts' have any independent existence outside the discourse which constitutes them? What are the grounds for deciding that what has occurred is 'plagiarism'?

As with decisions about whether or not to support political revolution in France, general philosophical commentary tends not to be very helpful, and a tutor would have to fall back on concealed commitments of various kinds in order to participate at all. Of course, no one could simply think any longer of these commitments as philosophically grounded sound 'foundations'.

At one hearing I attended, it was clear that the issue of interpretation, which so interests us as academic critics and which seems so difficult to resolve, so open to different approaches, was indeed going to be resolved, in a fairly unambiguous way, by four o'clock that afternoon. To be sure, some sort of simplified deconstructionist tactic was permitted to me (acting as prisoner's friend), and I was able to point to some ambiguity in the working definition(s) of plagiarism in student handbooks and in the suspect essay: my finest moment as a defence attorney came when I was even able to suggest that our working definition of plagiarism was itself plagiarised from a neighbouring and more prestigious institution. I thought of, but did not cite, Barthes' dictum that there is no original work anyway.

Inter-textual references, to other famous court scenes in films and TV programmes, were interwoven, occasionally rather embarrassingly, with the performances of all the participants. Reflecting on the matter afterwards, there was also some guilt about this on all sides, unassuaged, in my case at least, by any consideration of the postmodern self as beyond morality.

There were also clear limits to the interpretative activities going on which were 'outside the text'. There were some emergent qualities to the discussion, some developments which were effects of the discourse itself, but we were not proceeding exclusively on the basis of the pursuit of free signification, creative *bricolage*, or some artistic avant-garde exploration of meaning. Our activities were reified. We were limited by the suspect text itself and the way it became treated as some kind of evidence or data: the issue turned in the end on which of only two interpretations would be accepted ('unfortunately naive scholarship' or 'deliberately attempting to represent the work of others as one's own'). We were also limited by the context of the meeting and its social functions (not to pursue Derridean insights about the interplay of *la politique* and *le politique*, but to establish guilt or innocence), and by the relative power and authority of the participants, which rendered the utterances of the student as 'evidence' and those of the Chair as 'a ruling'.

It is relatively easy to think of examples like this, and to rebuke philosophers for their other-worldliness and political disinterest. There is the excellent survey of postmodernism, the textual metaphor and conservative politics in Norris (1992) that keeps a running commentary on the course of the Gulf War as a constant criticism of the excesses of Baudrillard in particular. Baudrillard wrote some articles claiming that the Gulf War would not happen, and then that it had not 'really' happened! What he probably meant, of course, was that we had been saturated with television coverage as a kind of simulation before, during and after the actual events. Norris goes on to trace the source of such absurd excess and political indifference in the whole tradition of work which we are to examine here, and offers a much more technical commentary from a more 'committed' viewpoint and at a more advanced level than I do in this modest introduction.

Perhaps the best example, for me, remains in the crushing comments made by Sivanandan (1990) on the new 'post-Marxist' tendency in Britain to push the metaphor of the text-like nature of everyday life. To paraphrase, you would need to be a very remote and indifferent commentator to want to see the cardboard boxes in which some homeless people of London sleep as an interesting 'text', a witty way to signify poverty.

Yet, Sivanandan's remarks are themselves 'textual', based on a superb rhetorical and committed style. Or a gloss: the very existence of 'Cardboard City' underneath Waterloo Bridge is somehow held to be compelling empirical evidence for those commitments, and Sivanandan is, in effect, daring us to break faith with him as a respected and admired activist, urging us not to give any comfort to political enemies, as much as offering any systematic refutations.

It is certainly possible to feel, with some frequency, the tension between a desire to be engaged in art, music, films and politics and the experience of the social constraints of the everyday reality clearly 'outside'.

How do we cope with these tensions and dilemmas? For some analysts, most people cope with a mixture of nostalgic regret and alienation, or a new playfulness and sense of liberation and creativity as the old responsibilities seem to apply no longer.

This has led, in some British cultural studies, for example, to fairly uncritical celebrations of youth cultures again, this time not so much as 'resistance' but as 'grounded aesthetics' (Willis 1990), or as the product of 'popular cultural capital' (Fiske 1987). The joyous pursuit of the goods on offer in the cultural supermarket, whether they be Madonna videos, surfing equipment or video games, is held up as a genuinely valuable cultural movement, an adequate new way to live in postmodernity.

However, we might want to see this value as added by the splendid writing that surrounds the descriptions in the accounts of these activities by the analysts and which serves to 'talk them up'. We could have here a kind of 'left-wing simulation' process, a mirror of the sinister activities of the culture industry described by Baudrillard in the manner we have discussed above, or, perhaps, the reverse of Sontag's complaint about the always-critical role of analysis. This time, the cultural studies professor 'textualises' everyday activities, with serious emancipatory intentions, no doubt, and fuses those textual manipulations with the activity itself.

This can lead to a kind of academic hyperreality where it is no longer possible to distinguish the interpretation from the real, and the account in the relevant chapter is somehow better than the activity itself. As participants read these accounts, or perhaps discuss them with the analysts, Baudrillard's 'implosion' could well take place between the 'spontaneous' meaning for the naive participant and the professorial gloss: perhaps this is why the semiotic analysis fits so seamlessly the ethnographic data in something like Willis's work?

The search for some resolution beyond the tactical accommodation to cultural 'McDonaldisation' persists in some 'serious' quarters, though. Habermas is one famous opponent of French postmodernism who wants to preserve some genuinely universal cultural and political interest beyond the contingencies of modern culture. As we shall see, this involves him in trying to postulate some 'ideal speech act' as a kind of referent or standard against which to judge actual distorted or strategic forms of communication. In this 'genuine' form of communication, the main activity is to question the claims to legitimacy of actual utterances or cultural activities, and, classically, doubts can be raised by any participant about the truth, sincerity or social appropriateness of any such claim.

This is, if you like, what 'real', unconstrained, undistorted communication would consist of, and, although it is an ideal, it can always be used tactically (which is what I think Habermas means when he says it can be 'asserted counterfactually') to judge the legitimacy of any actual communication – say, to evaluate the extent to which video games really do allow the player to 'participate', 'author' his or her actions, 'communicate' with the machine or with the software designers. Luckily, this sort of potential, to construct at any moment a challenge to legitimacy, is inherent in human language itself, and this helps Habermas to ground his analysis in a revived set of universal interests.

This project is still appealing, and it influences much of what follows in this book, but it is difficult to avoid being struck by its resemblance to intellectual or even pedagogic activity, and we can seem close to the old fantasy that the postgraduate philosophy seminar somehow speaks for all of us, and represents Life itself. Whether the undoubted potential for critique could ever be realised and turned into a practical programme of discussion so organised as to mutually 'unblock' all the channels to full participation is in doubt, and those of us who have tried to organise more modest discussions with real, tired, overworked, distracted, drunk, lazy, hostile or cynical persons, while trying to avoid hijack by the more experienced and better organised ones, might be forgiven for having reservations.

There is something too in Lyotard's suspicion that the whole thing could look rather like one of those political re-education sessions where the group turns terroristically on an individual and demands full disclosure, confession, repentance, and there is zero toleration of any evasion, euphemism, gloss or any other opacity: one can see only the powerless submitting to such treatment.

There is also activism, including some varieties of feminism, which has claimed to operate in a way which makes it immune to postmodern scepticism. We shall be discussing these claims below, but they seem to turn on the peculiar combinations of experience, political practice and theory which somehow offer a suitable solution to the dilemmas raised above – by providing us with clear and legitimate criteria to permit choices among theories or cultural and political processes. Whether these criteria avoid foundational claims that want to privilege either 'experience' or 'practice' as activists is much more in doubt, however. As with other kinds of cultural and practical politics that one wants to support, one experiences those tensions again between critique and commitment and perhaps it is not surprising to find a widespread silence and hesitation here, among male critics especially, who do not wish to harm progressive politics and who seek refuge in silence and deferment. In this sense at least, postmodern critique has had a conservative effect, and it is probably staff as well as students who have lost interest in politics.

## CONCLUDING REMARKS

I hope the discussions we have had have shown that there are no simple ways to describe modern cultural practices. Activities which look spontaneous or creative may have ties (perhaps unconscious ones) to the very social contexts from which they appear to want to distance themselves. The trend towards cultural differentiation and the separation of cultural activities, driven by intellectuals and specialists, is by no means as unidirectional as it seems: strong commercial and political interests can be detected which serve to 'embed' these activities once again. As the specific discussions of film or sport indicate, doing concrete analyses of actual examples is going to reveal some of these contradictory possibilities: confident predictions about overall general trends are easier if one stays with the safely abstract.

Widespread instrumentalism or cynicism is, perhaps, an equally

significant mechanism in any moves towards 'postcultures', operating to strip away original contexts of meaning to 'liberate' old
cultural fragments as signs. This is a rather gloomier analysis of
the usual story of the ironic playfulness of youth, however, and
one which offers far less resistance to the culture industry (unless
one sees deep apathy as a form of resistance, as Baudrillard
implies).

These points help us to become sceptical about the textual
metaphor, perhaps. We have pursued some obvious 'political'
issues here, but we return to some more technical ones in what
follows.

The political aspects are still important. No doubt some people
are able to liberate the playful and creative consequences of
cultural forms, but the old constraints have not gone away. More
areas of social life might be available to be lived as a text, but
everyday life is still permeated by the old contexts of inequality
and the play of power in what Foucault calls 'disciplinary technologies'. As a result, 'postculture' can look increasingly like a rather
reduced option, a form of deviance permitted only to those in the
cracks of the social system.

# 3

# Discourse theories and critical cultural analysis

Any critical cultural analysis must incorporate some sort of attention to linguistic analysis, some account of discourse and how it works. The general advantages of doing this have been explained in Chapter 1 – such a move is one way to bring Marxism to bear upon modern cultural activities and processes that have been transformed by linguistic activity (in its broadest sense). To be blunt about this project, using linguistics enables us to pin down the transformations away from the basic context provided by classic Marxist analyses of the mode of production.

## DISCOURSES AND CRITICAL ANALYSIS

In the traditions we are going to examine in this chapter, discourses can be defined as 'socially situated speech', according to Thompson (1984), and it is easy to tease out some pertinent implications from this basic definition. The intention is to rely largely on Thompson (1984) and Macdonell (1986) to guide the discussion. A social situation implies more than one participant, and therefore a social orientation of the speech, some relationship between speaker and listener(s), for example. Naturally, Marxist analysts are especially interested here in the type of relations involved and how the conduct of the discourse influences it – how a power relation is maintained, or how the real interests of the speaker are hidden or represented as universal. As we saw in Chapter 1, other types of analyst might wish to pursue more 'functionalist', integrating, consensual or *nomic* mechanisms in discourses – but it is easy to see how a critical, Marxist agenda might be pursued instead.

The social situation of discourses also helps us to focus on the institutions in which speech takes place, and how their organ-isation distributes power to different participants to join in dis-courses, or be forced to be addressed by them. In the terms of this chapter, organisations like hospitals or even entire education systems embed acts and sequences of communication and the positions and viewpoints permitted in them: 'institutions . . . prompt people to speak . . . and store and distribute the things that are said' (Macdonell 1986: 4).

These concrete embodiments have a history, of course, and it becomes possible to analyse it – how discourses replace each other in public life, for example, and how the institutions in which they are embedded develop and change. This provides another insight for Macdonell: particular discourses bear traces of rival discourses in them, since they are often shaped by the need to oppose earlier ones, or address earlier agendas, or distinguish themselves from earlier or competing contemporaneous ones.

Focusing on discourses as units of study, therefore, seems to promise much progress. Speech (including writing, of course) is not being seen as simply determined by an economic structure or class position, but is granted some autonomy, creativity and effects of its own, including an ability to operate 'between classes', in Macdonell's phrase. On the other hand, linguistics is being combined with critical social investigations instead of being an abstract study of the structural relations between signs.

The latter development explains why early developments were seen as 'poststructuralist', since the whole analysis shifts away from general structures of language and meaning in structuralist linguistics to specific concrete languages or 'sociolects', the actual words and expressions found in concrete texts, rather than some 'grammatical ideal', as Thompson puts it. We can now study 'concrete forms of differing social and institutional practices' rather than 'language', for Macdonell. We have progressed to-wards sociology or Marxism, in other words, compared to the more general change towards the 'new semiology' in Barthes (which we examine in Chapter 4).

Finally, although we have not discussed it at all here, there are the benefits of the much more general 'linguistic turn' in social theory: briefly, studying language in use is more promising in several ways than trying to study individual consciousness if we are interested in the effects of ideology or culture (see Bernstein 1985 on critical theory's variant). However, there is no need to study such language in use formalistically, purely as language, as abstract linguistic rules. Instead, we need to rethink the relation between linguistics and sociology or Marxism.

## Discourses and social classes

The work of some discourse theorists can be connected to Marxism without much additional work, as Macdonell explains. It is quite easy (still within a Marxist problematic for the moment) to see, for example, that social class structures and limits the discourses that commonly occur and that the different social classes use words and expressions differently. Obviously 'political' discourses offer a chance to see this clearly, and two rather elementary empirical experiments are insightful. The first one is discussed in some detail by both the writers we are using as guides.

Pêcheux and his associates asked a small sample of students to read and interpret a particular policy document to reveal how words like 'planning', 'political change', 'radical reform' could be incorporated (rather artificially, I thought) into quite different political 'corpora'. A 'corpus' is a new linguistic term referring to a cluster of language, so to speak. It is 'constituted by a series of discourses ... which are assumed to be "dominated" by stable and homogenous conditions of production' (Thompson 1984: 239; for the original, see Pêcheux 1982).

The terms used in this document permit this kind of ambiguity because they bear traces of past political struggles over them and, as Macdonnell explains, this led Pêcheux *et al.* to suggest that this residual ambiguity could be reactivated, so to speak. This leads to a more optimistic possibility than had been granted in Althusser's famous work on ideological state apparatuses, which stressed the overwhelming power of those apparatuses. Now, those 'hailed' in particular ways by the apparatuses do not have to conform to the identities on offer but can 'counteridentify' (a kind of inversion in our terms – see Chapter 2) or even actively 'disidentify' (a more radical kind of break involving a rejection of the whole mechanism).

The other experiment was carried out using the work of a Marxist linguist from a different tradition, but we can use it to make a similar point. According to Woolfson (1976), Volosinov's work also traces class struggle, and the effects of a partially separate 'sign community', in the 'multiaccentuality' of the sign.

These persist, despite struggles by various ideologues to remove these traces and the contradictions they produce. Woolfson proposed to demonstrate these linguistic struggles and their effects on experience by asking Glasgow Corporation bus crews to read some press reports of political events and record their discussions. Woolfson claims to have found the effects of hegemonic ideology, but also some limited potential resistance, in the critical remarks made by the workers, the way they both used and challenged and reinterpreted the clichés of the reports, and performed a kind of 'counteridentification' by inverting and playing back terms like 'parasites' to refer to ministers instead of workers.

This kind of work, mixed rather curiously with a sociological study of political deviancy, led to some well-known early explorations of the television audience and its ability to resist or even oppose the 'codings' found in news or 'current affairs' programmes (see Harris 1992).

Other linguistic work cannot be absorbed so easily into Marxism, though, and has to be supplemented or reinterpreted. Both Macdonnell and Thompson perform work of this kind on different discourse theorists (including, in Thompson's case, ethnomethodologists and some sociolinguists interested in educational discourses), although Macdonnell favours Althusser and Thompson Habermas to provide different integrating frameworks. One mystery arises for me in this integrative work, in that some obvious sociological studies of social class and language are omitted – those of Bernstein, for example (see Atkinson 1985 for some clues about how this work too might be subsumed into more general critical concepts).

## Critical linguistics

One study cited by Thompson does make progress in terms of detail, however, compared to the rather preliminary pieces in Pêcheux and Woolfson, which are designed to integrate Marxism with linguistic concepts rather than to do much concrete analysis. Fowler and others (for example, Fowler *et al.*1979) offer intriguing analyses of a number of actual strategic texts (to use the terms we introduced earlier), including materials deployed by 'middle management' on a management training course.

The language used orders the peculiar and contradictory social world of the middle manager, Fowler *et al.* argue, preserving a certain tactical ambiguity about their precise roles, for example (by pursuing two kinds of terminology referring separately to 'who is called what', and 'who does what', or by preferring the abstract noun 'management' and using passive verbs instead of nominating precise agents and active verbs). You might find local examples, perhaps, and I have one here which reports that 'Change was welcomed by the Registrar's Department . . .'.

In another example, one very close to my own experience in scores of consultations with staff in various educational organisations, Fowler *et al.* note that 'spatialisation of the ideological problem [of control and its legitimacy] pervades the syntax' (1979: 88) leading to the plethora of management diagrams and charts, or the widespread use of the 'line-management' metaphor to describe who reports to whom exactly. Such apparently harmless obsessions help to conceal the real issues of where decisions are taken and by whom.

The chapter goes on to list various techniques found in writing and speech to represent 'management' as a benevolent group who happen to have emerged to fulfil vital abstract functions – pronouns like 'we' are preferred to 'they'; 'modal verbs' like 'can' or 'think' (as in 'We think we can grow our college in the future', to take another local example) give a nice ambiguity to the issue of whose permission has been sought, and whether or not decisions have actually been taken yet. Various 'distancing devices' (like 'that would be difficult if . . .') or 'stalling devices' (including the very fashionable slight stutter at the start of spoken replies) both give the speaker time to think and create an impression that 'an extra amount of editing was applied by the speaker to the bit of speech that follows' (1979: 92), and, one might add, it alludes to an upper-class upbringing or participation in elite schooling, in Britain at least.

Detailed analysis follows of the substantial amount of ambiguity that expresses itself in the avoidance of the present tense, for example (endlessly deferred futures or cautious subjunctives are common in my experience): 'linguistic equivocation mirrors the tension of the real situation' (Fowler *et al.* 1979: 92). I also like the process referred to as the 'reclassification' of the 'syntactical problem' in management-speak, especially the way descriptions become activities, so that describing oneself as a manager becomes self-sufficient, a term requiring no further investigation or elaboration, one which takes on a sense of importance and status immediately.

Later chapters examine the ways in which various communication professionals deal with 'awkward facts' or anomalies when they construct press releases or television news programmes. What the authors call 'modal' activities can use indirectness and distance to code power relations, for example, while various 'transformations' can hide or displace agency, objectify events, classify actors in various disputes, and 'raise' or emphasise particular marginal aspects of a story. Very simple linguistic variations are used to perform these transformations: in one example, a story beginning 'South African police shot several black demonstrators today . . .' is transformed into the much more passive and objective version: 'Several black demonstrators were shot today in South Africa . . .'.

Of course, considering television (and film) introduces other possible ways to analyse discourse in this sense, and we have discussed some of the issues about visual representations and cinematic narratives in earlier chapters. We also know of newer work on the television audience as 'active', which raises new possibilities for research in Fowlerian critical linguistics. Do the actual readers of middle-management texts or organisational diagrams fall under the spell of these techniques, or do they too 'resist' in any of the ways we have described? Is there a growing cynicism among those 'consulted at'? Can we see the emergence of charismatic management seminar styles or documents as a response?

There is also another highly detailed study in Thompson (1984), this time of political discourses associated with Nazism, as analysed by the French theorist Jean Pierre Faye. This one is of special interest methodologically speaking as well as substantively, and, while re-reading it recently, I found many implications to pursue beyond the immediate ones for Nazism. Faye compares very favourably with the well-known studies of Thatcherism in British cultural studies (in Hall 1988, for example), and offers a much more rigorous theoretical structure and one which demonstrates a clearer grasp of the connections between political narratives and actual events. One can also compare Faye's approach with the similar-looking 'topographical' analysis of Disneyland in Marin (1977) (to which we shall return in the last chapter).

Faye offers an analysis of the complex and developing narratives used to consolidate the power of the various groups in German politics in the emergence of Nazism. The narratives develop in response both to the raw materials available and to external events. The linguistic raw materials include various sets of terms used in political oppositions (such as 'conservative' and 'revolutionary', or *völkisch* and 'Semite'). Linguistic practices available to the developers of narratives include transformations and weavings of these terms, so that Hitler is able to label himself as a 'conservative revolutionary' and claim the middle ground, or Goebbels is able to identify the narrow interests of the far right with some sort of mass sentiment.

As narratives change and develop, they influence actual events. One example concerns the Nazi 'economic miracle' engineered by Schacht as President of the *Reichsbank* (Thompson 1984: 223–4). The spoken discourse embraced by Schacht apparently stressed the virtues of personal constraint and savings as a source of recovery, while his actual practice involved secretly channelling large sums of money to the armaments industry. This could be glossed as expenditure on 'public welfare' eventually. Such glosses permitted this expenditure, which was a real element in the economic recovery of Germany, of course, and one of the main causes of the subsequent war. In this way, 'texts' do not just exist in some ahistorical way, as a universal feature of human life, but are located in and transmitted along 'lines of force', in Thompson's phrase (1984: 231).

## Thompson and 'depth hermeneutics'

Thompson's own position develops out of these detailed readings and critiques, and from his own earlier (1983) work, which centred largely on Ricoeur and Habermas. His position is of particular interest to us since it offers a firm rejection of the notion that social life is best studied as a variant of linguistic behaviour, and it goes on to develop a thoroughly sociological or materialist account, based on an extension of Giddens with liberal helpings of Habermas.

The problems with linguistic approaches can be sketched by reconsidering work like that of Fowler *et al*. Although it is insightful (and even rather amusing or rather useful in helping sceptics to perform exposés of current managerial practices), it is very abstract. The grammar of the sentences is the major focus, rather than the contents themselves. As we have seen before, content, a social context, a position of power and domination are smuggled in, so to speak, with the chosen example of management-speak. We know the context already, as indeed we do with the example developed by Faye (or, for that matter, those analyses of advertising developed by Barthes). The same combination of an implicit context and a focus on a specific linguistic feature (grammar, syntax, narrative or semiotic for the 'structuralist' examples) affects much of the work we have reviewed so far.

What results is a kind of partial methodology – the specific linguistic features somehow generate the effects of the examples without any further analysis (or with only limited analysis in the better examples). Thus 'modalisation', or whatever, is implicit in the power relations of management, narrative explains the acceptability and thus the rise of the Nazis, albeit in a very complex manner.

We can anticipate a little and invite readers to consider whether or not Barthes or the postmodernists operate in the same way, this time with largely (post)structuralist linguistic terms. As a clue, Thompson (1983) argues that the formal split between connotation and denotation in Barthes' analyses of modern myths (discussed in the next chapter) is not sufficient on its own to explain the persistence of concrete ideologies, while our own later chapters consider whether the mere flourishing of terms like 'intertextuality' is sufficient as an instant analysis of actual films or videos. There is usually an implicit social theory lurking somewhere in these exercises, of course.

Thompson (1984) suggests that we need a far more explicit analysis both of discourse and of social structure if we are to undertake a critical analysis of ideology (whether postmodernists have abandoned this project altogether is something we shall discuss). His own model involves a further development (after a critique) of Giddens's 'structuration' approach which we outlined briefly in Chapter 1. It seems we now need to develop a three-fold model of everything to go beyond Giddens's radical dualities, and we need much more concrete analytical tools to specify the effects of social structures in particular.

Thus Thompson offers us a three-fold model of the social system with the levels of 'action' and 'social structure' in Giddens supplemented by a definite level of social institutions. Giddens's split between 'virtual' and 'systemic' dimensions is replaced by a more concrete division at each level. Thus we have actions as both reflexively monitored general flows of activity and as concrete actual action-events, institutions as both 'specific' (for example, the University of London) and 'sedimented' ('the university system as such'), and social structures as both the elements necessary for any social life (a production system) and specific social formations (capitalist production) (Thompson 1984: 129).

Power is still built into the model, and takes different forms at each of the three main stages: an ability to act (at the level of action), a capacity to act (institutional level), the conditions which limit the range of institutional variations (structural level). These specific types of power replace the Giddens notion of rules and resources, which, we have already argued (Chapter 1), are too general and too dependent on Giddens's own root metaphor (the use of a language – see Thompson 1984: ch. 4 on Giddens). Here, we reinstate properly specific sociological categories.

Having cleared the ground, we can now see how ideology works, mainly to obscure the relations between the concrete and the general levels of action, institution and structure we described in the penultimate paragraph. It is in the interests of domination (expressed in the 'systematically asymmetrical' conditions for action associated with the class system, but also with race and gender and with rather vaguely specified 'other' forms) to legitimise existing actions, institutions and structures. Dominant groups also dissimulate (conceal or block knowledge of processes or possibilities) and reify (by offering no concrete histories of the structures which exist).

We must pursue our enquiries by analysing these forms of domination at the three levels; and here we can usefully incorporate people like Goffman on the situational specifics of action, or Bourdieu on the institutional contexts (of educational institutions, for example, to pick up one of my favourite topics). Marxism or Gouldner's critical sociology seems to be useful at the structural level. Although this is impressive, one cannot help thinking of the pursuit of the complex (which we have discussed in others) by 'bolting on' additional layers and analyses, however.

We can also analyse discourses. Here, analysis of narratives could be useful (not only as in Faye, but also in Barthes on myth – and, presumably, in some of the examples of ideological narratives and representations we discussed in the previous chapter). Thompson also wants to include critiques of grammatical structure as in Fowler *et al.* (1979) and something that looks rather like what came to be known more fashionably as 'deconstruction' – the interrogation of texts and the exposure of their 'contradictions, . . . inconsistencies, . . . silences and *lapsus*' (Thompson 1984: 137).

Thompson wants to go beyond such 'internal' discursive efforts, though, and to revitalise Ricoeur's 'depth hermeneutics' here (which we met, very briefly, in Chapter 1). This interprets existing discourses in a much less formal 'structural' linguistic manner than some of the alternatives discussed above, and keeps open the possibility of the explanation of discourses (by refusing to stay exclusively inside the text, by going out to the structural and institutional contexts outlined above).

As we saw, this draws upon the production contexts of texts, their socio-historical locations (ibid.: 134) and 'lines of force', and what might be termed the 'social existence' of texts after they have been written. They come to take on an ideological (for example, legitimising) role as when different readings are quietly privileged by dominant groups. Thompson refers again here to the specific report discussed by Pêcheux which we considered above, but we might think of the plagiarism example in the last chapter (where a student essay was rendered as 'evidence' for some judicial interpretation). To take another specific example, a struggle is underway in a local school to organise a debate about opting-out of local government control: one party wants to take a statement of government policy as some 'factual' or 'naturalistic' text apparently without a (party political) history, to structure the necessary meetings with parents as mere 'information sessions' where they can learn about this neutral text, and to manage rival policies as 'outside disruptions' to this impeccably non-political exchange of information.

Finally, Thompson is well aware that analyses of this kind are clearly 'political' themselves. There can be no attempt to pretend that we are doing social science here. Nor can we pretend that a neutral 'philosophical' or historical critique can be allowed to slide over into a political one in the hope that no one notices (not an uncommon development in my experience). Thompson moves on to the ground staked out by Habermas to suggest that the only real way to ground such critical work is in some idea of genuine 'generalisable' or universal interests, (briefly) ones that would be generated if all the participants concerned were able to discuss matters freely and without any external constraint.

As with Habermas, Thompson realises that this is going to look rather an empty and abstract procedure, and that there are going to be real problems in using this sort of procedure to connect to complex actual political situations. Certainly, no theorist can simply expect any political action to follow immediately from the analysis, and, in situations where there are asymmetrical power relations already which would simply prevent any chance of unconstrained discussion, the only option seems to be a rather defensive 'counterfactual assertion', an insistence that there is another way.

However, these issues haunt any such endeavours, and at least we have an explicit discussion. An 'aversion against the universal' in Lyotard, say, pours scorn on the possibility of unconstrained discussions to establish generalisable interests, but that leaves only an abstract and formalistic way to ground analysis – some support for a general pluralism, some attempt to 'fuse' in some unclear way some activities with an indefinable 'différance' or to claim them as alluding to the realm of the sublime, as we shall see.

## FOUCAULT, DISCOURSE/PRACTICE AND DISCIPLINARY TECHNOLOGIES

The problems for critical discourse theory are also focused nicely in the discussion of one of the best-known practitioners – Foucault. Here, Thompson actually offers no sustained discussion (Macdonell does, however), but Foucault's work has been seen as rather uneasily compatible with Marxist interests in the networks of power and domination dispersed throughout society.

Poster sees Foucault as offering an account of a much needed 'mode of information' to complement Marxism's 'mode of production' and to analyse the new 'forms of language experiences that now inhabit our social landscape' (Poster 1984: 167) (including new forms of electronic surveillance and interactions with computers). Foucault is exactly the person to pursue the project at the centre of the work in this chapter – to 'make intelligible a level of analysis consonant with emergent ["linguistic"] forms of social relations' (ibid.: 168). However, as we shall see, these enterprises have other consequences, including the need to abandon much of the usual material on power, ideology, domination by classes, the classical subject, and a good deal more.

We end this chapter with Foucault as a transitional figure, in other words, like Barthes, one who shows some of the less-desirable consequences, for Marxists, of attempting to develop new forms of 'linguistic' analysis. He will also serve as an exponent of 'poststructuralist' writing, which we discussed briefly at the start of this chapter. To borrow from Poster's discussion again, we can define this approach as offering readings that insist on the preservation of differences or discontinuities (between the past and the present, for example, or between different processes at work at the same time).

This leads, in turn, to a reflexive awareness of the way in which conventional readings (including Marxist or Freudian ones) impose unities and smooth out differences. Poststructuralists are sceptical about what might be seen as the politics of such orthodox readings which claim to act in the name of some universal reason or subject but which find themselves complicit in new forms of domination. Referring to Marxism, in Poster's work this leads to a number of problems, including intellectual elitism, the privileging of the claims of the proletariat over those of other equally oppressed groups, and an unfortunate alliance with the very forms of dominating reason (like liberalism) that were allegedly transcended (Poster 1984: esp. ch. 2).

Foucault's own attempts to avoid these dominating readings are not always successful, argues Poster, especially when he refuses to account for the specific positions, contexts and politics of his own work – a refusal of the function of author is no real substitute for such analysis. However, there is an attempt to develop a suitable style of analysis which keeps to poststructuralist tenets, and the development of suitable concepts, especially 'discourse/practice' as the unit of analysis rather than some essentialist category like 'man' or 'mode of production'. This partly explains the strange and frustrating nature of Foucault's descriptions too, as a number of commentators suggest (for example, White, in Sturrock 1979, to whom we have referred already).

With those warnings in mind, let us begin with a look at some attempts to borrow Foucauldian analysis for a more general Marxist project. He has been seen quite frequently as providing the means to both concretise and 'elaborate' the basic Gramscian concept of 'hegemony' in British 'cultural studies', for example, to  extend and modernise such analysis, and to fight off the problems that came to attach themselves to Marxism after the early attacks by postmodernism (see Harris 1992 for some examples).

In one of the clearest and most readable cases, Hargreaves (1986) uses Foucauldian themes to explore the ways in which discourses about sport, fitness and athletics, and their organisation can be seen as 'disciplinary technologies' designed to enforce some suspect concept of a 'normal person' in a peculiarly contemporary manner – by persuading people to regulate, manipulate and police their own bodies in a revisited version of the Protestant work ethic.

This example, apart from giving us all good reasons never to visit the sports centre again, gives some idea of the tremendous detail of description of the mechanisms in Foucauldian analysis to which we return below. Yet there are problems in such 'elaborated Gramscianism', as a former exponent later came to realise. Bennett (1990: 246) argues that 'the theoretical assumptions from which Foucault and Gramsci proceed are so sharply contrastive as to belie any significant points of contact', and goes on to list the main differences: Foucault abandons the 'ideology/truth' problematic of Gramsci (and, one might add, the purely negative prohibitory or 'juridical' concept of power), advocates a 'grid' of power relations as fundamental to social life, rather than the 'State/civil society couplet', denies the possibility of a 'unified source of opposition' as opposed to the Gramscian 'project of counter-hegemony', and so on. For Bennett, Foucault does share with Gramscianism the need to attend to concrete detail, however, although even here one might still entertain doubts about whether the point of the detail is to confirm a (very flexible) concept of hegemony, or to protect difference and deny totalisations.

No one discusses what might be called 'local domination' in quite the same specific way as does Foucault, but then his objects of study provide wonderful levels of detail themselves, and perhaps the credit should really go to the designers of the disciplinary technologies and apparatuses in the first place, and the records they have left of the principles they have used. We can illustrate the range of the approach with reference to the example of prisons and punishment. The other main 'applied' example – sexuality– appears briefly in our discussions of sexual identity in later chapters.

Bentham might have used dubious abstractions in his general theory, but he displayed a wealth of detailed planning and insight in his plans for a rational prison system. *Panopticon* was a system designed to keep every prisoner under individual surveillance and control from a central position (which accounts for the characteristic star shape of some of the older British prisons like Pentonville), and to offer detailed ways to modify and shape their behaviour, including maximum opportunities to repent in isolation, and a system of providing mattresses graded in thickness and comfort and awarded according to progress made towards repentance and reform. Embedding indeed!

In a way which inevitably evokes later work by Goffman on 'total institutions', all creature comforts were administered in this close 'payment by results' manner in order to shape the behaviour (and the intentions) of prisoners towards the desired end, and Bentham included detailed costs and procedures to inform the conduct of the administrators of the system. The whole system is a triumph of bourgeois rationality, as good as any in Weber's work on the Protestant ethic, and, of course, a triumphant demonstration of Bentham's utilitarianism.

Foucault argues that such technologies did not appear as an obvious alternative to the earlier system, nor is there a tight link to social evolution or to changes in the mode of production. Instead, we have the emergence of a more general discourse/practice in its own right, so to speak, one which appeared in other areas of social life too. This discourse/practice not only reflects conceptions of punishment; it activates them, calls them into being, generates the actual prisoners and regimes it describes. Finally, we are to see these developments as perfectly rational in their own terms, with obvious critical implications for our own systems of discipline and punishment – perhaps these are equally historically relative, equally dependent on a discourse/practice that appears normal to us.

Bentham was also an educational reformer, and he produced plans for a rational teaching system, based on a number of precedents and other people's systems, but again developed to an amazingly detailed extent. In *Chrestomathia* Bentham proposes a thoroughgoing simplification and rationalisation of school subjects, for example, as well as detailed designs for a rational teaching scheme involving the older pupils teaching the younger ones, with periodic testing and with seating in classes ranked according to merit. The scheme would be more fair and rational than the brutalised and scandalous teaching regimes in existence in Bentham's day (which involved a good deal of flogging, for example) and far more cost-effective.

Nearly two hundred years after this sort of proposal, I have argued elsewhere (Harris 1987b), Bentham's design is coming to fruition in the modern forms of 'individualised teaching', educational technology, and above all in features like modularisation, continuous assessment regimes, and the electronic monitoring of a range of student activities such as attendance at lectures or library use (all of which will be coming to your university soon, if they are not already in place, I predict). These changes were foreshadowed in discussions long ago in establishing early 'distance education' systems like the UK's Open University, I have argued, where again a well-meaning interest in the problems of educating effectively combines perfectly with an interest in cost-effective management.

Other writers have pursued the tracks of *Panopticon* into modern industrial practices, into attempts to manipulate intentions and behaviours in 'just-in-time' regimes, for example (see Sewell and Wilkinson 1992). Thus the labour process becomes more visible in such regimes partly because the drastic reduction of stocks 'reduces the scope for workers to "hide" any defect' (Sewell and Wilkinson 1992: 279), and because 'management must erect a superstructure of surveillance and control which enhances visibility and facilitates the direct and immediate scrutiny of both individual and collective action' (ibid.: 282). Sewell and Wilkinson include 'the impact of teleconferencing on managerial self-discipline' (ibid.: 286) as a further example of a 'mechanism of *Power/Knowledge* which can bring out the minutest distinctions between individuals' (ibid.: 287).

This sort of analysis works perfectly well within Marxism (indeed, I drew upon 'critical theory' in my critique of educational technology rather than Foucault), but Foucault cannot be assimilated entirely, as we have seen. Macdonell (1986) rebukes him for his inconsistency on important issues (such as whether the class system and class struggle do lie behind all the specific cases he examines). Without a consistent position, she argues, we have a rather arbitrary shift of positions from one analysis to the next, and, to pick up on a major problem noticed by other commentators, no real account of organised resistance either.

On the last point, the work of DeCerteau became popular, in cultural studies at least, for offering an account of activities such as 'poaching, tricking, reading, speaking, strolling, shopping, desiring' (see Frow 1990 for a critical discussion) as techniques of resistance to the disciplinary technologies. We have already seen Fiske's development of this kind of argument. Poster (1984) cites additional studies of prison life which provide even more detail and which do include prisoner resistance (including the formation of prisoner subcultures, to make a link with an earlier chapter).

Foucault's innovations include an 'archaeological' method and a form of historical research he calls 'genealogical' (defined succinctly in *Two Lectures* in Foucault 1980, or in Poster 1984). This is a method of using the radical difference of past practices to undermine the rationality of the present, as we have suggested, and neither of these is the kind of rigorously Marxist materialist analysis Macdonell would like, of course. Nor does Foucault's specific analysis of power (or rather power/knowledge couplets) lead to organised Marxist politics, as we have seen, but points instead to more localised struggles to expose the workings of disciplinary technologies and to permit the excluded (prisoners, nurses, patients) to speak. This can look excessively 'pragmatic' or opportunistic to Marxists.

Foucault suggests, as we have seen, that Marxism (and all the other grand theories) are discourses themselves, however. Although intellectuals, in France at least, went along for years with the assumption that the categories of Marxism simply did connect with the real state of affairs, that they represented the real class system, the real mode of production and so on, Foucault withdraws that belief. As we shall see in our discussions in Chapter 5, Marxism seemed much less coherent and plausible, and much less able to defend itself against this new doubt than many people thought. Local analyses of domination began to seem much more plausible than the attempts to link up with wider structures.

Secondly, French Marxism in particular was every bit a disciplinary technology as any bourgeois discourse, partly because Marxists were keen to embrace the title of 'science' in the bourgeois tradition (and to enjoy all the fruits of public recognition, university posts, and so on). Foucault (1980: 85) wants to ask the usual questions:

What types of knowledge do you want to disqualify . . . [by this] demand? Which speaking discoursing subjects – which subjects of experience and knowledge . . . do you then want to 'diminish' . . .? Which theoretical-political *avant-garde* do you want to enthrone?

You can see that this sort of questioning will lead to the familiar accusations that Marxism ignores feminist struggle or non-class political movements. Foucault means to include victims of clinics or prisons too, however, and refers to the disinterest of his Marxist colleagues. The French Communist Party dominated Marxist thought at the time with its own suspect political agenda and its association with tainted Soviet practices (such as using psychiatry to control political dissidents). This sort of work fits my own arguments that British Gramscian Marxism also ended with an uncritical adoption of the disciplinary conventions of the university (although it can be absolved from any involvement in the Gulag, of course).

However, the argument is not all simply critical of Marxism – Foucault himself seems to need to refer to the class system as the final embedding mechanism to explain the precise course of dominant discourse about sexuality, for example, according to Macdonnell, and perhaps to overcome a certain acknowledged lack of integration or 'discontinuity' in his work. We have here the old problem, in other words, of wanting to address the major struggles in society while refusing to provide any compelling theoretical reason to do so.

Why not study any discursive struggle, why not continue to amass further isolated studies of 'subjugated local knowledges' in institutions like local cricket clubs, churches or garden centres? Foucault knows why: it would make his work look 'fragmentary, repetitive and discontinuous', a mere scholarly indulgence, 'a typical affliction of those enamoured of libraries, documents, reference works, dusty tomes, texts that are never read . . . [an addition to the] . . . great warm and tender Freemasonry of useless erudition' (Foucault 1980: 79).

## CONCLUSION

We have reviewed a number of approaches in this chapter which can help us to see the problems and prospects of extending Marxist analysis into the area of modern culture. The attempts involved various linguistic theories designed to analyse 'discourses' in this rather special sense of 'socially located speech'.

Various options were discussed which attempted to deploy and control such analyses, to combine them with materialist (Marxist or critical sociological) analyses of social structures. The attempts have generated work of great interest and some considerable ability to grasp the detail of the practices of cultural or ideological domination.

We have also hinted at a dissatisfaction with this sort of work, though, most specifically via the work of Foucault. He exemplifies best of all in this collection of work the problem, in that to fully grasp the specificity of modern cultural forms of domination a new beginning seems necessary, the deployment of new concepts and new interests. In the next chapter, we shall see another highly influential writer – Roland Barthes – treading the same trail away from Marxist problematics altogether. There is a sense in which we have tested Marxist approaches to destruction in this chapter: it is not so much that we have refuted them decisively, but rather that we have exhausted them, perhaps.

## Forget Marx?

Poster's (1984) commentary on the links between Foucault and Marx begins with a critique of Marx's approach which has become familiar. I came across a similar critique first in the work of Habermas (1972: ch. 2, esp. 33–40, and 1974: chs 1 and 6, for example), in fact, so it might be possible to extend the discussion slightly into his work too. There are serious problems with the labour theory of value, for example, in explaining modern societ-ies. We have outlined the basics in Chapter 1, and many sociology students will be familiar with the usual criticism of Marx's work – that it is 'economic reductionist'. This is not just a political flaw, though, which privileges the politics of class over, say, those of gender. It means that Marx's main explanatory devices and schemas no longer work.

The reasons are not too difficult to spot. Wealth these days is produced in a variety of ways apart from the classic mode of labour producing surplus value in manufacturing industry. There are problems arising from the widespread deployment of ma-chinery which add value in their own right. There are also ways of creating wealth that do not seem to depend any longer on the direct exploitation of labour. A recent scandal in Britain uncovered the astonishing world of currency futures, for example. Banks went into currency markets initially, it seems, to facilitate international trade, as a service or supplement to industry, and, of course, bought currencies for the future in anticipation of demand from traders. That function would cause few problems for Marxist analysis – but banks then began to realise that they could make a great deal of money by speculating in foreign currencies as an activity in its own right, by buying currency futures at the current price in the expectation that those prices would rise. We know from the Barings Bank scandal that the sums of money involved ran into hundreds of millions, possibly even billions of pounds, far outweighing as a source of wealth the 'normal' service functions of the banks.

If the exploitation of labour is no longer central to capitalism, neither can be an analysis that is based upon it as a central motif. The effort needed to ground and conceal the exploitation system in legal and ideological systems becomes more marginal, possibly (although notions of private property and free trade were well to the fore in the Barings scandal). The classes generated by exploitation need be central no longer, and other forms of division and inequality might emerge: apart from anything else, this leaves bankrupt the Marxist account of the inevitable end of capitalism as the proletariat comes to be aware of itself as an active political agent, a 'class for themselves'.

More technically, the model of domination based on alienation, commodity fetishism or the exploitation of labour ceases to be the main organising concept for the analysis of ideology, of culture or of discourse. We need new models of communication as well. In Poster (1984), Foucault supplies just such a new account of the 'mode of information' as we have seen.

Habermas, somewhat earlier, had already turned elsewhere, to bourgeois (American) sociology, to symbolic interactionism, and later to Parsons. He was able to insist that these writers had correctly identified a separate sphere of human life, an interest in interaction or communication in its own right. This sphere could not be collapsed back into a Marxist interest in 'work' or production, where communication was more instrumental, so to speak, more purposive rational (to borrow Weber), more ideological in classic Marxist terms.

We have seen this tactic before, though, and we know that it seems to stave off one problem, only to raise others. We are left with rather uncomfortable-looking lists, or models of different levels. Above all, we are left with a suspicion that analysts have grasped complexity at the expense of incoherence covered by some of the devices we discussed at the end of Chapter 1 ('bolt-ons', for example, involving the quiet tactical switch into another discourse altogether).

In Habermas, this worry led to a massive effort to synthesise the different approaches. To be terribly brief, he was to argue, at a fairly early stage, for the existence of three separated universal 'interests' which defined the human condition: 'quasi-transcend-ental human interests' in work, interaction and emancipation or critique (as in the famous Appendix to Habermas 1972). Each of the different approaches in social science could be fitted into the scheme as pursuing interests in work or interaction, as we have hinted, leaving critical theory uniquely qualified to pursue the third.

This rather evasive system was to give way to a scheme based on types of communication, however. Communication offers, after an evolutionary process at least, a universal capacity to reflect upon different types of knowledge in different spheres, to think in terms of different sorts of validity for that knowledge, and above all to question the claims to validity of specific utterances and arguments (McCarthy 1984 and Dews 1992 offer much fuller summaries). This system too is highly controversial, and we have hinted at Lyotard's critique already (we shall see his alternative in Chapter 5).

Marxism, and its characteristic interest and critiques, fits into this scheme but it is no longer the dominant approach. Marxism is not just plainly wrong or limited for Habermas, of course – apart from certain philosophical errors, especially the way in which Marx deals with Hegel (see Habermas 1974: ch. 4) – it is partly that in Marx's day the other types of communication were 'clamped' to production and exploitation much more firmly than they were. Habermas leads us back to some of the discussions we have had on culture in (post)modernity here – the spheres of culture have become much more autonomous since the early days of capitalism.

We can link these points to later work on 'embedding'. This would be far too technical and neutral a term to describe the ways in which ideas are connected to social practices for serious Marxists, of course, but it enjoys a certain current popularity. The sort of analysis we have pursued with Thompson's 'depth hermeneutics' or with Foucault represents the high points of attempts to describe how social life is embedded in a general structure of domination.

Many writers now feel that is the wrong level upon which to operate, that general social constraints have become attenuated in complex and pluralistic societies. This is one sense in which culture is now thought to be 'disembedded'. However, there is still lots of work on what might be thought of as more local concrete embeddings, in institutions, in organisations or in discourses, and I have tried to outline some of the more interesting examples. These show considerable variability, but we are still far from the picture of complete drift and disembedding, the playful relativism that some see as characterising social life.

## Forget Foucault?

As we saw with Foucault, however, general theory is not easily left behind, even if we wanted to run the risk of endless repetition and incoherence, and it tends to be smuggled in, especially at the level of choosing examples to analyse in the first place. It should also be said again that none of the alternatives is without problems. The work reviewed here offers some of the clearest recognitions of some of the major problems of analysis. In many ways, those problems have also not been transcended or resolved in the newer approaches, but have been just left aside in a flight from 'seriousness' and the model of the severe and responsible analyst operating with an awareness of a wider political context.

For Baudrillard, for example, all these serious endeavours are passé, and for that matter so is Foucault's whole corpus of work (and Marx's of course). We are simply best forgetting them, since the game has already moved on, away from all 'productivist' theories, designed to create meaning and system. Foucault described the mechanisms of power in tremendous detail, and was right to emphasise its positive side – but his clinging to emancipatory politics, even in the form of a role for intellectuals in 'sapping' disciplinary technologies, is politically and methodologically naive.

Just like Marx, he failed to realise that the critique of power only helps to validate it. Indeed, constant talk about power and constant minute analysis of it are about the only things left holding everything together for Baudrillard – the real system has long ago declined into a mere simulation of power. The painstaking reconstructions of Foucault or Habermas (and others, like Deleuze), and their connections with the real remind Baudrillard of the relation between beautifully produced and detailed pornography and actual sex: pornography does not simply represent actual sex, but informs, initiates or even constructs it.

Constant argument about the productive (as in 'world-producing') role of power/knowledge, discourse, desire, economic production or universal pragmatics is at best a gesture – an 'accumulation against death'. In political terms, fascists were the last to develop such a fascination with power and to try and mobilise it on a total scale, to impose their political will on reality, according to Baudrillard. The implication, of course, is that Foucault and Habermas are conceptual fascists, and like many of Baudrillard's provocations, this is hardly new – both writers have long recognised the dangerous connections between cognitive and real domination (to phrase it in the terms of Adorno's critical theory).

We end, therefore, with Baudrillard promising a philosophical position of great abstraction, able to fit grand theories together, to reconcile, for example, Marx and Nietzsche (see Kroker 1985) and to show the fundamental similarities between thinkers who had thought themselves opposed. Let us just anticipate some of the further discussions in Chapter 5, if only to deny Baudrillard some triumphant 'last word'.

From a participant's point of view, we have also reached absurdity. Here is a great French thinker who can see no differences of any importance between pornography, fascism and Habermas's social theory. Baudrillard's comments seem so unattached and remote as to be pointless, far too clever and innovative to be dispensed with, but irrelevant, simply to be left to one side while the rest of us get on with our lives.

In his interview with Lotringer, Baudrillard shows all his remoteness and brilliance. We discuss his evasiveness in connection with sociology in Chapter 4, and he is apparently equally unconcerned about feminist analysis: 'I consider women to be the absence of desire. It is of little import whether or not that corresponds to real women. It is my conception of "femininity"' (Baudrillard and Lotringer 1987: 95). And what can and should one do with statements like: 'The drama of love is entirely in men, that of charm completely with women' (ibid.: 96)? I know, of course, that we are meant to grasp these generalisations as poetic, but if we play Baudrillard's game back and take them literally we are left with something that really can be safely forgotten.

Baudrillard's interview also contains much insight into the dangers of taking his sort of radical 'coolness' to excess: 'The giddiness I'm talking about ended up taking hold of me . . . I felt I was going totally nuts . . . Dying doesn't do any good. You still have to disappear' (ibid.: 81–2).

Let Lotringer have the last word: 'I wonder if there isn't a kind of "skidding" endemic to theory. When theory manages to complete itself, following its own internal logic, that's when it disappears. Its accomplishment is its abolition' (ibid.: 127).

# 4

# The textual metaphor in Barthes's 'new semiology'

This chapter pursues a different sort of structure from that of the others, and a word of explanation is necessary. Instead of offering a number of short summaries of the work of several main authors, I have chosen to discuss in some detail in this chapter three short essays by one – Roland Barthes – all in the collection Barthes (1977).

I have chosen a more detailed analysis of Barthes's work, because it has been the most influential in introducing 'structuralism' to British students of cultural studies and media studies. As is often the case, the basis for Barthes's status as a major analyst among this readership arises from the inclusion of his work in certain foundational texts.

One key text has been Hebdige (1979). Among other themes in that best-selling book, Hebdige fills in some of the history of British cultural studies developing at the University of Birmingham's Centre for Contemporary Cultural Studies (CCCS). The Centre began life with strong inputs from a kind of committed literary analysis, but had taken a turn towards Marxism and Gramscianism especially (see Harris 1992). Barthes's work seemed to offer a suitable synthesis between a congenial structural linguistics and Marxist analysis, especially in his analyses of current (ideological) myths and their structure (Barthes 1973), and thus offered some sort of immediate affinity with CCCS themes and interests. Some examples from that tradition, showing Barthes's influence, are discussed below.

As an aside, it might be added that other high-status French thinkers had already been grabbed by rival approaches in Britain – Lacan by 'Screen theory', for example, which had launched an attack on CCCS approaches (Coward 1977) – while Althusser's work seemed far too tied to the operations of a strong communist party for the liking of British activists. And there can be no doubt that Barthes is very readable, and that therefore he offers a much more appealing introduction on pedagogic grounds, certainly when compared to Metz, Derrida or Deleuze, say.

For media studies students, a famous Open University course – *Popular Culture (U203)* (Open University 1981) – pursued the same pedagogic approach with the same author (hardly surprisingly, given the strong continuities between CCCS and the OU Popular Culture Group). A central 'block' of *U203* (especially Martin's Unit 13) introduces core concepts that have since become familiar to all media students, gathered from across the range of Barthes's writings – types of signs (iconic and arbitrary), levels of significa-tion (connotation and denotation), codes and their different types (hermeneutic, proiaretic and the rest), narratives and how they work across time and space to deliver particular effects. We discuss how some actual analysis has been based on Barthes's work as we proceed.

When students (mine at least) refer to 'semiology' as an approach to the study of film, youth cultures or recreation, they often seem to mean something like the OU's pedagogical construction based on Barthes's work. It is sometimes hard for them to detect changes in Barthes's work, his own responses to some of the arguments we discuss in Chapter 5 (under the 'crisis of representation', for example). It is convenient to focus attention, therefore, on some short and highly readable pieces which do introduce some of these problems. They also happen to be essays which are often cited in debates about 'postmodern sensibilities' or identities – social and cultural life itself is moving from patterns that look like 'works' to those that look like 'texts'. There are also several rehearsals in these essays of arguments that have become familiar in any account of postmodernism and which we encounter again in Chapter 5 – the refusal of 'depth' or 'centre' to ground readings, for example.

Discussing these pieces helps me pedagogically, to reflect upon textual metaphors again, in other words, and to raise problems of their application to everyday life. Barthes is especially helpful here, of course, even if rather atypical, since he does attempt such applications and does not remain exclusively at the 'philosophical' level. However, 'applications' of this kind are not straightforward, and it is possible to criticise Barthes here for falling between two stools, as we shall see: briefly, when it comes to attaching signs to real referents, so to speak, he refuses both the (philosophical) implications of a 'poststructuralist' analysis and fails to develop an adequate (sociological) account of social practices.

Finally, I am not concerned to judge Barthes specifically here, and thus I do not see any need to be 'fair' to him specifically. I do not intend to offer a summary of Barthes's work before and after the pieces I have chosen; for example, I shall not pursue his answers to the criticisms I shall make. There are excellent summaries of Barthes's work which do this, such as the readable accounts in Martin's unit (Open University 1981), Sturrock (1979) or Culler (1976a), and there are the specific commentaries in other philosophers' works which you will encounter.

I do want to discuss these pieces critically, to encourage a re-reading. Because they are so short and accessible, they are particularly suitable for student readers to practise their own critical readings. Of course, my discussion is more than just a straight review of the three essays, and I have gone beyond a close reading of them in a way which probably does them a little violence. It might well be rather unfair to choose three separate essays and then to look deliberately for incoherence between them. I am aware that I am offering a rather prosaic, perhaps even a nit-picking analysis, rather than the more poetic reading which is sometimes on offer (in Young's collection, for example, which offers a more systematic commentary on Barthes and reminds us that he, like Foucault and Derrida, deliberately plays with words and their meanings, which is bound to appear as inconsistent: 'in Barthes's essay, the word [text] enacts its own meanings, a wandering of signification which is, precisely, text' (Young 1981: 31)).

## BARTHES ON TEXTUALITY

Perhaps the best way to proceed is to begin with a very short summary of each piece. Obviously, this summary is not going to be an entirely innocent one in terms of the critical discussion which is to follow. I hope it is clear where I am also offering comments or asides on my summary as I proceed.

### 'The Death of the Author'

First, the piece offers an uncompromising argument for the 'death' (or redundancy, to use an equally frightening metaphor) of the concept of the author. It begins by noticing the disappearance of the narrator in modern writing . Balzac's *Sarrasine* is the example here, later to be the subject of a much larger piece by Barthes (1975) (the dates refer to different English editions of Barthes's work, and are not reliable as a guide to the actual sequence of the writing). Perhaps something like Martin Amis's *London Fields*, with its switches between different narrators, might be more appropriate an example for the modern reader? The effects of surrealist or Brechtian experimentation are also cited, as steps on the way, so to speak. There is an insistence that even autobiography is not about real life coded in writing but the other way around – for example, Proust reconceptualised his life after or during writing in order to make it a 'work for which his own book is the model' (Barthes 1977: 144). As Sturrock (1979) reminds us, Barthes wrote his own autobiography in the third person.

Secondly, as structuralist linguistics tells us, texts do not express the subjectivity of their authors – they are better thought of as 'fields without origin', 'multi-dimensional spaces', 'tissues of quotations', 'never original' (Barthes 1977: 146). This point applies to all kinds of mundane feelings of 'authorship' as well as actual novel-writing. The inner self that we experience as the 'real us', so to speak, is 'only a ready-formed dictionary' – so life imitates books.

There are no fixed meanings or privileged ones: 'writing ceaselessly posits meaning ceaselessly to evaporate it' (ibid.: 147). We should see the act of writing as 'performative'. As a result, conventional literary criticism, designed to uncover the 'real' meanings of novels, expressed by 'real' authors, is also abolished and that's good, because, in its arrogance, such criticism used to ignore the reader and also selectively overlook the 'phatical' bits of texts (designed to involve the reader).

The reader is the missing term in conventional criticism – the multiplicity of the text is focused in the reader, not the author; the unity of the text is in its destination. '[T]he birth of the reader must be at the cost of the death of the author.' Yet, to raise a point which we shall discuss below, 'the reader' is also an abstraction 'without history, biography, psychology' (ibid.: 148). Really, of course, it could not be otherwise for Barthes: it would be inconsistent to abolish the (actual) author while retaining the (actual) reader.

## 'From Work to Text'

This piece begins with an interesting comment about the effects of a move towards interdisciplinarity 'when the solidarity of the old disciplines breaks down – perhaps even violently' (Barthes 1977: 155). We now have an escalating pattern of change, where the classic 'breaks' (attempts to re-found Marxism, Lacanian Freudianism and structuralism) have relativised our knowledge of the world, and changed our notions of the relations between writers, readers and observers. There will be further changes in the basis of knowledge, a new 'epistemological slide' rather than a break (ibid.). (Althusser had claimed to have found an 'epistemological break' between humanist and structuralist Marxism in Marx himself, a break that inaugurates a new 'scientific' Marxism.)

For Barthes, the new (literary and cultural) analysis will not be a new, tightly ordered discipline, but should be seen as necessarily speculative, employing 'not argumentations but enunciations, "touches", approaches that consent to remain metaphorical' (ibid.: 156), rather than an attempt to read off meaning from a metalanguage. Methodologically, we are told (ibid.: 164):

> the discourse on the Text should itself be nothing other than text, research, textual activity, since the Text ... leaves no language safe outside, nor any subject of the enunciation in position as judge, master, confessor, decoder. The theory of the Text can coincide only with a practice of writing.

We see here one of the ways in which Barthes is shifting to a radical kind of textuality, then, one which 'goes all the way down', as Norris (1992) puts it, and one where Barthes, like Lyotard, heads into a denial of any other criteria by which to judge events or accounts of them. We get to the heart of Barthes's argument when he tries to distinguish 'texts' and 'works'. The distinction is not a matter of location in time or of value or quality. Works might have different qualities among themselves, but this is not the proper topic for a critic: 'there is no difference between "cultured" reading and casual reading in trains' (Barthes 1977: 162). By implication, for Norris, there is also no difference between works in history or economics either.

Works are designed to be consumed with *plaisir* (roughly defined, a rather conformist pleasure delivered by a work, gained from following the narrative to its delivery point and responding as intended to the 'phatical' bits). Works are 'filiated', closely connected with social practices like those in the world of commercial writing, including literary criticism and notions of authorship, ownership, copyright and the law. (This point is made in Foucault's own announcements of the 'death of the author' – collected in Bocock and Thompson 1992.)

By contrast, texts are distinguished by their 'methodological fields' rather than by anything substantially or concretely different about them or their contents. They are performances, 'limit works', existing at the limits of 'enunciation, rationality, readability etc.' (ibid.: 157). Texts are radically symbolic, 'off-centre, without closure' (ibid.: 159), playful, offering *jouissance* (an ecstatic pleasure in language that escapes the devices of the narrative and rejoices in the experience itself, a kind of literary orgasmic release – see Heath's discussion in the introduction to Barthes 1977). Texts help us glimpse a 'social Utopia . . . [a] . . . transparence of linguistic relations if not social ones', a 'space where no language has a hold over any other' (ibid.: 164). Texts operate via 'serial movements of disconnections, overlappings, variations' (ibid.: 158).

Texts are networks (rather than discrete entities or 'organisms' with a history and parentage like works), opening out to readings well outside the author's intentions. Such openness blurs the conventional differences between reading and writing (ibid.: 162). The reader and the text both play with meaning, rather as a musician plays with a score, both to reproduce it and to embellish, to perform. There is here a clear preference for texts, of course, and a way of denying any claims to sufficiency advanced by any mere works (and see the discussion on Lyotard and 'the sublime' in Chapter 5).

### 'Change the Object Itself'

The old critical project, as in Barthes's earlier classic *Mythologies* (Barthes 1973), has to be altered. That earlier work followed an 'inversion model' (common in Marxism, but subsequently attacked by the Althusserians), which saw connoted ideological meanings as a base for the denoted literal meanings of cultural phenomena. In this way the meanings of advertisements, performances, cultural activities of various kinds naturalised capitalist ideology.

As an aside, it is worth looking at some of the pieces in *Mythologies*, perhaps. My personal favourite concerns a very brief analysis of what became known as the 'structure of apology'. At the most specific level, the piece entitled *Operation Margarine* features an analysis of an advertising campaign for margarine which cleverly acknowledges and then incorporates the consumers' perceptions of margarine as an inferior product (modern readers might think of substituting junk food, say, for margarine in order to locate themselves in the politics of the piece).

Apparently, the advertisement began with a 'cry of indignation against margarine: "A mousse? Made with margarine? Unthinkable!"' (Barthes 1973: 42). A narrative then developed which revealed these perceptions as misguided and ill-informed: 'And then one's eyes are opened, one's conscience becomes more pliable . . . The moral at the end is well known: "Here you are, rid of a prejudice which cost you dearly!"' (ibid.). Barthes sees this sort of structure operating in the wider society: 'It is in the same way that the Established Order relieves you of your progressive prejudices' (ibid.). He finds the principles at work with discussing the Army or the Church, for example (ibid.: 41) (and implicates some popular novels in the process):

> [on] the Church: speak with burning zeal about its self-righteousness, the narrow-mindedness of its bigots, indicate that all of this can be murderous, hide none of the weaknesses of the faith. And then, *in extremis*, hint that the letter of the law, however unattractive, is a way to salvation for its very victims, and so justify moral austerity by the saintliness of those whom it crushes (*The Living Room*, by Graham Greene).

This sort of analysis had made Barthes very influential, and perhaps it is easy to see why from the example above: a mundane advertisement is made to yield some concealed truth about capitalism after a skilled and sceptical reading which refuses simply to follow the account of the world on offer, but which imposes its own. Now, to return to 'Change the Object Itself', Barthes feels it is time to move beyond this sort of analysis of mythology as a mystified or an upside-down world, as inversion. This analysis was drawn from themes in the young Marx, but we can now progress to those in the mature Marx (another specific reference to Althusser's project here, Barthes 1977: 169).

Mythology still works in the same way, but we now have a new science of reading it. Also: 'any student can and does denounce the bourgeois or petit bourgeois character of such and such a form' (ibid.: 166). Denunciatory discourse and demystification have been routinised, have become a mere 'stock of phrases', orthodox, even mythological themselves. As a result, properly academic and critical analysis must go further and 'shake the sign' itself, just as French psychology has moved on: that began by listing the symbolic contents of dreams and so on, and 're-inverting' them only to find that being done these days by mere dabblers, the 'psychological vulgate' (ibid.: 167).

The task now is not to reveal latent meanings but to 'fissure' meaning and its representation; not to destroy myths ('myth-oclasm'), but to splinter the smooth connections between signs ('semioclasm'); not to critique just French society but the whole of Western civilisation and its unifying 'regime of meaning' (ibid.). This is a project to dissolve any 'works' back into 'textuality', in other words.

Apart from being made possible by the new methodological work available, this shift is necessary because the signs of advertisements no longer point to products or to political ideologies as simply as they did. The whole world is already playing with signs: 'endlessly deferring their foundations, transforming signifieds into new signifiers, infinitely citing one another' (ibid.: 167–8). The issue now is not one of 'critical decipherment' but of estimating the 'levels of reification of various languages, their phraseological density' (perhaps a reference here to Durkheim on 'moral density'). We have an interest, then, in the extent to which these different 'languages' can appear as fixed, immutable, natural and compelling, as 'works' making claims to be sufficient, to use the terms we developed above.

This is a shift from a more obviously 'denunciatory' stance, with its problems of separating out the error of the myth from the truth of its analysis. In a way, Barthes is anticipating here the failure of the Althusserian project, perhaps, which was the last great attempt to clarify the basis of Marxism's claims to be able to offer a 'science' to help us identify 'ideology' or 'myth' (one of the last great metanarratives in Lyotard's terms).

Myth is still universal in our societies, affecting 'inner speech, newspaper articles . . . political sermons, [running] from the novel to the advertising image (i.e. all *the imaginary*)' (ibid.: 169). We need new concepts to grasp it, not the old ones of sign, signifier, signified, connotation and denotation, but 'citation, reference, stereotype'. We need to offer an 'antidote to myth', and its reifications, languages which are 'airy, light, spaced, open, uncentred, noble and free' (ibid.: 168), a 'new semiology'.

## DISCUSSION

These pieces have been very influential, and they are superbly well written and plausible. In a few brief pages, we have discovered strong arguments for a shift towards textuality as the task of cultural analysis. The (concrete) author (and reader) and the academic study of them as actors in a social environment have disappeared, leaving only texts. Language itself has become more fluid and less concerned with representations of objects or ideological systems, and we cannot study its effects as once we did. This fluidity is now an everyday phenomenon and texts are increasingly replacing works on a global scale, as society itself becomes caught in an endless flux of signification. Disattending to some specifics, for a moment, these essays can be seen as capturing all of the issues we have been discussing, in other words.

Barthes's position still presents several puzzles to the reader, however. Of course, we are not really invited to discuss these pieces too seriously by Barthes himself: he says the discussion is speculative, metaphorical and can only be pursued by a kind of textual strategy, a certain attempt to conjure meaning not in the old plodding, logical manner of empirical science, but by engaging with the metaphors, intertextual references and ambiences of the writing itself. I must confess I have never been very good at this sort of literary reading myself, although I am able sometimes to appreciate it, and even find a kind of academic pleasure in it. Let us refuse this sort of poetic engagement for now, and read the remarks as arguments after all. Let me begin with a few 'phatical' comments of my own, designed to bring in some reservations which you, the reader, may have felt on reading my summaries.

The earlier essay on the 'death of the author' gives us a clue to the shift of object which is taking place in the other pieces. Clearly, it is not real authors who are really dying, but 'the author' as a theoretical object, the thing (or 'function', in Foucault's terms) which is in fact a construct of an old tradition of literary criticism (and of other social practices). Using familiar sociological terminology, we might think of the author as an 'ideal type' used to try and explain the central meanings of a novel, to fix meaning. Much literary criticism tries to construct both author and text in a kind of circular process of interpretation. As objects of criticism, however, neither is a simple empirical object, simply 'real'.

In this sense it is possible for the old concept of the author to disappear or 'die' as new forms of interpretation develop which do not require an author. Barthes is suggesting that the old sense of 'text' can no longer be held either – that we need a new theoretical object. Unfortunately, this new object still shares the same name as the one used in the old interpretation to refer to novels or films, although perhaps giving the name a capital letter ('Text') helps to remind us of the change (although I am not sure this usage is consistent in Barthes's essays). As we shall see, this phenomenon of (theoretical) objects 'disappearing' became even more widespread – the (usual notion of the) 'reader' also disappears (or becomes an abstraction), Barthes tells us, and he hints that so will 'the individual' and, as we shall see, so will 'society'. In the normal world of 'everyday consciousness' this sort of rhetoric can look inexplicable, excessive, even absurd.

All will be well, though, even if a little strange, as long as analysts like Barthes remain with theoretical objects. It is understandable if inexperienced readers still get confused by the use of terms like 'text' or 'author', and think that what is being referred to are actual books or particular writers, but once you get used to the special usage that confusion should evaporate. However, clarity might emerge, only to be followed by doubt: why should analysts develop new theoretical objects like this?

Here, we find several arguments. A strong motive for the change appears to be 'theoretical'. Barthes wants to develop and take part in the new ways of reading, to contribute to the new linguistics and the new semiology. These new developments look exciting and seem to be making real progress towards rigour and explanatory power by pursuing a particular approach which gets beneath empirical variability to the underlying scientific concepts that account for that variability (and Lévi-Strauss's work, which we have discussed in Chapter 1, is also cited by Barthes, in another essay in the collection. Sturrock (1979) further explores the link). Althusser and Lacan at that stage also seemed to be merely extending structuralism, perhaps.

You also get a sense that things have moved on in the academic world and in Barthes's own career, that the old ways of doing things (analysing modern ideologies, for example), are a bit routine, even slightly common and vulgar, as in the references to what 'any student' now does, or to the 'psychoanalytic vulgate'. French psychoanalysis and French Marxism are making new discoveries using new methodologies, partly in order to separate themselves from such vulgarity, and it is time for cultural analysis to join in the exciting new research programmes and do the same. This will be an attractively expanded project not just to demystify myths but to interrogate the very structure and function of signification itself.

All this is understandable, but still rather parochial and academic, perhaps. Why should anyone outside the academy worry about these great shifts in theoretical objects? In England, very few people did, although there was a brief popular controversy over the non-appointment of a prominent advocate of the new reading to a professorial position, and the public got to hear of some of the apparent absurdity of refusing to distinguish between (concrete) texts on the grounds of quality (the lack of any 'difference between "cultured" reading and casual reading in trains': Barthes 1977: 162).

This early appearance of the famous 'collapse of internal differentiation' led to controversy, because journalists, politicians, elderly academics on appointment committees, and several others clearly felt that professors *should* be interested in these everyday mundane matters, in common definitions of objects and interpretative problems, and not in the rather specialised theoretical tasks and objects that Barthes and his followers were proposing to research which apparently intended loftily to ignore them. This rebuke is still likely, of course, and seems to have affected just about all the commentators on this topic: intellectuals, especially in Britain, perhaps, are expected to be engaged with the 'real world' and its objects, as we have seen before.

Methodologically speaking, there is no going back, however. The old goal of offering authoritative, fixed readings is no longer attainable. One sort of reply to accusations of irrelevance is to point to the fundamental flaws in the old attempts to be 'relevant'. This sort of critique became famous later as the attack on the 'emancipatory claims' of orthodox social sciences (discussed in the next chapter), which, after decades of the pursuit of 'relevant' knowledge of how to run welfare states, or to expose the ideo-logical evils of British television (or whatever), simply failed to produce the goods, passed into history, and left the field to accountants, careerist politicians and writers of viewers' guides.

In Barthes's pieces specifically, the enemy is the old literary criticism, which promises to deliver relevant or emancipatory knowledge using the old techniques such as telling the reader about the author as a person in order to explain how the texts can best be understood as the imperfect unfolding of some inner personality. Politicians and journalists (and students) might be grateful for this sort of labour as offering them a quick fix on a complex text, but it will not do for Barthes, as we have seen – not only is the category of the author itself a construct, although this is hidden, it is a particularly uncritical kind of construct 'the epitome of capitalist ideology' (Barthes 1977: 143). It is not even a helpful category, especially since much actual writing in modern narratives deliberately sets out to write from different positions, via the construction of fictional narrators, for example, or the construction of different points of view, or other attempts to hide the author. Of course, the notion of a single author is particularly hard to apply to collectively authored pieces, which clearly includes most movies.

It is simply impossible to escape a focus on textuality, then. There are no 'given' categories outside the textual processes of interpretation and construction, the fixing of meaning by writing. It is naive to think that even autobiographical novels reflect some 'real life' outside the text. To the contrary, someone like Proust never simply puts his life into words but rethinks and retextualises his life in order to make it into 'a work for which his own book was the model' (ibid.: 144). We have here a much expanded version of textuality. Texts are not just those avant-garde ex-plorations which cross generic boundaries or deliberately play with language at the limits of communication: those pieces indic-ate what is now a much more available tendency, so to speak.

## Expanded textuality and disappearance

Let us move in a slightly more technical direction. Barthes makes much of the distinction between 'works' and 'texts', and these distinctions have been used as metaphors to describe the cultural shifts from modernity to postmodernity: the former are much more closed, for example, and offer only a rather conformist and limited form of pleasure in reading them (*plaisir*), while the latter offer more playful pleasures, 'symbolic liberation' less tied to (embedded in) the old social patterns. How useful and coherent is this distinction?

Despite his denials, Barthes could be accused of offering a re-run discussion of the differences between 'high' and 'low' culture, or so it seems to an English eye: artistic objects belonging to the latter have long been despised by the English bourgeoisie for their limited and conformist meanings, their 'two-dimensional' qualities and, of course, their association with 'work', with an impure interest in production and (heaven forbid) making money. Echoes arise too of Bourdieu's discussions of high bourgeois aesthetics which focus on form rather than content to define themselves against the popular taste. The problem is, I suppose, that Barthes never discusses in any detail the referents for his terms, and so it is always possible to suspect connections like these.

Further, and rather confusingly, texts are also something much more mundane and omnipresent, the name for the routine processes by which we make sense of our lives, and the differentiating functions of the term are lost. Indeed, textuality in the expanded sense goes further than this, since texts constitute us as individuals – they are our lives, and nothing is outside them.

The expanded version serves to justify the interest in texts as theoretical objects, then, and to avoid accusations of merely qualitative analysis, since there can be no other objects: the usual notions of 'the author' and 'the reader' are really reified textualisations. They all disappear into the broader category of text. Let us explore this notion further.

Not just the author and the reader but the concrete book or play or whatever itself disappears too: there is no need to allow the mere existence of a physical object like a book or a film to intrude into our theoretical analyses, since meanings clearly flow around, behind and in front of those objects, in unities constituted by readers. Following Barthes, Bennett and Woollacott (1987) identify the influence of both 'production teams' and 'reading formations' as generators of meaning in James Bond films, and neither formation exists in the physical sense in the images captured on the film. They reside elsewhere (in the texts and social formations of the production team and the viewers, in the film posters and publicity), and yet they are crucial. It makes no sense then to confine analytic attention just to the films – the text (or is it work?) as the only object of analysis has disappeared.

Incidentally, Bennett and Woollacott (1987) also pursue some of the other implications we have raised. Briefly, they argue that the Bond movie can no longer be seen, in the spirit of *Mythologies*, as a container for ideology, produced by the interplay of ideological 'codes'. They had themselves offered an analysis of Bond like this in their unit in *U203* (Open University 1981), but had gone on to recognise that a good deal more went on in the text than merely connotation and denotation. The production team themselves had detached the signifier of Bond away from its original function of representing British imperialism and sexism and had developed a more flexible signification process. Now, Bond films cited other Bond films, and offered ironic or parodic elements about the myth of Bond itself, for example. Similarly, the viewers had become more open to these elements and, as the signification process developed over time, were able to read Bond ironically or 'inter-textually' (see Chapter 6 for a further discussion of the 'active viewer'), to find their own pleasures in the Bond texts instead of just having to await those delivered by dubious demonstrations of the superiority of masculinity or 'Englishness'.

Sociologists may be more familiar with the famous announcement of the 'disappearance of the social', in Baudrillard, say (to anticipate some discussions in the next chapter). Smart (1990) summarises this argument as suggesting that, for example, the old conception of societies as contiguous with nation states is radically undermined internally and externally. Internally, 'civil society' or the public sphere 'implodes' as mass media communicate directly with the masses, and they 'respond' in the form of opinion polls or plebiscites. Externally, the autonomy of nation states dissolves as multinational companies and supranational political organisations construct new social networks. The old theoretical objects called 'societies' therefore disappear, sink back, and new ones are required.

There is a problem of reintroducing some kind of foundation again, however, where the underlying textualisation that constitutes all life appears as some sort of privileged concept really at the heart of things. Did it emerge as a concept independently of the textualising practices of the new semiologists? If so, something lies outside the text. If not, the conception must itself be a fixing or reification of textualising practice, no different in principle from the reifications of the old criticism, but quite unable to claim any simple status as a final trump card.

The triumphalist use would need to be supplemented by a proper discussion of the grounds for using it. Instead, the expanded notion of textuality seems to be deployed as a constantly repeated *leitmotif*, as a kind of solemn warning against the tendency to take things too simply or literally. Insisting that 'social life is a text' seems to be a standard gambit to weaken older traditional theoretical categories and then to begin with newer ones. Whether the concept has a practical use at all, beyond the tactical or the rhetorical, is much more debatable, and we would require much more detail on the processes by which the potentially limitless textuality of social life actually becomes realised or 'reified' in actual social practices. How do 'works' arise? Will they continue to arise despite the new free-flowing textuality? What we get for answers to such questions in these Barthes essays seems to involve Marxism after all, via coded references to Althusser or Lacan. As Culler (1976a) suggests, Barthes's interest in the mechanics of meaning generation never quite displaces an interest in actual meanings and their social functions. The latter are introduced quietly, via evaluative comments on actual clusters of meaning (or works).

## The reader revisited

Similar, if more specific, problems arise in discussing the reader. Given that someone has to fix the flux of meanings, at least initially, for any social life to materialise at all, it is clear that it should be the reader, not the author, for Barthes. The role of the reader has been ignored too long in the old criticism, it is argued, and 'the birth of the reader must be at the cost of the death of the author' (Barthes 1977: 148). This 'must' could contain theoretical, methodological and/or political imperatives, of course. In this usage, 'the reader' is clearly an abstract theoretical object or function again, as we have seen.

It is not at all clear if this means that the open, fluid textuality we were discussing above is found only after a reader (or the reader Barthes himself) has so constituted it, however. In some ways, the very category of readership sinks into general textualising practice again: there are no substantial differences between reading and writing, we are told, for example, since both express a 'single (universal? foundational?) signifying practice' (ibid.: 162). In other areas, though, readership is a separate practice that does have specific effects, as we see when Barthes discusses real readers, and here there are some important qualifications.

Not all (concrete) readers are equally competent, for example – some seem unable to read in the required unreified way, 'to produce the text, open it out, set it going' (ibid.: 163). Who these people are exactly has been the subject of debate in social science for a long time, and the issue returns in the concrete discussions we are going to have about consumerism, for example, and whether or not consumers can 're-read' advertising in this 'open' way. These debates inevitably reintroduce contexts of cultural competencies or capitals, or of class, gender and ethnicity.

In recent cultural studies, after years of seeing proletarian children, housewives, recent immigrants or other undesirables as such incompetent readers, it has become quite fashionable to spend some time and effort in discovering 'active readers' among these groups, as we have noted on several occasions. Fiske (1989a) sticks quite closely to Barthes's arguments about readership being the same sort of signifying practice as authorship, for example, when discussing the active player of arcade video games, and arguing against the usual view of such players as 'addicts' or 'victims'. Authors are never as creative as they appear to bourgeois critics, Fiske argues, and nor are games players the passive zombies of bourgeois moral concern. Both operate creatively, as participants in a common signifying practice, within a structured environment. To paraphrase, we might suggest that Fiske is arguing for the structural similarities between writing *Pride and Prejudice* and playing *Mortal Kombat II* as a more streetwise version of the indifference between 'cultured' and 'railway' reading. Whether it is a theoretical reader or player who 'must' act like this, or an amalgam of real readers/players that Fiske knows, is far from clear.

Barthes himself occasionally is unable to read actively the more culturally remote classics (which must remain as 'works', therefore, implying that the whole distinction is based in readership – see Barthes 1977: 163). The opposite can also happen as Barthes (along with many other critics) reads a good deal of complexity into modern practices and (concrete) texts. We know from his earlier analyses, as we have seen, that he can find immense textual labour and cultural significance in margarine advertisements, strip-tease performances, the depiction of Romans in films, words used to describe detergents, or a host of other matters (Barthes 1973). These banal works too can be opened out and made to disclose something about signification itself.

More usually, however, Barthes is able to accept the invitation to encounter his preferred texts in a much more relaxed and unstressed way, one which has little to do with the circumstances in which students encounter them, incidentally: 'at a loose end', 'stroll[ing]' as if in a strange landscape with half-identifiable elements in unique combinations (Barthes 1977: 159). Nevertheless, he still prefers some landscapes to others, despite his structuralist indifference: he clearly admires Proust, Genet, Brecht and Balzac, for example. He also clearly gains pleasure (*jouissance* even) from a wide range of textual encounters, but then he is (or rather, was before he died) an eminent academic and polymath, and he no longer has to grind through texts in order to write assignments, prepare lectures or bolster research proposals, perhaps as you, the reader of this chapter, have to do.

This raises the recurrent question of the origin and context of Barthes's readings again: are they in the text, or in the reader, so to speak; are they the product of a leisurely, cultured and bookish reading formation, or are these readings claiming a more universal status? Can anyone read like Barthes does, or do you have to have had years of experience in literary criticism, Marxism and philosophy?

This is what lies behind Culler's insistence that a 'competent reader' (or a 'competent writer' for that matter) cannot be omitted from Barthes's work (a part of the reaction to structuralism that Freund describes as 'reader-response theory').

Of course, we have seen that 'the reader' does appear in those essays of Barthes that we have cited, but it is an 'ideal reader' or 'super-reader' (Freund 1987) who largely (not exclusively) opens texts. The same reader appears in the 'activist' material in cultural studies, in Fiske or in Bennett and Woollacott, we have argued. What about readers who close texts, who refuse the chance of *jouissance*? Jameson (1992) appears to be one of those: he describes the attempt to resist the open, playful textualisation of what he takes as the ultimate example of Barthesian texts – experimental video (we discuss this example in Chapter 6); and I have already implied that pedagogues and students often need to do this sort of closure too.

This theme arises in Giddens's work as well (for example, Giddens 1979) in his general insistence on the importance of semantics rather than semiotics, the activities and practices (as opposed to merely the abstract possibilities or rules as in Culler – Giddens 1979: 42) of producing meaning. Giddens mediates the gap between text and reader, in other words, exactly as he does for the gap between 'structure' and 'action', as we saw in Chapter 1. In his case, however, this is how social systems are generated out of virtual structures, or 'works' out of 'texts', to put it in Barthes's terms. Such processes help us to resist the strangely evolutionary drift of Barthes's work, some sort of model of increasing textuality which we explore in the next section.

## Barthes as a sociologist?

Barthes does not confine himself to literary texts as the theoretical objects of a new reading, or to theoretical debate alone. He refers to social trends and developments as having something to do with the theoretical shifts he is keen to pursue. Some of the earlier social commentary and ideology analysis persists, even in the new theoretical endeavours, and we find another characteristic of recent 'postmodernist' commentary in the assertion that not just French society, or even the 'whole of Western civilisation', but the 'whole world' is somehow converging with the theoretical interests he has outlined. We can interrogate these sections at least from a sociological point of view.

Somehow, then, social trends confirm the validity of the theoretical transformations: possibly Barthes is suggesting that his (and others') perceptions of the social changes around them have somehow pushed them into new theoretical labour. In this case, the 'texts' being developed by 'the whole world' are better understood as having some independent existence, rather than being constructed in and by theory alone. This is fine, and it restores the relevance of the debate to people outside the academy; but to argue that events outside somehow themselves compel theoretical changes looks a little empiricist. Such a view also renders the new approach open again to the old critical questions, such as how typical these new social trends are, and whether they must be understood differently.

But perhaps the emergence of worldwide textuality has happened the other way around: has the concept of 'text' constructed by the new semiology escaped the laboratory and seminar room, and acquired a real existence, rather like a conceptual virus? Or is some world-wide essential process at work, moving in mysterious ways to alter both French theory and the activities of advertising companies in, say, Los Angeles? The problem is that all the possibilities are forbidden by Barthes himself: the old empirical approach is a flawed attempt to fix meaning, as is essentialism (which, in its Christian guise, is also accused of being repressive).

The virus possibility has been discussed in a way in Feather-stone's (1991) account of 'postmodernism' as a concrete term, gradually articulated, developed and transmitted by a definite group of scholars and critics in France and the USA, and then reimported, ready-reified so to speak, into British academic life. This seems close to confirming the view that the whole exercise is of significance mostly (exclusively?) to academics and other cultural gatekeepers.

If the concept of 'text' is going to be used to grasp real texts, then these issues cannot be deferred or glossed by refusals to do any more than sketch in outlines. Barthes ends his piece on works and texts by arguing that no other approach is possible, as we have seen; that (theoretical) texts by their very nature cannot be captured by any metalanguage, since '[the Text] ... leaves no language safe, outside, nor any subject of the enunciation in position as judge, master, confessor, decoder' (Barthes 1977: 164). This leaves the analyst in an impossible double-bind again: if we try to say anything about texts we fail to do justice to the never-ending fluidity of them, but if we remain silent about them we risk isolation and marginalisation and we vacate the field for more vulgar interpreters. If we just sit there and marvel at the endless deferrings of meanings, we can gain real pleasure (not to be underestimated as a motive for academic work, I have suggested), but we can never lose the feeling of fiddling while Rome burns around us, and our external audiences will lose patience with us.

This is where we can return to an organising theme of our own. If there is still to be an interest in analysing concrete social practices or systems, it will not do to try and produce these solely from some single process like textuality. That process has to be operationalised, energised or given expression by agents oper-ating in social contexts. Again, this is glossed in Barthes, as we have suggested (and, I have no doubt, in Baudrillard or Lyotard too). The existence of works (or concrete social systems or practices) is taken as read: fashion houses, Disney sites, cultural eclecticism, James Bond movies or whatever are criticised without being explained. This gives a strangely 'parasitic' and backward-looking tinge to much of this sort of criticism, and opens it to the charge of relativist indifference, an inability to prioritise or to see much difference between TV coverage of the Gulf War and a 'virtual reality' video game (to cite Norris's 1992 example).

We shall examine some work which still attempts to explain these works in terms of 'market forces', 'reification' or 'strategic communication' in due course. We can again rely on Giddens to pick up some more methodological points (not made specifically against Barthes, but useful in the whole critique of the 'textual metaphor'). Briefly Giddens (1979) uses the notion of social practice to give an account of many of the processes that we have found to be so problematic: the relation between signifier and signified is produced in practice; practice produces the coherence of signs in actual codes or works (which denies the need to focus strictly on the relations between signifiers). These points help us to break out of the strange abstractions of formal linguistics, while losing none of the critical power of Barthes on the in-adequacies of the concept of the author (for example). Thus, in Giddens (1979: 43–4):

> a text is not the outcome of an 'intention' . . . it should be studied as the concrete medium and outcome of a process of production, reflexively monitored by its author or reader . . . meanings are never 'contained' in the text as such, but are enmeshed in the flux of social life . . . in the enactment of social processes more generally, *the consequences of actions chronically escape their initiators' intentions in processes of objectification* (original emphasis).

## Epistemological sliding

Those of us reading the Barthes essays in 1994 also know something of the sad fate of the attractive new programme alluded to in the closing sentences of 'Change the Object Itself'. Barthes refers on several occasions to Althusser and the emerging programme for 'scientific Marxism', and likens the stages of development of semiology to the progress in Marxism. An early 'inversion' phase characterised the attempt of both to break with conventional depictions of social life and restore the correct relationship between culture and the 'economic base'. The Althusserian reading of Marx (which we discussed in Chapter 3) suggests that the real break with conventional depictions, the break into real Marxist science, came at a later stage, with the elaboration and deployment of novel concepts, not just inversions of conventional ones (and see the discussion on inversion in Chapter 2).

The Althusserian reading of the break introduced a good deal of vigorous Marxist analysis and much discussion, as we shall see, but a major aspect of the substantial critique it attracted turned on very similar aspects of the relations between concepts and referents that we have followed above.

After some early suspicion, for example, Althusser's new, more rigorous and 'scientific' Marxism attracted the attention of some British Marxists who were very keen to employ it in their own analyses. I have filled in details elsewhere (Harris 1992), but, briefly, the usual combination of theoretical, methodological and institutional academic reasons had made a rigorous-looking Marxism a pretty desirable property in Britain in the late 1970s. Marxism began to be 'applied' to a number of more concrete analyses – to the education system, for example, or to media, or to the study of deviance.

Problems soon arose with these 'applications', though. For example, Hirst (in Taylor *et al.* 1973) argued that one could not simply treat objects or events like crime as if they were 'real' or empirically given. Such empiricism would make the mistake of ignoring the processes of production of these 'objects' and their location in rather dubious bourgeois practices like policing or record-keeping or moral and political activities. It was an error made by sociology to take over these defined objects as if they were unproblematic (even if the discipline then proceeded to explain them quite differently), and Althusser himself had criticised such empiricism (and other erroneous accounts of the production of objects of study as in 'idealism' or 'historicism').

To be sure, there were commentaries in Marx's work on crime, law, jurisprudence, civil society and the like which could be seen to support a radical politics of crime and deviancy (wanting to politicise the whole issue, and seeing the capitalist system itself as criminogenic). However, these concepts were deployed in Marxism before the break into mature science, while Marx himself was still under the influence of reified definitions derived from other disciplines. Marx uses those concepts politically or morally, rather than analytically, so to speak (although even then he is rather scathing about crime as a form of political protest). The concepts of the mature scientific phase – 'mode of production, the class struggle, the state, ideology etc.' (Hirst, in Taylor *et al.* 1973: 204) – do not refer to crime as their objects, and cannot be expected to do so rigorously.

This sort of critique seems still to be pertinent for much contemporary 'applied' analysis. Much of it seems still to proceed via simple 'recognitions'; for example, as when one reads Barthes on textuality and 'recognises' the concept in certain of the characteristics of modern films, say, or even music videos (discussed in Chapter 6). The free-flowing signification practices of such products can be grasped and understood as (theoretical) text-like, and, as with Barthes, somehow the existence of such music videos buttresses the claims made for the general analysis.

There are many examples of this sort of argumentation which combine theoretical concepts and empirical objects as if they were simply the same thing. It is not uncommon, for example, to find articles which discuss the concept of gender and then provide some empirical data on patterns of women's work as if the one were just identical with the other, or as if the last simply confirmed the first, 'without remainder', to borrow Adorno's term. There is always a remainder, though, an element of non-identity, if only at the level of what might be called 'definition': is 'gender' being defined in the same way in empirical study and theoretical commentary, and does it mean the same thing?

Is it helpful to single out the signifying practices of, say, music videos (which are fairly easily 'recognised') and to ignore the production and reception contexts? Should music videos be classed as texts along with, say, a Bataille piece, a Godard film or a Mondrian painting? Do the signifying characteristics and practices of these pieces outweigh all other considerations and values?

Returning to Althusser, further twists were to develop over the years as the 'trajectory' of the British commentators (Hirst and Hindess) matured. In one phase, a thoroughgoing critique was developed of the processes involved in (conventional) social sciences of 'applying' theory to concrete events and practices. To be brief, none of the main approaches succeeded in doing this rigorously. Concrete events were just attached to theoretical concepts via some dubious procedure such as 'recognition' or 'identity thinking', to change the concepts for a moment, as some sort of speculative or more dogmatic attempt to force concrete events into a conceptual mould. Or arguments were manoeuvred tactically or incoherently, with slippages of the kind we have suggested between theoretical objects and empirical objects which happened to share the same names.

The main thrust of the argument for me concerns the wholesale rejection of 'epistemology'. What 'epistemology' means here is a philosophical endeavour that concerns itself with establishing correct relations between empirical objects and theoretical concepts. It is common to hear arguments from a wide variety of sources (and the bedfellows here can be very odd indeed) that this relation should be as tight and as rigorous as possible. As Hindess and Hirst have argued extremely well (see Macdonell 1986 for a good summary), theoretical objects and empirical objects belong to different domains or discourses, and can only ever be related in one of the three ways outlined above: theoretical concepts can apparently emerge from empirical events (but this is empiricism); some worldwide essence can express itself in both (essentialist and ultimately theological says Hindess); or some production process can generate a connection (the groups of critics discussed in Featherstone 1991, or Althusser's production system). The problem with the production-model approach is that the connections are forged on 'impure' or 'nonrational' grounds, and can be seen as giving a lot of ground back to the notion that ideas have authors and origins, in groups if not in bourgeois individuals.

As implied, even Althusser fails to escape the critique, and there is a careful analysis of the dogmatism and incoherence in his work. There are some specific issues raised, like those we shall discuss below, arising from the particular claim in Althusser merely to be discovering his approach in the work of Marx. The main problems arise, and in a recognisable form, however, when Althusser wants to mix general 'philosophical' criticisms with substantive ones. There are all sorts of lines of critique stemming from this analysis that could be applied to Barthes, perhaps.

Again to be very brief and to side-step the very technical and detailed level of Hindess's (1977) critique, Althusser offers an analysis of substantive (concrete) empirical analyses (largely those of economics) as specifically 'ideological', arising from some flawed view of the relation between 'objects' and the concepts that allegedly describe them. Althusser wants to use the term 'science' for the correct relation. Although he sees the work of Marx as mixed, he 'symptomatically' reads Marx, claiming to be clarifying what is there, bringing out the implicit scientific relation, so to speak. This is quite different from the treatment he gives conventional economists and writers, whose substantive work is read as an 'index' of an irreducibly ideological framework (or 'problematic', in Althusser's terms), and is simply junked.

In doing so, Althusser is clearly smuggling in a distinction not found in Marx's work and reading, using this prior distinction in order to stage-manage the 'discovery' of science that he wanted to find all along (between signs of the mature science and signs of earlier problematics). This distinction arises from some of the 'nonrational' interests Althusser possesses, therefore, including various 'practico-social' determinations from his involvement in active struggles of his own. The vaunted 'mechanism of production' of Althusserian knowledge is clearly constrained in such a way as to produce a dubious coherence between Marx's work, Althusser's prior distinctions between science and ideology, and the 'practico-social' interests which inform the distinction.

To cut a long story short, there is no coherent or undogmatic solution for Hindess and Hirst. Discourses produce their own objects and knowledge(s) about them. They cannot and need not be judged by attempts to make them coherent with the objects and knowledges produced by and in other discourses.

Applying this to Barthes – and he himself seemed to want to see a connection between his work and Althusser's in the pieces we have read – we are left with an irreducible split in disciplines such as 'the new semiology' between the theoretical discourse, with its special objects like 'texts', and empirical or 'practico-social' practices (as found in the 'whole world') with their objects like (concrete) texts. A person can operate at these two levels, but not rigorously or entirely rationally: I can read, enjoy and criticise Barthes 'abstractly' or 'theoretically' within the frameworks of his own discourses, but 'applying' them is a matter of calculation, interests, my personal ideologies.

Much depends on whether one wishes to be bound by the formal logic of 'scientific' discourses and the strict rules of application which govern the relations between the objects of those discourses, as in the Hindess and Hirst approach. We know that meanings do leap across discourses in various nonrational (strictly speaking) but nevertheless common ways in practice.

Barthes himself has done much to clarify these fuzzy processes, using terms like 'metaphor' and 'metonym'. Briefly, metaphors allow meanings to leap out of one element of a narrative into another (for example, a shot of a cloudscape in a film permits one to draw inferences about the 'emotional atmosphere' of a scene), while metonyms permit a necessary 'nesting' (not Barthes's term) of elements to take place, so that, say, a long conversation can be recalled when a key word of it appears in another conversation. We have already mentioned (in Chapter 1) analogies and abduction, too, both of which are common in academic analysis.

To complete the list of coping strategies, it is necessary to add some less plausible methods of joining together objects of different discourses. We have already discussed 'slippery pronouns', for example, which might be fitted under the more general strategy, with which Barthes is so unhappy, to unite differences in the wonderful subjectivity of an author. There are also commercial and other strategic practices designed to manipulate and influence rather than enlighten: the way in which advertising tries to unite healthy, glamorous people with particular, often rather tacky products, for example (Barthes 1973 has splendid analyses). There is the dubious unity imposed at a 'deep' level in bourgeois realism, which has attracted so much critical attention (again, signalled in Barthes's essays, and discussed later) or the 'eclecticism' rejected by Lyotard which simply collects together, uncritically, visiting McDonald's and attending the opera (although perhaps Barthes would be less happy with this distinction among works).

A strong Marxist tradition, still evident in Barthes at this stage, criticises the unifying trends of the market, of course, where everything is reduced to its exchange value, and it becomes possible to manage the production of weapons, spray-on chocolate cream topping, sexual or religious fulfilment with equal indifference. Capitalism incorporates and thereby recuperates or mythologises any subversive independent or critical areas: none knows this better than modern academics, in fact.

## CONCLUSION: ARE 'SOCIETIES' 'TEXTS'?

How can we evaluate Barthes's contribution overall, as a promise to deliver a new way of looking at social life, as textuality? Are his arguments convincing and coherent enough to persuade us to adopt the metaphor of 'text' for the key areas of modern social life, with all the openness and 'performativity' that implies for concrete texts, readers and authors?

I hope I have suggested here and elsewhere that the metaphor of the text is appealing but by no means without difficulties. The methodological difficulties that arise with other metaphors, especially the organising ones of conventional social science, cannot be banished (and, indeed, will return in the next chapter). But to withdraw into 'pure' linguistics, to consider only the play of signifiers, without referents, as in 'pure' textuality, is to risk an abstract formalism and a relativism that means a deep indifference to actual social practices, despite attempts to conjure them back into the analysis.

What exactly is a text in this writing, for example? Does the term refer to an avant-garde experimental piece or to all mundane 'objects' produced indifferently by an underlying process of textuality? Where exactly are the open liberating qualities of texts located: in the objects themselves, in the processes of textuality, or in the skilled reading of those materials by analysts such as Barthes? I must say I find Barthes's work less than satisfactory in providing answers to these questions. The ground seems to shift from one possibility to another in order to avoid the familiar dilemmas we have discovered again: in order to claim relevance and possibly to deny elitism, the 'expanded' versions of textuality are deployed, but then the original distinctions between 'works' and 'texts' fall, for example; or it is acknowledged that the skilled reading of these pieces is what makes them text-like, but it is also asserted that 'the whole world' tends to read that way anyway.

Perhaps the argument is a sociological one, suggesting that real social change, some version of (post)modernity is taking place and that this has forced us to respond as analysts; but there are problems here too, as we have seen. How widespread is the kind of playful signification being described? Exactly what kind of relation is being suggested between 'real' playful signification and the theoretical impulses which lead us to change our old concepts?

As I have suggested, social science, especially in cultural studies and media studies, has learned a lot from Barthes (and the others). The problem is to be able to detect the 'good' and 'bad' sides of what might be called discourse-swapping, or 'de-differentiation', or the demolition of internal boundaries (of logic and of traditional practices) between academic disciplines, such as linguistics and sociology, to return to the main focus. Marxist or bourgeois sociology can be cheerfully blended with literary criticism or philosophy, or any other disciplines, but either in 'good' creative, exploratory, critical ways, or in manipulative, recuperative, 'lazy' or reductive ways, we have suggested.

Are internal boundaries always 'bad' anyway? We are no longer under any illusions that to some extent the boundaries around academic disciplines are 'pure', merely cognitive ones, uncontaminated by any social and political interests. Yet nonrational grounds for choice need not be entirely cynical or self-serving. There are still cognitive interests, and good reasons for working within these boundaries: they help to generate knowledge; they offer researchers some sort of reason for commitment to research or critique (to paraphrase an argument of Kuhn's); the power they provide can be used to positive ends (to paraphrase Foucault); and they appeal (on the grounds of what can only be seen as a preferred aesthetic) by permitting rational involvement according to ability to engage the public conventions, regardless of one's prior ascribed identity: disciplines are more open than personal hierarchies.

As the focus on Barthes has implied, the alternative often seems to be to base one's analysis around the insights of an academic guru able to articulate their findings only in a personal charismatic, poetic manner, which mere mortals can hope only to catch. Such individualised floaters or 'strollers' run the particular risk of being rendered as star individuals, domesticated academics; living representations of a comfortable image of artists and intellectuals. Social commentary, analysis and critique run the risk of being reduced to a kind of personal poetics, delivered by the unwinding of an inner knowledge encountering some open text, albeit one conceived in terms of performance of textuality itself, rather than individual personality.

No one will be able to distinguish between statements delivered by famous philosophers with a long scholarly tradition to support them and the similar-looking statements of journalists, media folk and other *zeitgeist*-surfers. I realise I may risk being seen to do a little academic boundary-maintenance here to stave off 'the vulgate', just as did Barthes, but it is not uncommon to find pieces like one which ran: 'After years of hairy-chested stereotyping, Tom Jones is swinging in many new directions. Is this man a postmodernist?' I want the relativists to discuss whether it is just the name at the front that is to distinguish such pieces from works by Baudrillard, Lyotard or Derrida.

Finally, it seems clear that even those philosophical *tours de force* are performances which are parasitic upon the production of the more work-like concrete texts which the performer weaves together, which indicate a deeper reliance upon those more concrete disciplines than has been acknowledged: could there have been an Althusser without a Marx, no matter how epistemologically flawed, or a Hindess without an Althusser? Unless postmodernism really does wish to end history with itself, and to disappear in its turn when its raw materials are exhausted, can it cope without a continuing commitment to modernism, pursued by underlabourers, perhaps, unable or (thankfully) unwilling to trade *plaisir* for the higher delights of *jouissance*?

## The end of 'the social'?

We could quite justifiably take a stern, purist's position, like Hindess and Hirst, and simply refuse any implicit claims that such analysis somehow replaces and demolishes the claims made in more conventional sociology. It is common to find postmodernist analysis wanting to appear as benevolent and mature critique, helping any naive sociologists to clarify a few of their assumptions, often by repeating some sort of variant of the 'society as text' theme. I am not at all sure, however, if there are any sociologists left now who have not heard this sort of cautionary advice and have not abandoned long ago any naively positivist or empiricist procedures.

What are we to make of Baudrillard's remarks (in Baudrillard and Lotringer 1987: 84), for example:

> Well let's be frank here . . . My point of view is completely metaphysical . . . I'm . . . certainly not a sociologist. The only 'sociological' work I can claim is my effort to put an end to the social, to the concept of the social.

No doubt, this is a remark intended to be playful or witty rather than taken seriously. But let us refuse the jest for a moment, and consider it literally, much as Baudrillard himself suggests we handle irony by a grinding literalness. Baudrillard's 'society' is either a theoretical (metaphysical) or an empirical object, or some incoherent mixture of the two doing some tactical work. If it is an empirical concept, it could be tested (and perhaps found wanting) against the empirical standards of sociology, the conventions of gaining evidence for generalisations and the like. No one would see this sort of discussion as purely cognitive, of course, and vested interests would soon emerge, but they would not be confined to just the one side, and they need not dominate the agenda.

If Baudrillard's concept of 'the social' is not at all an empirical one, but purely metaphysical or theoretical, valid only in a specific discourse, one could suggest that there can be no rational implications flowing from it for the status of sociological concepts located in quite another discourse (or at least none that could resist Hindessian scepticism). There will almost certainly be no agreed 'epistemological project', surely, which can unite the two sorts of concepts in some kind of hierarchy (so that Baudrillard's concept is more valid, reliable or 'better' than, say, Durkheim's).

At the level of high theory, and with high levels of generalisation in mind, we might allow an abstraction and an indifference to suggest that the interesting thing about social processes is that they are all 'textual', in the senses of either Barthes or Baudrillard, but it is just as suitable (at least) for participants to 'assert' that the relation is best thought of as the other way round – that (concrete) texts, including philosophies, are produced by specialists embedded in social processes in social contexts.

# 5

# Postmodernism, anti-foundationalism and the aversion against the universal

There are several ways to begin to discuss the issues raised by 'postmodernism'. This account tries to address the debates with the interests in mind of sociologists and analysts of popular culture, implying, as the Introduction suggests, a wariness towards what can look like philosophical excess. This chapter is instead pitched at a different level and with different interests, and it is also necessary to remember the student audience for this book: you will be pursuing these issues in a rather different context from those professors who discuss issues in interviews with their peers, say.

There is clearly a danger of offering such readers 'bad' simplifications, that distort and mislead and permit a kind of 'soundbite' approach to theoretical work. But there are also 'good' simplifications that act as initial frameworks to bridge relative newcomers into theory, and I am obviously trying to construct these here. Despite the esoteric nature of some of those discussions, I believe it is possible to encourage student readers to ask their own questions based on their own interests as they read some of this material.

I should also point out to you some excellent collections of pieces on postmodernism that you will need for further researches (for example, Docherty 1993). I especially like the conference papers such as those in Appignanesi (1989), and various 'special' journal issues on postmodernism like *New German Critique* 33 (1984), or *Theory, Culture and Society* 5, 2–3 (1988), or *Journal of Communication Inquiry* 10 (1986). I also refer to specific articles from those collections in the Bibliography. Lechte (1994) has a series of superb and brief summaries of the work of many of the authors we are discussing in this book

To begin, then: according to Featherstone (1991) the term 'postmodernism' refers to:

- certain artistic developments in architecture, writing and film, video and television;
- social changes (a wide variety of things, taking in changes in work, leisure, urbanism, global patterns of finance and control, but above all, cultural changes);
- the experience of living in such societies (the good and bad feelings of change such as those we discussed in the Introduction, the senses of liberation, uncertainty, choice, insecurity, freedom to experiment and to enjoy life).

The last aspect is better addressed in the last four chapters. To begin to grasp the issue, though, it is also necessary to refer to a particular philosophical development. The obvious place to begin is with Lyotard and Baudrillard.

## LYOTARD AND NARRATIVITY

Perhaps the most influential account of the importance of narratives in social science appears in Lyotard (1986) (there is an excellent Introduction by Jameson in the edition I have cited, which foreshadows many of his own thoughts on postmodernism that were to appear later as Jameson 1992).

Lyotard begins with some remarks about natural science which will probably be familiar to many sociologists. As anyone with a working knowledge of the sociology of science will know, the debates triggered by Kuhn (1970) brought about a realisation that the development of natural science was heavily influenced by various social processes and conventions condensed into 'paradigms', in Kuhn's term. It was naive to see science as a simple attempt to get to 'the truth' and to represent it in logical concepts (the first appearance of the 'crisis of representation' which we shall discuss below). This realisation, together with the development of certain approaches like quantum mechanics, 'chaos theory', the emergence of uncertainty in scientific measurement and so on, led to an abandonment, even among scientists themselves, of the old views of science as the logical workings of the human mind confronting some fixed reality, some universal model for thought itself.

Instead, Lyotard argues, scientists legitimate what they are doing by using narrative strategies. These involve using locally agreed conventions ('language games') to shape reality as well as to develop concepts, so that science manages to become 'a story which science is bound to verify' (Lyotard 1986: 60, borrowing from Medawar). This '*de facto* legitimation' is acceptable because science is no longer interested in pursuing some deep philosophical truth, based on some 'metaphysical consensus' (ibid.: 61) but justifies itself instead on the grounds of 'performativity' – its ability to deliver knowledge. Rather than spending time on the 'grand narratives', the search for overarching theories of truth, the pursuit of the answer to mankind's ills, or the development of science into a coherent system with strong boundaries, scientists devote themselves to pursuing 'little narratives' to 'do science' at a more limited and local level.

Clearly, this is what those who fund science want too, but this is not an account of how capitalism distorts science. Lyotard insists on the 'good' aspects of this rather pragmatic approach (in the philosophical as well as the everyday sense of 'pragmatic'): there is no alternative, since the old metaphysics is discredited, and the pursuit of 'little narratives' generates new ideas for scientists themselves. The 'blindspots', the arguments where there is no rational consensus, are the source of innovation and the spur to research: local little narratives are the 'quintessential form of imaginative intervention' (ibid.: 60). Science progresses when it pursues 'paralogy': 'making the known unknown, then reorganising the unknown into an independent symbolic metasystem . . . The specificity of science is its unpredictability' (ibid.: 100).

There are several implications for this argument, stretching beyond natural science. Social science offers different possibilities compared with natural science: less of an emphasis on performativity in the sense of developing a technology, perhaps, and much more of a tendency to claim legitimation under the other main metanarrative (the 'emancipatory claim', the interest in the liberation of humanity from various social constraints). Yet the general crisis of representation is clearly in evidence, as 'social reality' refuses to be grasped by simple concepts, and the narrative solution, so to speak, is still the only one available. In what follows, we can see these points developed in much greater detail, albeit from a slightly different critical stance.

Lyotard is particularly critical of Habermas's project, which we outlined briefly in Chapter 2, and to which we return in the

Conclusion. To be very brief here, Habermas still holds out hope for a process of arriving at rational consensus in a 'discourse community', involving some universal interests behind all the little narratives and language games. For Lyotard, the version available in the 1980s seemed to have the potential to limit freedom and playfulness, to police and stifle creativity, and he roundly condemned it as naive and politically repressive. We should celebrate ambiguity and heterogeneity instead, and devote our political efforts to widening opportunities to gain access to knowledge in order to let people pursue their own narratives – a kind of prescient advocacy of the Internet against the alternative commercially provided 'information superhighway'. Whether this sort of optimistic pluralism can triumph is in doubt, however: in the Appendix to the book (reproduced in Docherty 1993), Lyotard himself warns us against mere 'cynical eclecticism', as we shall see.

It is possible to perceive here some implications for education too, and these are also developed in Lyotard's book. Once more, formal education has been challenged to legitimate itself, and Lyotard notes that performativity is being demanded increasingly by licensing and providing bodies (as in the turn towards training and vocationalism, for example), and that this will bring universities into competition with other providers of such knowledge (including databases and 'invisible colleges' – networks of people attending conferences or reading the same journals). Lyotard sees little future in defences based on some old claims that universities are pursuing universal and disinterested knowledge, or that their activities are somehow essentially linked to the emancipation of humanity as a whole. Instead, the university should justify itself in terms of access, as facilitating access to circuits and networks of knowledge.

This example gives us entry into the debate, of course, since 'we' are readers, students and teachers, and it might produce a little reflection on our own surroundings. As a quick example, I am certainly aware of the crisis in legitimation for the subjects I teach, and of the increasing pressure to claim some kind of performativity, either in the form of desirable transferable skills for students, or as tangible research outcomes (publications) for me. You may be aware, perhaps, of the effects of narrativity more locally, as you listen to your own lecturers negotiate their way around the welter of competing perspectives, paradigms, approaches and theories while contriving to make it all into an interesting story or a manageable narrative to retain your interest (and presence), and to get you safely through the assessment scheme.

## BAUDRILLARD AND HYPERREALITY

Implicit in what we have been discussing are several important social implications, and it is time to move away from the more abstract issues in order to consider them and then to return to discuss an earlier theme of a turn towards textuality as an organising metaphor. Some famous issues arise from Baudrillard's particular version of the linguistic turn as it affects Marxism, for example. Briefly, the argument here involves a rediscovery of the signifying powers of commodities: commodities circulate in culture as well as in markets. One particular aspect, we have seen – the dominant one these days in the case of Baudrillard – is the use of commodities to signify qualities about oneself: wearing the right sort of trainers, or driving the right sort of car, or eating the right sort of food. These signifying activities are at the heart of modern consumerism and the modern economy, and make Marx's analysis highly limited (to a particular stage in social development) and largely redundant (since it never really went on to the issue of symbols but stayed analysing 'objects' and 'production' in a literal sense).

It is too technical a matter to pursue here (try the selection appearing in Poster 1988: ch. 3), but Baudrillard begins by trying to complete Marx's analysis of 'use-value'. Commodities are used not in some unknown 'personal' way, but according to a cultural system which constructs apparently personal needs (and the subjects who carry these needs, of course). Baudrillard is able to go on to argue that, in this sort of way, objects function fundamentally as signs, containing exchange values, use values and sign values. Disentangling the relations between these involves pursuing an 'homology' between classical Marxism and structural linguistics, an equation between the dualism of exchange value and use value in Marx, and the dualism between the signifier and the signified in structuralism. This in turn helped Baudrillard to extend and radicalise both Marxism and structuralism and to uncover a common structure or 'code' linking the two, and moved analysis on to a new topic: what might be called (at this fairly early stage) the topic of systems of ideological communication and how they work.

We have already discussed Baudrillard on hyperreality and simulation, which represents a more mature stage of the argument. Signs become fused with their referents in 'simulacra', seen best perhaps in the creation of deliberate 'fantasy worlds' like Disney theme parks, but extending to include all aspects of 'reality', as we suggested in the Introduction.

As Crook *et al.* (1992: 31) argue, this fusion of signs and referents leads to Baudrillard's famous predictions about the 'end of the social', which have been discussed briefly before: 'the effectivity of culture is so increased that only the relations between ... its "signs" have force ... The social ... is merely absorbed.' Thus Baudrillard goes further than Lyotard who holds out hope that 'at best, flexible networks of language games provide localized capacity for resistance to performativity ... at worst ... a totally steered society becomes a reality by the mechanism of computerization' (ibid.)

However, the 'methodological' issues are what we are interested in here: 'it is now impossible to isolate the processes of the real or to prove the real ... [for example] ... all hold-ups, hijacks and the like are now as it were simulations ... inscribed in advance in the decoding and orchestration rituals of the media' (Baudrillard 1983: 41–2). In other words, there is nothing 'outside' hyperreality.

Much else follows from this analysis: political and academic analyses based on attempts to criticise the 'distortions' or 'lack of realism' of cultural representations of events have had the ground cut from under their feet, and political theories based on these critiques (or, indeed, political activity itself) naturally lose their point. Baudrillard puts this in his usual polemical and excessive way when he urges us to 'forget' all those analysts who have devoted their lives to exposing the ideological and cultural masks and mechanisms of political power in capitalism – above all Foucault (Baudrillard and Lotringer 1987).

The development of hyperreality can be traced in various artistic movements, beginning with realism and surrealism, and developing through various ways to 'empty out the real' in increasingly abstract and isolated signs. At the end of the process, we have 'binarity ... digitality ... minimal separation', and an overwhelming interest not in depicting reality but in reproducing representations 'for their own sake'. Indeed, 'The very definition of the real becomes: that of which it is possible to give an equivalent reproduction' (Baudrillard 1983: 145).

In more abstract terms, meaning itself 'implodes' since it becomes impossible to spot the gaps between appearance and reality, or between cause and effect. Apart from anything else, the sort of empirical research undertaken by social sciences on people's 'opinions' is wrecked in this implosion. Asking a question – about opinions of an election result, say – assumes that what is spoken by the respondent as an 'answer' is an opinion which arises from their 'own' interpretations: but that assumes that there is still a gap between 'real events', the question about them, and the answer. This is a 'tactical hallucination' (ibid: 117): the question itself immediately calls forth the answer by demanding a suitable and instant 'opinion', and the inescapable media representations of the election flood the perceptions of the event drawn upon by the respondent, leaving no room or time for 'an interpretation'. A similar fusion operates between the media's interrogation of events (or any academic interrogation, including psychoanalysis or ethnology) and the 'events themselves' which immediately 'reply' according to the required structure of the question. This is another variant of the interest in reproduction mentioned in the paragraph above: the fusion neatly reproduces the reality and confirms the validity of the concepts used to interrogate it. In this rather special way the real world has become 'like a text, to be read or deciphered' (ibid.: 121).

When I outline these arguments to my own students, or discuss them with colleagues, a number of objections can arise, especially among those still committed to some kind of political critique of our society. We can finish this section by considering these objections (and you can, of course, list your own). Let us start with some obvious 'political' points.

For Baudrillard, most of us no longer know or care whether the America represented in Disney World's American Pavilions, say, is more or less real than the cities which lie outside it. That 'real world' outside Disney's EPCOT (or outside any other fantasy versions of it) is disappearing anyway. In fact, massive efforts are needed to talk up the fast-disappearing real as we have seen: 'The cool world of digitality . . . the principle of simulation wins out over the reality principle' (ibid.: 152).

Most of the familiar politics of representation debates – whether or not America, Britain or France is accurately depicted in EPCOT, whether or not social classes, races or genders are fairly represented in movies like *Pulp Fiction* – becomes similarly pointless and meaningless. The real pleasure lies in being able to play along with, to engage in 'an aesthetic pleasure, that very one of reading, and of [following] the rules of the game' (ibid.: 150).

As with other critiques, especially Marxist ones, academic criticism of a denunciatory kind runs the risk of actually serving a positive function for the culture industry, acting as a sign of the 'democratic' openness of capitalism, partaking of a secret deal between the industry and academic criticism which keeps both going, or, above all, holding out some notion of the real again, nostalgically usually. Academics find themselves as the allies of big business and politics in wanting to talk up the real.

Of course, we might want to object, cultural objects are still consumer goods, produced in an industry, which is exploitative and out to make profit in the end, and there are still 'repressive spaces', even for Baudrillard (1983: 138). But why are these aspects so important as to dominate all the possible ways to analyse consumption? What is being claimed exactly: that the conditions of production outweigh all the other aspects? Can all the specifics of, say, the wearing of trainer shoes used in the peculiar cultural displays of male youth be read off from the one origin, in a capitalist system of production? Shifting consumer objects and analysts for a moment, Eco (1987: 148–9) has pointed out some obvious problems:

a firm produces polo shirts ... and it advertises them. A generation begins to wear the polo shirts. Each consumer of the polo shirt advertises, via [the logo] ... this brand of polo shirt ... A TV broadcast, to be faithful to reality, shows some young people wearing the ... polo shirt. The young (and the old) see the TV broadcast and buy more [brandname] polo shirts because they have the 'young look' ... at this point, who is sending the message? The manufacturer of the polo shirt? its wearer? the person who talks about it on the TV screen? Who is the producer of ideology? ... There is no longer Authority, all on its own (and how consoling it was!). Shall we perhaps identify authority with the designer ... or the manufacturer ...? Or those who legitimately agree to wear it and to advertise an image of youth and heedlessness or happiness? Or the TV director . . .? Or the singer . . .? All are in it and all outside it: Power is elusive . . .

Clearly, some highly problematic foundational and emancipatory metanarratives still operate in Marxist critiques of consumerism, and we are about to explore some difficulties with these. For a while, it was possible to make the original foundational concepts in Marxism, say, stretch to fit behaviour such as consumerism, but now it is much less certain that we can or that we need to do so. (Chapter 7 discusses some implications in more detail.)

This can cause insecurity among those who have devoted their lives to Marxist politics or to a sociological career. Students too can sometimes feel that they have only just grasped an approach like Marxism, and that to undermine it would risk being at sea again.

It is even possible still to find students who are shocked by the apparent indifference of postmodernists to politics. Generally, though, Baudrillard feels that students display 'no real mourning for the absence of [critique], as could have happened in the universities after 1968' (Baudrillard 1983: 156). Jameson also points to the generational nature of the debate, using the terms in Barthes we discussed in the previous chapter: what is perceived as 'postmodernism' can often appear to offer a refreshing break into creative 'textuality', away from the 'work'-like nature of 'modernist' analysis, especially when modernist works (Marx, Freud and so on in this case) have been 'reified' in university syllabuses (Jameson 1992: 317).

Instead of pursuing political (or Marxist) critiques here (Jameson appears in more detail in the next chapter), let us return to the technical and 'methodological' focus, and try to explore in more detail the bases for these serious challenges offered to social science and political commitment by Lyotard and Baudrillard.

## POSTSTRUCTURALISM

Lyotard's and Baudrillard's famous arguments arise out of a much broader context of argument, analysis and debate, which we can refer to as 'poststructuralism' (see Dews, in Appignanesi 1989, for a useful but critical account of how poststructuralism turns into postmodernism). I'd like to discuss that development, so that you can begin to see in full the issues for sociologists and Marxists (and thus for analyses of popular culture based upon these perspectives). Roughly, what we have is another excess, escalation or tragic development, rather like the ones we discussed in earlier chapters. Poststructuralism involves the kind of linguistic or textual turn we have seen in Chapter 3, with its potential to dissolve, or to make 'disappear', conventional social science. This led to a lot of deconstruction of other people's arguments. Initially, these were controlled or directed under a Marxist, feminist or some other kind of critical politics. We saw some examples when we discussed what came to be known as 'discourse theory' (including Foucault's work) in Chapter 3. Culler (1976b) offers a good, clear discussion too.

That deconstruction easily turns to the kind of trenchant anti-foundationalism directed against all positions, including Marxism and feminism, which we are going to discuss here. All you need to add in order to get to Lyotard's postmodernism, for example, is what Honneth (1985) calls 'an aversion against the universal', the abandonment of the claim to be speaking in the name of science, and thus of humanity in general, the realisation that there are in social life many equally valid 'little narratives' which can be organised no longer under the old 'grand narratives' of Marxism or (social) science.

There is also a notion of excess or escalation arising from growing cultural autonomy, its textualisation in forms like simulation, and the sort of cynicism and vertigo that results, as we discussed in Chapter 2. Those trends lead you to something like Baudrillard's postmodernism, or, more modestly, to the newer work on 'postmodernity' which we shall be discussing in Chapter 7. I suspect that the kinds of technical 'philosophical' arguments we are about to examine are the crucial ones for these theorists in the conviction that we cannot return to the old ways of doing social science, together with the general disconnection of social theory from the centre of political life that Bauman (1987) describes.

## Foundationalism

We have already tried out the claim that postmodernism is not only a new and better term to describe the social and cultural changes listed above, it is the only possible way to describe them. All earlier theories and techniques are redundant, discredited, fundamentally flawed. These earlier and flawed theories include all the major theories in the social sciences – Marxism(s), Christianity/ies, feminism(s), Freudianisms, bourgeois sociologies, psychologies and histories, film theory, English Lit., community studies.

These subjects will not disappear immediately, of course, but, for the most sceptical analysts, they will not be able to claim any necessary privileges: they should admit that their foundationalism and emancipatory claims are as unfounded as those of any others – that is, that they are just 'ideology', or 'strategic communication', or 'productivist' accumulations against death after all. Emancipatory claims are important in the current demands that education makes for public expenditure, so the future looks interesting: most university academic subjects are doomed as universally applicable paths to truth, and so are universities for that matter, in so far as they claim any privileged rights as communicators.

This is alarming and depressing for those struggling to acquire qualifications from those very universities, perhaps; but if your attention is engaged by these threats, let us proceed to examine the basics of the debate. Foundationalism is the attempt to establish some sort of discipline or 'science' on some secure foundation of privileged concepts. This often involves an emancipatory claim: that possession of these privileged concepts will deliver superior political insight too, enabling a sophisticated political plan to be developed that is rooted in proper theory. As Crook (1991) argues, this goal of linking theory to adequate political practice is central to the very development of sociology as a subject, in Durkheim as well as in Marx.

We have already discussed some brief examples of analysis from Marx or Freud in Chapters 1 and 2, and it is clear that they are plausible and can seem powerful, but they can also be seen to derive their appeal precisely from being reductionist, incoherent and dogmatic. Marxism in particular was interrogated very closely by a number of critics in Britain, including the 'post-Althusserians' Hindess and Hirst, whom we discussed in Chapter 4. Crook (1991) offers a good review of this material as well.

## FOUNDATIONALISM IN MARXISM

Let us apply a basic critique to the concept of 'dominant ideology' in Marxism, for example (a thoroughly critical discussion is available in Abercrombie *et al.* 1980):

- Incoherence can creep in when the term dominant ideology is applied to a range of belief systems (professional values in media, teachers' beliefs, party political propaganda) and to a range of practices and structures (which are usually analytical constructs anyway, 'discovered' by researchers and critics and often unrecognised by the participants). Sometimes the term is used in more 'scientific' discourses and sometimes in more 'political' ones. The term gains its power by being applied to all these diverse objects, but is this consistent, or does the meaning tend to change slightly every time it is used? Only very close readings of the originals can help you decide.
- Dogmatism can arise to cover the imprecision mentioned above. For the true believer, dominant ideology simply must exist, as part of their entire outlook. There is a tendency for such believers to do 'lazy Marxism' as a result, where any set of ideas and practices that are not immediately appealing must be dominant ideology – including postmodern critique. Instead of analysis, we have rhetorical devices like appeals to authority, exhortations to stop thinking and just believe, threats of political persecution, *ad hominem* denunciations, splits, schisms, witch hunts, and much self-absorption and pursuit of party purity.

Foundational concepts tend to reduce the complexity of actual cases and see them simply as further examples of something old and familiar: postmodernism must be simply the old 'post-industrial' thesis, for example. This reduction is also a partisan one – in this case, we reduce everything in such a way as to validate Marxism. Other foundational concepts are excluded, as well as postmodern scepticism.

Your experience as a student will reveal, exposed as you are to a number of different major approaches, that one problem with foundationalism is that there are other equally plausible alternative foundations on which to base an analysis. No one can agree about what the foundational concepts should be: dominant ideology? conversational competencies? Freudian metapsychology? patriarchy? God's will? Before postmodernism came along, foundationalism was in trouble from other foundationalists! We

have no choice but to be sceptical about all foundational claims –
we've seen all the best ones confronted with or undermined by
rivals already. Incidentally, Mannheim said all this long ago in his
neglected classic (1972).

It is easy to dismiss work produced a long time ago, of course,
and in fact generational arguments can be seen as examples of the
tactical manoeuvres which riddle modern Marxism (and classic
Marxism) and which are used at crucial moments to gloss, to
persuade, to appeal, to argue rhetorically. I have identified
some of these in my own analysis of Gramscian cultural analysis
(Harris 1992).

Marx himself used a wide variety of these manoeuvres, including personal attacks – for example, on the devastated Proudhon
(Marx 1956) – sentimental appeals, fiery denunciations, and a
range of irritating metaphors, often at crucial moments (such as
at the very end of the famous 'methodological' Introduction to
*Grundrisse* (Marx 1973)). It can make Marx a good read, but it is
not science (that is, it isn't coherent or undogmatic). For Hindess
and Hirst, all the founding fathers of sociology, and all their major
disciples, used the same sorts of manoeuvres – sociology is not a
science but a series of plausible stories (see Hindess 1977).

## Foundationalism in Freud

The basics have been discussed already in Chapter 1, but it is
important to realise that Freud has always had a greater significance for Continental thinkers than for analysts in Britain. Social
theorists tend not to bother much with the actual work on
neurotics or with the practical outcomes and 'cures', but to focus
instead on the general theoretical issues. Freud can be read instead
as a writer who developed a general theory about the way human
beings construct meaning, and as the inventor of a method to
understand subjective meaning.

There are probably several models, in fact (see Wollheim 1971,
for a readable introduction). Freud wanted to generalise away
from abnormal individuals to found a theory that would explain
routine and quite normal phenomena too. Some recent critics have
suggested, however, that he did not generalise enough, and
remained within an unexamined context provided by Western
capitalist societies in the early twentieth century, and that he

should be re-read as offering an embryonic general theory of desire as the main mechanism that animates human action.

It is clear that 'normal' behaviour is analysed too, especially dreams, jokes, politics, art and parapraxes – the everyday slips we make in speech or writing or in mishearing others. In fact, in his own accounts of his work (Freud 1974a, 1974b), he introduces his models of the psyche by taking us through some analyses of parapraxes and dreams before getting on to the hysterias, obsessions, fetishisms and perversions.

This is clearly very interesting material, and, as with Marx, Freud demonstrates a close familiarity with story-telling devices, including the deployment of excellent narrative skills and ways to involve the audience: phoney dialogues, crushing rebukes to his rivals, self-serving accounts of his heroic struggles towards the truth, and so on. We have the same interweaving of science and rhetoric, then. This may not matter, of course. It is appropriate to explore the arguments in more detail in order to decide. I have chosen one of the models in Freud to pursue the argument.

The normal everyday view of the personality sees the conscious, rational part of the mind as the dominant aspect – the part that is engaged in ordinary conversation, that manages ordinary life, plans out the day, and apparently governs most of our normal behaviour. Occasionally, we are aware of a higher sort of ego too, that talks to us and reminds us of our duty, of morality and the higher things of life – the superego. If we are honest with ourselves, we can also detect a darker side, a kind of fringe of semiconscious (preconscious for Freud) thoughts trying to intrude, and these are often far less respectable, certainly by the standards of Vienna in the early twentieth century. These thoughts, wishes and desires are bubbling up from a substantial reservoir (or they are visitors from another, much larger room, to use one of Freud's metaphors) – the unconscious.

By definition, the unconscious is not routinely available for our inspection, but it is vitally important in understanding our psychic lives. Its existence and power can be demonstrated in dreams, Freudian slips and mental illness, but only after we understand the mechanisms at work. Very briefly, the unconscious offers a source of powerful pre-rational, pre-verbal thoughts in the form of images. Flows of energy (the drives or instincts – basic pre-rational wishes and desires) connect (cathect) these images to our conscious and rational thoughts, often in apparently mysterious ways. Visitors from the unconscious have to struggle past a censor to get over the threshold to the preconscious, and then wait to be noticed, sometimes almost randomly, by the conscious. Psychic phenomena thus have a rational, conscious element 'at the surface' and an unconscious tap root leading us back to the unknown depths. Actual examples from psychoanalysis can involve long and detailed analysis. Let's take some simple and common ones from Freud's own introductory lectures and focus on the material on dreams.

It is this sort of work that has been used in the analysis of culture more widely, such as images in film (see Gledhill on melodrama, in Cook 1985, for a brief discussion). For the beginner, the knowingly 'Freudian' sequences in *Blue Velvet* offer little challenge. There are several dreams in the film, and perhaps the whole film is itself one. There are many of the elements appearing in dreams – Dorothy finds herself naked in respectable company, for example, while the virginal Sandy dreams of a flood of (red) robins bringing love to her world in an obvious reference to loss of virginity (and possibly to menstruation). More generally, Jeffrey witnesses some adult sexuality between people who call themselves 'Mommy' and 'Daddy' in a filmic version of Freud's 'primal scene' (where infants stumble across their parents making love, with occasionally dire consequences). Later, Jeffrey hides in the same cupboard with a large gun at the ready and shoots the father-figure Frank, in a clear Oedipal reference.

Returning to real Freud, dreams of flying or floating, for example, represent half-censored sexual desires, often energised by some event that has happened in conscious life recently. Flying or weightlessness is connected with sexual arousal in men, since erection gives the male organ that floating, gravity-defying feeling. Male organs are also represented by sticks, pins, umbrellas, the number three, fire-arms (large guns), watering cans, reptiles, fishes, hats, overcoats and cloaks. These are some of the famous 'phallic symbols'.

Female bodies are represented by houses with balconies, vessels and bottles, cupboards, rooms, wood, snails, fruit in general, jewel cases (and, in one actual dream, a clock – back to menstruation again). Parents often appear as royalty; children as vermin or small animals; dying by a journey; masturbation by 'piano playing ... gliding ... sliding and pulling off a branch'; sexual activity by walking upstairs and getting out of breath, dancing, riding, climbing, being run over, or 'certain manual crafts' (Freud 1974a: 186–9).

In these examples, we can see that the contents of dreams are symbols, and the dream work does the symbolising, taking the real but hard-to-express wishes and desires (for example, sexual desires), and representing them in a way that permits us to experience them as dreams. Further, dreaming is complicated by two additional processes:

- *displacement*, which occurs when the 'psychical accent is shifted from an important element on to another which is unimportant, so that the dream appears differently centred and strange' (ibid.: 208). Freud's running example in the *Introductory Lectures* concerns a dream where a woman's dissatisfaction and regret at an early marriage is displaced on to an absurd arrangement for booking theatre tickets for another married couple;
- *condensation*, since the original unconscious material (the latent dream) can often be reduced in the translation, as it were, into the actual (manifest) dream: the easiest example, perhaps, concerns the composite figure in dreams – the threatening stranger is both your father and your examiner. Puns, including visual puns, often contain condensed meanings of this kind.

Dreams show us the difficulty of representing our unconscious desires, laid down before we had adequate language to depict them. Imagine trying to represent the contents of a newspaper by pictures alone, says Freud – and under the close eye of a censor too. The resulting dream is a wonderful testament to human ingenuity (and to the flexibility of language and symbolism), and a great challenge to the interpreter.

Clearly, the interpretation can be questioned in terms of its coherence and rigour. Freud was attacked long ago as offering us a series of self-justifying arguments that can never be falsified. Sometimes the elements of dreams are to be taken literally, sometimes they are symbols, and sometimes the symbols have to be supplied by the analyst. Sometimes the causes of dreams or illness are biological and predisposed, and sometimes accidental (or traumatic), or both, as in Freud's notion of a 'complementary series'. At different times, Freud supports his analyses with all sorts of references to biological theory (including then-fashionable material on the links between the evolution of individuals and of the human species), and also to linguistic theory. His examples are empirical case studies derived from his clinical work with patients – but also elements of poems or literary works.

On a methodological note, the very subtlety and creativity of the capacity to symbolise causes problems: interpretation could proceed *ad infinitum*, as chains of displacements, condensations and other transformations are pursued. The clinical setting disguises some of the problems here: we can apparently fix and check our interpretations by getting the dreamer to confirm the meanings. However, the status of the patient's insights are contradictory. In neurotic patients, for example, Freudian interpretations are often fiercely resisted, we are told, but this is to be seen as a part of the illness, as evidence of the very correctness of the diagnosis. Further, it is clear that the patient is to be involved in a fairly close relationship with the analyst, essential if the necessary transference is to take place.

Classically, understanding and cure take place after a kind of intense personal psychodrama that involves the patient and the therapist acting out conflicts between the old (infantile) irrational elements in the complex and the strong wish to avoid the contradictions in them, and the rational (mature male, paternal) understandings of them. Deep feelings involving sexual and ego developments are awakened. Great struggles take place. Denial, abuse (verbal), scorn, bitterness, and admiration and sexual attraction for the analyst are common, Freud tells us.

This highly personal and emotional process is hardly capable of being made to appear as a mechanism to test out the validity of different readings. Those who still disagree with Freudian diagnosis could be written off as still neurotic. Freud was not above using his skills to diagnose the psychic flaws in his academic critics too (and vice versa).

This sort of procedure is at the heart of Foucault's (1979) critique of Freud too. Foucault notes the similarities between Freud's demands that patients disclose all to the therapist (and agree with his analysis), and the techniques of confession developed in the Catholic Church well before psychoanalysis appeared. This connection helps Foucault to make a more general point about Freudian discourse as merely occupying one position in a long line of discourses about sexuality, all of them claiming to be therapeutic and emancipating, but all of them serving to construct human sexuality, and 'talk it up', while fixing it in a context of social regulation and discipline (we shall discuss this in slightly more detail in Chapter 6). We have here a classic poststructuralist argumentative ploy, then: to expose the elements of irrationality, repression or control in the very heart of discourses that claim to have 'broken' with them.

Freud's work developed in a special way following Lacan's re-reading of his metapsychology to connect it with then-fashionable structural linguistics. The famous aphorism: 'The unconscious is structured like a language' has a number of implications which we cannot pursue here (Lechte 1994 has a particularly good summary). Essentially, this built on the linguistic concepts and psychological mechanisms already in Freud (symbolism, puns, representation, condensation and so on), but rewrote them in the new concepts – metaphor, metonym, paradigm/syntagm, signifiers and signifieds, codes and so on. But above all, the new reading reconnected Freud's work into the social order, the linguistic and political context of the 'individual personality' which became the unconscious material beyond the reach of individual rationality.

A methodological maze is also apparent, however: metaphors can be used to extend meanings infinitely, and individual egos and analysts are faced with a struggle to fix and stabilise meanings, and to trace them through a labyrinth of metaphorical connections. We also discover in this struggle a possible pathology: schizophrenia arises when meanings cannot be stabilised in chains, but appear only in isolated and disconnected segments. This diagnosis also takes on a social form, and the term 'schizophrenic' became a fashionable label to apply to those experiences of instability and dislocation faced routinely by all of us at sea in hyperreality and the information overload of 'postcultures'.

As this example indicates, after Lacan, Freudian metapsychology could then be used much more generally: Lacan's work on the 'mirror phase' in infantile development, for example, where children come to recognise themselves as both subjects for themselves and as objects for others via their reflections in the literal and metaphorical mirrors surrounding them, was used in fields as diverse as Marxist politics (as we have seen already with Althusser on ideology and how it 'hails' individuals) and film theory, especially feminist variants (see Buscombe *et al.*, in *Screen* 1993). Of course, Habermas and Apel, and many Marxist writers before them, saw Freudian theory as a model to explain the unhelpful ideological 'blocks' on emancipatory thought and practice (see McCarthy 1984).

Lacan, on the Oedipus complex as a crucial stage at which sexual differences emerge, spawned a whole generation of feminist work that tried to disentangle the connections between the infant's entry into the linguistic order and her falling under the control of male domination in the Symbolic Order. If this connection could be made, sexual difference would lie at the heart of the formation of the personality and the whole Symbolic Order, with clear implications for the claims to centrality of feminist analysis itself. In particular, this shift permitted feminists to analyse the system of differences in the abstract, as it were, instead of being confined to a mere critique of representation (see Merck's 1987 Introduction or Williamson's longer discussion in the *Screen* special on this topic).

The shift also helped to locate patriarchy firmly in culture rather than in biology. Perhaps the most famous deployment of the whole approach came in Mulvey's account (reprinted in Bennett *et al.* 1981 or *Screen* 1993) of the 'male gaze' in mainstream cinema, in the spectator and in the film, and how this system of 'looks' contributed to constructing women as passive objects in the narrative of the film. We have already alluded to this work in the previous chapter, via the work of Bennett and Woollacott on James Bond movies.

Problems with this thesis, with the emergence of other dimensions to sexual difference, and with a residual insistence on a biological basis for sexual difference even in Lacan (says Merck), led to a number of revisions. Lacan's analysis seemed to leave no room to escape patriarchy, except by retreating to some pre-Symbolic foundation for culture (see Kristeva, in Moi 1986, for an appealing and critical discussion). One way or another, however, this debate was to dominate feminist analysis of film for at least a decade.

## The crisis of representation

Let us return to a focus on a methodological aspect – the crisis of representation. To be schematic:

1 Signs express a relation between signifiers and signifieds. The signifiers (symbols in Freud) clearly represent something ident-

ifiably concrete, a signified (a concept) and a referent (some-times equated with the object itself) – as in the examples of the 'phallic symbols' listed above. Even here, however, in this simplified model of direct representation, what is signified is a concept, not a real object – signs never just connect simply to real objects, they are never simply the same as real objects.

2 Further, signifiers take on meaning by being connected to other signifiers, in processes of signification. A signifier like a word gets modified by other words in sentences or it takes on meanings from puns or allusions, or because of its own con-densed nature. Using more structural-linguistic terms, signifiers stretch away over time in sentences or codes, and leap across space, so to speak, via metaphorical connections with other signifiers. The latter leap is chronically likely: every signifier occupies a place in a whole set of related signs, stretching on either side of it.

3 To take a simple fictional example, a dream about a flight in an air balloon can involve a simple reading of the air balloon as a phallic symbol, as one would expect. But this simple meaning is not stable. The air balloon then does something in the dream, on its own, as it were, in a way not governed by its original function as a representation of a phallus – it triggers associations of World War One, perhaps, or of the Imperial War Museum in London as a repository of boyhood memories, or it decondenses and recaptures the sensation of wearing tight purple velvet loon pants in the 1960s. Pursuing a second-hand metaphor, the signifiying air balloon follows the title of David Niven's auto-biography (*The Moon's a Balloon*) and turns into a moon – or whatever. Signifiers float, drift away in currents of signification, free from any mooring in 'reality'.

The point is that it becomes very hard to trace back the meaning of signifiers to an original signified. Freud himself struggled to decide what the 'real' meaning of a dream or symptom was: in the most famous or notorious case, he prevaricated over whether the (very common) reports of infantile sexual abuse among his patients were representations of real events or just fantasies. The specific and general dilemmas are well discussed in Maccabe (1981).

More pragmatically, perhaps, the whole enterprise of 'centred readings' came into some disrepute. Basically, even if you could reliably trace back chains of signifiers to some 'real' origin, it would still not be clear why you wanted to do this – what's so special about a moment of origin? Why should the connection with the original signified assume such an overwhelming importance? Think of all the interesting meanings contained in the signification processes after that original moment – why should they be subordinated in some hierarchy, arranged according to some nontheoretical interest in practice? We see here a shift towards textuality, in other words, just as we saw in Eco's example (above), the polo shirt as an object of study in its own right.

Nor was this crisis of representation confined just to abstract or psychological analysis. To take one concrete example, Hebdige's mature work shows this shift in his analysis of youth cultures. The most popular Marxist explanation of youth cultures was as some kind of symbolic representation of the real conditions of life for the young (as in Hall and Jefferson 1976, for example). Hebdige was already identifying a shift away from this direct representational line in his famous study of 1979 (the Introduction charts a similar one in the work of Barthes, which we have discussed in Chapter 4). By the time he writes *Hiding in the Light* (1988) he is analysing inner histories of the signifier (the 'objects themselves' – scooters not Mods) to explain the significance of youth cultural icons, and we never hear again of the legendary 'class problematic' of the Hall and Jefferson material.

It follows that the crisis of representation is also a political crisis. The impeccably emancipatory intentions of Freudianism or Marxism cannot be grounded in a rigorous theoretical practice any more. Theoretical and practical interests no longer coincide, and as became clearly felt in the 1970s, after years of high-powered endeavour, they cannot be made to. Freud could not really rigorously explain how to cure people. Marxists or feminists cannot really do any better with pinning down the precise site of ideology or patriarchy. The whole 'epistemological project' is dead, as we argued in the previous chapter.

### Foundationalism in feminism?

To the extent that these problems of representation affect Marxism, Freudianism or structuralism, feminist approaches developed on these traditions will also import the crisis. I know best some of the earlier work that attempts to develop Marxist and

Freudian insights into feminist theory. I am aware that other insights crucial to the development of feminism seem to have come from women's direct experiences in the women's movement or more generally from being a woman (see Brunsdon, in Women's Study Group 1978) – and clearly I cannot claim any expertise there. I have also read some more recent work by leading female feminists on foundationalism in feminism (for example, those collected in Docherty 1993), although again I realise there is much I haven't read (Morris's piece in Docherty gives a large list of neglected commentaries on postmodernism written by women feminists). Some feminists have used and popularised Baudrillard's work anyway – such as Kaplan (1987) or Morris again. Fraser and Nicholson (in Docherty 1993) give a good balanced account of the foundational and anti-foundational elements in feminism, and I have tended to rely on that as a guide.

Feminism became of interest to me initially as a source of critique of foundational claims in Marx or Freud. This rather 'theoretical' interest dominates for me, rather than an immediate 'political' one, despite a general sympathy. I believe male academics should read feminist work primarily because it offers an essential corrective to the limits of classic work. Its great gains for male academics have been cognitive ones – we all now know a lot more about the world than we did. Certainly some fields I am interested in – such as cultural studies – have developed so well because they have been 'feminised' (Morris 1988).

Marxism was subject to a most impressive critique by writers like Beechey, Bland, Brunsdon and the other Birmingham feminists (see Women's Study Group 1978). Basically, Marxism was interrogated in some detail and found to lack sufficient explanatory power in key areas. Bland *et al.* argue, for example, that the workings of the labour market can only be grasped by considering a sexual division of labour too (a theme developed by Beechey, in Kuhn and Wolpe 1978) – that members of the 'reserve army' of the unemployed are disproportionately female, and that their labour has already been assigned a low status by families and more general ideological mechanisms. Detailed interactions between sexual and economic divisions of labour are needed to grasp the complexities: Marxism hitherto had just assumed rather than analysed some of the effects of the sexual division of labour.

More generally, family and kinship were connected back into economic analysis – seen as an important area of 'political' effects, not just a matter of consumption and distribution of rewards, for example – by breaking one of the boundaries between academic specialisms, exactly as Marx himself had done. Freud too came in for the same sort of critique and 'symptomatic reading'.

Freud's insights had been pressed into feminist service before, following a rejection of his biological mechanisms, and a rebuke for his feeble analysis of female sexuality specifically. The Lacanian re-reading seemed more promising (see p. 133) to overcome and generalise away from these limits and permit a proper account of patriarchy via the Oedipal moment. Burniston *et al.* (Women's Study Group 1978) review a number of classic pieces, including some by Mitchell and by Kristeva, and identify one problem with Freudian feminism of this kind: it is too abstract, offering some very general theory to explain patriarchy as such. When Freudians do get to the concrete level, it is to consider individuals. What is missing is an analysis of social structures, 'material practices' in concrete sites like families, media, work and education.

Some early arguments had simply tried to 'add women in' to existing conceptual schemes in Marxism and Freudianism. These critics, often men, had been guilty of foundationalism, assuming that the privileged concepts – mode of production, reserve army, Oedipal complex, mirror phase – could just be applied to women too. These feminists whom I have reviewed briefly argued that this was too simple, that the position of women had to be seen as a complex concrete one, the product of many determinations and concrete material situations and practices.

This anti-reductionist, anti-foundationalist stance still has difficulties, however, and even here foundationalism can reassert itself in two ways:

1 Not all feminist work has been as careful and as thorough as the material I have reviewed. Some of the more popular or polemical material uses foundational concepts like an unexplained and general 'patriarchy' in exactly the same flawed way as did advocates of 'dominant ideology' (see p. 127). It was everywhere, at the bottom of everything, from school curricula to Disney cartoons. It explained simultaneously both the oppression of women and their apparent liberation (as tokenism or incorporation). It fitted every case. Critics were guilty of a patriarchal blindness. 'Patriarchy' was biological in origin, or was cultural, or both. There is a clear danger here of incoherence

and/or dogmatism, in other words. Feminists in the tradition of Hindess and Hirst had little difficulty in applying their critique to a range of feminist work (see, for example, Kingdom's critical review 1980).

2 Even the more concrete analyses found it difficult to keep foundationalism out of their work. Another Hirstian (Adlam 1979) was able to argue that the concept 'capitalist patriarchy', for example, tended to slide between a Marxist and a biological foundationalism, and that, at the end of the day, all the concrete diversity of social relations still had to be reduced to one essential difference, some 'original signified', if you like, between men and women in feminist analysis. As with other radicalisms, this is partly because of an attempt tightly to connect theory and politics in an emancipatory narrative – 'scientific' interest in a coherent feminist theory, and the political need to build an activism around gender combine together to make sexual/gender differences into a privileged foundation. As with other Hirstians, Adlam suggests that a more calculative politics of alliances, some between men and women, some involving bases other than gender, needs to be developed instead.

McRobbie's (1994) interventions, from a 'cultural studies' perspective, sketch out some familiar problems too. Both politically and theoretically, gender has 'splintered' into a range of more complex identities and possibilities (black women, young women, married women, lesbian women, and so on) and is no longer so obviously a foundational 'condensation' or 'master identity' (see the discussion in Chapter 7). Nor is the feminist politics based upon this condensation so obviously suitable for all women. This can be liberating, when directed 'playfully', against those in power who would wish to use gender to control people in the classic way, but McRobbie is also worried about the fragmentation and relativism in the approach. Her answer involves a recognition of the challenge of postmodernist anti-foundationalism (as in 'a feminist "real me" was perhaps a necessary fiction in the early 1970s' (1994: 72) and a call for a new discursive articulation of these fragments, with a strategic interest rather than a theoretical one: 'an engagement with the politics of difference, as characterised not by pluralism but by lines of connection and disconnection . . . [via a quote from Judith Butler] "of expanding the possibilities of what it is to be a woman"' (ibid.: 73)

Here, a 'postfeminist' stance is being developed which bears a close similarity to 'post-Marxism' (which we discuss below), and which parallels 'postcolonialist' debates in matters of ethnicity. Certain difficulties are common to these positions too – whether that 'post' means a complete break or a partial one with what has gone before, and whether political interests can be harmonised with theoretical ones, as we shall see.

## Foundationalism in postmodernism?

If Denzin (1991) is correct, the usual source for a sustained critique of postmodernism is Jameson (1992) (the strange sequencing of dates here arises because of the dates of different editions of the works: Jameson 1992 contains essays written in the late 1980s). Jameson does indeed develop a powerful critique, but in two ways. Perhaps the most famous one concerns his attempt to explain the personal and cultural symptoms of postmodernism in terms of a process of 'reification', developing in a way that looks rather similar to Baudrillard's account of the increasing abstraction of signifiers and their increasingly trivialised and commercialised deployment in cultural markets and the mass media.

However, Jameson wants to retain a classic Marxist reading of this process of reification (not so much as a tendency for social relations to turn into things, he tells us, but in terms of an inability to relate objects to the circumstances in which they were produced, an 'effacement of the traces of production' (Denzin 1991: 314). This reification accounts for the lack of temporality, the immediacy or 'nominalism' of cultural activity, the lack of depth, the ceaseless 'renarrativization' and reordering of abstracted signs, and the growth of consumerism. This material process of reification follows the logic of capitalism itself, especially the advanced abstractions necessary for the global scale of the operations of 'late capitalism'. This is classically 'misrecognised' in everyday experience and in postmodernist writing which is 'the conceptuality that results' (ibid.: 375) from this massive globalised, abstract and virtually inconceivable system.

We shall be trying out this Marxist account later, in our more detailed discussions of 'lifestyles' (a word Jameson detests). It is difficult, however, to give the last word to the specifically Marxist thrust of Jameson's retort here. As we suggested in the Introduction, it is not easy to judge one approach 'externally', as it were, by using the terms of quite another. Crook *et al.* list Jameson with a number of other 'more-or-less' Marxist commentators who pursue a 'strategy . . . [running] . . . on well-worn tracks . . . to tame postmodernity and postmodernism by simply reasserting the priorities of modernist social theory' (Crook *et al.* 1992: 69), especially the supremacy of the economic or social level over the cultural one. On the other hand, Jameson insists on his right to 'name the system' (Jameson 1992: 415), and complains that post-modernism insulates itself against critique – 'it cannot be dis-proved insofar as its fundamental feature is the radical separation of all the levels and voices whose recombination in their totality could alone disprove it' (ibid.: 376).

We seem to be left with an impasse, or the need to opt for one system rather than another on some non-theoretical grounds. As we suggested in the Introduction, there is still room for an 'immanent' critique, however, whereby postmodernist writers can be judged against their own standards, especially in terms of their own prohibitions of foundationalism (or, as we suggest elsewhere, in terms of their consistency in their support of 'heterogeneity' or pluralism in political and aesthetic matters).

Here too Jameson offers a number of themes to begin with, many of which we pursue in more depth in this book. (Of course, they are not merely 'internal' or logical, but are connected with his overall Marxism.) However, we might consider problems arising from denying that postmodernism has broken with modernist narratives, for example; or the circularity in the way postmodernism points to a range of objects and practices as 'evidence' of its power, yet also claims to be somehow a result of tendencies already apparent in those objects, 'contained in the thing itself in embryo' (Crook *et al.* 1992: xii). We have mentioned specific problems like the ones involved in maintaining the distinctions between 'text' and 'work' (see Chapter 4), and there are many others scattered throughout Jameson's huge book: the need for a general theory despite an insistence on the specificity of individual practices, for example (Jameson 1992: 186–7) (a problem we discussed with Foucault's work, in Chapter 3). Above all, there is a contradiction (Jameson does not shrink from the term and all it implies) between the penetrating critical analysis of rival accounts (usually those of friends on the left, Jameson points out) and the uncritical stance towards the most banal equations of market choice with real choice, or of the celebration of heterogeneity and ethnic diversity (say) and the indifference of the labour market (or at best a liberal tolerance) towards *gastarbeiters* (ibid.: 341–57).

Moving away from Jameson specifically, as we have seen, it is by no means that easy to dispense with foundationalism. Post-modernism has unleashed a whole anti-foundational bandwagon, but it can be judged by its own creature. Some writers would say it must do so – that at the most general level, you cannot have a presuppositionless argument, that all arguments necessarily priv-ilege some concepts over others, despite the best attempts to work with origins that are unfixed, or ideals that claim to elude representation.

Crook (1991) argues this particularly well. The postmodernists also deploy privileged concepts, and they tend to reduce com-plexity to certain fundamental processes – 'monism', Crook calls it. Hindess and Hirst have a privileged kind of rigorous discourse in mind when they critique others for incoherence or dogmatism, for example.

Baudrillard has a privileged model, a kind of social evolu-tionary 'physicalist' process of explosion followed by implosion. Explosions of information via the media lead to 'the masses' becoming a saturated imploding 'black hole', indifferent to any more kinds of communication. Processes of social differentiation – for example, in modern consumerism – escalate into hyper-differentiation, and then collapse and reverse as they become so widespread as to lose any social meaning or significance. By contrast, Crook *et al.* (1992: 34) want to preserve a complexity arising from an interrelation between two major processes in modernity – 'The contradiction between hyperdifferentiation and monocentric organisation' – and we have seen some of the implications for popular culture especially (in Chapter 2). We have also seen Giddens's response to 'monism' in his insistence on a radical duality at the heart of social life.

Foucault also has a 'monist' foundational process – the 'micro-physics of power' – at the heart of his work, says Crook. Lyotard has been accused of deploying a new metanarrative of his own (Callinicos 1985; Jameson 1992; Habermas, in Dews 1992) under the guise of a scepticism towards all metanarratives, and we can see traces of that in our short discussion above: liberation for Lyotard lies in some essential heterogeneity.

Norris (1992) develops this point in a clear and readable manner too, in his critique of Lyotard on 'the sublime' (see esp. chs 4 and 5). We have seen how Lyotard uses the concept of the sublime, the 'unrepresentable', to deny support for mere commercial eclecticism masquerading as postmodernism, but it appears too in a more political discussion about historical accounts and whether we can choose between different versions of, say, the Holocaust. Lyotard apparently wants to deny revisionist versions of the Holocaust that deny that Auschwitz existed as a death camp – but on the grounds that 'history is always a "sublime" referent ... [hence] ... differing [accounts] cannot be resolved *either* by appealing to "the facts" ... *or* by invoking established concepts of truth, justice or ethical principle' (Norris 1992: 81). This is Lyotard's version of the manoeuvre we discussed with Barthes's turn towards textuality (Chapter 4) as some ineffable unreified play of language against which to judge the pretensions of mere 'works'. For Norris, this use of 'the sublime' is a wrong reading of Kant (a point taken up by Dews 1992 too), and leads to 'some dangerous forms of moral and political obfuscation' (Norris 1992: 81). More in line with our interests in 'immanent critique', though, Norris sees Lyotard using 'the sublime' to support 'radical hetero-geneity' and yet, in practice, to disqualify particular 'language games' or 'phrase regimes', those which do not insist on criteria of 'appeal to the known or discoverable facts of the case' (ibid.: 78).

Dews (1992) also summarises Habermas's work on post-modernism to point to substantial reductionism, in Lyotard's work especially, to match that of Jameson discussed above. To be brief, the legacy of Enlightenment rationality is reduced to discus-sions of science and 'instrumental rationality', and then opposed to an equally suspect excessive human subjectivity and playful-ness, just as in the most banal 'common sense', or even as in neo-conservatism. Lyotard does not accept the politics of neo-conservatism, of course, but he does share the analysis. These notions are actually a product of modernity anyway, argues Habermas. Apart from other problems, this sort of valorisation of excessive subjectivity helps us merely to shock the reader while systematically denying any rational grasp of the possibilities (see also Habermas 1984 on Bataille). Habermas's own views are summarised in the Conclusion, by comparison.

We have not considered him in any depth, but Derrida has not escaped 'metaphysics' and 'centring' (Ree 1984), despite his critique of others, and Dews (1987) provides a particularly useful analysis of Derrida's notion of *différance* as an origin (or foundation). Overall, says Dews, Derrida's efforts to maintain a foundationless system that also tries to account, with 'textual' concepts alone, for actual concrete meanings must be logically incoherent, 'an interminable attempt to subvert and evade a structure of thought which must perpetually renew itself' (Dews 1987: 36).

A particularly famous and influential critique comes from Bourdieu (1986) too. His attempts to chart the nature of (petit) bourgeois aesthetics make a neat link with postmodern aesthetics. The description of postmodern experience in someone like Vattimo (1992) celebrates the cultural diversity, the liberation of local 'dialects', the displacement of absolute value-systems by relative ones, the centrality of 'communication', as everything becomes 'cultural', and the joys of experiencing 'freedom as a continual oscillation between belonging and disorientation' (Vattimo 1992: 10). For Bourdieu, this sort of playfulness is characteristic of bourgeois aesthetics; it is embraced largely by the economically and financially secure, and its social use is to distinguish itself against the relative certainties and immediacies of both popular and 'official' taste. We have a classic case, in other words, of special tastes and interests being elevated into allegedly universal ones, then used as a foundation for analysis.

Constant vigilance is the only guarantee against foundationalism for Crook (1991); but even this runs risks, principally of inviting back in philosophical deconstructors and anti-foundationalists as some kind of beings blessed with superior insight, Habermas wants to suggest (in Dews 1992). As we shall see, for him only a permanently open commitment to rational discourse, where the validity of any claim can be challenged, would prevent foundationalism and its consequent philosophical idealism and excess. A modesty and self-awareness, rather than rash claims to have invented new sciences, to have made major breakthroughs, to have made all previous knowledge redundant, or to have founded a new liberating politics grounded in the truth, would be welcome.

One solution, then, leads to a kind of academic avant-gardism. Just as radical film-makers like Godard wanted to make the audience aware of the artifices needed to construct a film, some writers (Derrida and Baudrillard are often cited here) attempt a sustained openness in their writings. On a more mundane note, it might be possible to insist that academics also be required, if necessary, to 'lay bare the assemblage' of their arguments, to cite an older debate (see Harris 1987a). An account, and justi-fication, of our privileged concepts might be required, a grasp of the ironic ways our work turns out to have consequences which we did not intend.

Feminist writers have pioneered some of the techniques here, and some classic writers have been better at it than others – it is not altogether absent in Marx and Freud. The danger is that this self-reflective approach also turns into a mere style at the end of the day, one designed to disarm the critic, give the appearance of openness to involve the reader and prepare them for the strong claims of 'prime knowledge' at the end, after all the modesty, doubt and irony (see McLaren and Smith on the techniques of 'televangelism', in Giroux *et al.* 1989, or Lasch 1982 on the sinister aspects of irony and self-effacement).

At the same time, however, the excessive clarities of pedagogic writing are also suspect, as we saw in the Introduction. As Kamuf (1991: xii) says: 'Standard notions of clarity or "correct" style . . . must be seen themselves as obscurantist since they encourage a belief in the transparency of words to thoughts, and thus a "knowledge" constructed on this illusion.' Of course, no one wants obscurity for its own sake or as a distancing device.

## Post-Marxism

In the section above, we have criticised Marxists quite a bit, or side-stepped them, and it is interesting to see how they might have responded to all the attacks on foundationalism, the linguistic turn and the other critiques. I want to concentrate on British Marxists especially here (which means the Gramscians in cultural studies again, largely). We have seen something of the dilemmas of French Marxists in earlier chapters, and in Chapter 3 traced Marxist approaches in their relations with other systems, includ-ing Foucault's. I also want to use the discussion to highlight some possible difficulties facing postfeminism, although I have not foregrounded these particularly. Perhaps there are some general principles from this discussion of post-Marxism which could be tried out on postfeminism, but I shall leave it to my readers to debate this.

A series of debates in *New Left Review*, including a bitter controversy between Laclau and Mouffe (1987) and Geras (1987, 1988) serves as a good introduction to the issues. Hebdige (1988) and Grossberg's (1986) interview with Hall also have good discussions, and I have ventilated the debate in Harris (1992). Bennett (1990, esp. ch. 10) offers another useful critical discussion of the Laclau and Mouffe position.

Briefly, 'post-Marxists' like Laclau and Mouffe wanted to take seriously the criticisms of Marxism and the turn to the textual metaphor, and to rethink various approaches to Marxism as discourse theories. This rescued and modernised Marxism, and recognised the flaws in the old conceptions quite openly – the old essentialism, the dubious causal models and determinist accounts, where everything was rooted in the commodity form and the economy in the last instance. But it meant that Marxism had to take its place as a mere discourse, not as a science, and to be prepared to take on more linguistic forms of analysis to stay credible (a project already begun by Gramscians keen on Marxist linguistics anyway). The main goal of Marxism becomes a political one, and the old 'scientific' pretensions have to be abandoned in favour of a more pragmatic interest in establishing a suitable unifying and articulating discourse for the 1980s – more or less as we have already discussed above, via 'calculative politics' and McRobbie's proposals for feminism.

In this project, massive amounts of critique have been admitted. All that seems to be left is some central belief in 'struggle' to change the system, vaguely in the interests of 'everybody'. Everything else in Marxism, including the major interest in the proletariat as the agent of change, or, indeed, even class struggle itself, is displaced as central. We have discussed this sort of proposal for drastic revision before, in Chapter 3.

As always, such revisions are 'good', because they mean that post-Marxism is no longer tied to the old projects of the past, and can have a voice in modern struggles (around women, black people and the environment). But there is the embarrassment of making Marxism look like a kind of refurbished, all-purpose doctrine or label that must survive at all costs, an opportunistic politics not really different from any other (not all that different from the once-despised and short-lived Social Democratic Party in Britain, for example). There are additional problems too, so Geras says. We have mentioned Geras before, but in summary:

- everything is now 'politics', admitted by the new post-Marxism. Any discourse about any issue can involve 'struggle', including disputes between two neighbours over an uncut hedge;
- any attempt to deny interest in 'trivial' struggles involves making some extra-discursive claim about the 'real' issues – which smuggles in foundationalism again, or, at the least, those bits of Marxism which are supposed to have been replaced. Why should we be interested in the particular struggles of women, black people and environmentalists especially? Because Laclau and Mouffe tell us they are important and 'progressive' and assume that any sensible person will agree. An undisclosed set of political values has set the agenda in practice, of course;
- the shift to discourse theory has problems of its own anyway. It still runs the risk of foundationalism, this time with 'discourse' at the heart of all analysis (we saw this with Crook's discussion. The notion of 'articulation', at the centre of the new role for socialist intellectuals constructing new political blocs, is also incoherent: how can disparate political issues and struggles be articulated exactly? What do they have in common? If they share some 'real' features before skilled politicians articulate them together, there is some 'real' level to politics after all, and it is not only a matter of skilled discursive articulation. If disparate struggles have nothing in common before someone comes along and articulates them, on the other hand, then the attempted articulation merely seems arbitrary or opportunistic and will be ineffective. Is there a real basis to the longed-for alliance between black people, women, disabled groups and sexual minorities, or is it all wishful thinking and abstraction in the minds of activist academics?

In my view, this ambiguity runs through much work on articulation. In some fairly recent work on black identities, for example (Hall 1993; Hall, in Donald and Rattansi 1992): 'blackness' seems to be both an element that can be articulated in various ways with other identities (as in full-blown discourse theory) *and* some kind of special master identity with some special reality above, beyond or 'outside' the discourses that energise it. It could be purely a tactical matter, based on appeals to the reader to join in some apparently agreed project to found a new cultural politics or on exhortations to share in a new beginning, involving perhaps what McRobbie (1994) refers to as 'strategic essentialism' – but this too is risky.

As with the other examples, it seems difficult to escape foundationalism by embracing discourse theory, and then escape the relativism of discourse theory by opting back again. Post-Marxist analysis and commentary could become a matter of smuggling political priorities back in, once we were assured we were safe in communities of like-minded people, but staying cool, ironic, detached and indifferent in more critical company. Such tactics could only work in the short term, however, and they risk the audience (and the activists) becoming cynical. As Bennett (1990: 251) puts it: 'To suggest, in these circumstances, that socialists should "fake it" too reduces politics to a contest between big black lies and little white ones.'

## CONCLUDING THOUGHTS

This has been a rather demanding chapter, in which we have outlined some of the basic tenets of postmodernism through its most commonly cited spokespersons. I have then tried to explore some of the more important 'methodological' implications via an exploration of the attacks launched against conventional social sciences and its 'foundationalism'. These alone demand respect, and prevent us from simply asserting the tenets of conventional social science back, as it were; reclaiming postmodernism under Marxism, say (Lasch comes pretty close to doing this, and we explore his approach in Chapter 7). Nevertheless, it is possible to isolate some problems with postmodernism from within an 'immanent' critique, and I hope I have illustrated some. They run parallel to those discussed in Barthes's influential work (see Chapter 4).

The rest of the book goes on to discuss these matters in more detail. Applying terms like 'postmodern' to the specific areas of everyday life, tourism or film and television will reveal a concrete dimension to these rather abstract discussions. Here, we encounter a strong suspicion that postmodernist commentary has abolished the class system or the micropolitical structures of everyday life only in thought (to borrow a phrase from Jameson).

We already know from our preliminary discussions in Chapters 1 and 2 what to anticipate. Real films and TV programmes resist any simple analysis, however (and so do music videos, as we shall demonstrate). The debates about them lead us into questions about the whole validity of the textual metaphor: when we analyse these pieces merely as texts, we have to struggle with further problems; for example, if we wish to choose between them on the grounds of worth. When we discuss the audience in any sort of concrete way, and I shall be suggesting that we must, issues arise revealing the 'struggle for meaning' that can occur, and we eventually arrive at issues of power again, as an 'outside' to texts after all.

We now go on to consider 'everyday life', identity and 'lifestyles': do people 'do' a kind of free-floating textuality there? Are those areas best considered as 'postcultures', as 'societies of signs'?

# 6

# Film and video and
# 'postmodernist sensibility'

Chapters 6 and 7 both review some material on personal identity in modernity. The issue of identity is at the heart of many discussions of modernity and its impact, and it is one area in particular that gives postmodernist analyses their force. We rehearsed the argument in the previous chapter: postmodernism is not just an abstract philosophical debate, but it has applications to everyday life. Somehow the term seems to capture really effectively something of the experience of life in societies like ours at the end of the twentieth century.

Identity is a convenient topic to choose to try and focus some of the debates because it is also central to work in classic sociology (where it tends to be found among discussions of socialisation of various types and at different levels). It is a major theme too in cultural studies, and here the work concerns what might be called the politics of identity, the cultural processes which construct it, and the ways in which people manage to resist, or to develop, identities against the cultural flow, both generally and in specific encounters with actual films, TV programmes, shopping malls or any other institution.

Somewhere in here are the materials that could be used to generate a considerable research programme. The different arguments tend to stay rather separated at present, however. Sociological work has emphasised face-to-face contacts and settings for the construction of identity, which has underplayed less immediate contexts (like the identities constructed for people in films). Where these have been studied, there has been a tendency to pursue social policy goals (as in studies of the effects of the media on the violent behaviour of the young), and such 'effects analysis' has often been accused of missing the specifics of the experience of watching film, and the extent to which the audience interprets, constructs and even resists the main 'messages' of the film. For their part, film analysts have also placed too tight a boundary around their special interests, and have shown an indifference towards the social identities that viewers bring to a film and how their past socialisation has affected their readings.

Some recent sociological commentaries on identity are also very abstract: we have trailed this criticism of Giddens's work before (Chapter 1), and we shall examine it in more depth in the next chapter. Giddens is being singled out there as an example, of course – we could also apply the same criticism to some of Bauman's recent work too, for example. In my view, this sort of analysis is just far too simple, easy and 'lazy' – a general concept of 'identity' calls to and confirms the occasional throwaway remark about a film or a current social pastime (and vice versa) in that circular 'poetics' which we have noted before.

There is need of some work, then, to pull together studies in sociology and in cultural studies, and to use concrete studies in both fields to flesh out and criticise the very general and abstract discussions commonly found. Goffman's work is a rare exception to the trends I have been describing, and we shall consider it as we proceed. No one could fail to be aware of the immense methodological problems involved in such a labour, and it is not surprising, perhaps, that no one has really made an attempt at such a major synthesis. My own goal is much more modest: to exhibit key examples from the range of work available in order to re-open debates, especially to resist the spreading view that (all? most?) identities in modernity can simply be described under slogans like 'nomadic subjectivity' or 'postculture'. I hope this does not break my implicit contract with you, the reader of a textbook, to help you to package and manage this material. I have not abandoned all structuring devices, as you will see, but I offer lists of topics and debates rather than any tight conclusions.

We have to start this process somewhere, and this chapter focuses on film and television and the debates within media studies and cultural studies about them. In the next chapter, we concern ourselves with the more classically 'sociological' interests – socialisation, primary groups and consumerism. This division between the two chapters is really only a device to permit manageable chapters in a textbook, and the hope is that readers will find relevant material in both.

To introduce the study of films in this context might still be a little problematic, of course. Can films really construct or confirm an identity for the viewer? We can begin our investigations with some classic early debates.

## POSITIONING THEORY

The problem of identity in films was studied in one tradition through Marxist concepts of ideology and the subject. We have already mentioned some work here (in Chapter 1). Some analysts used Gramscian concepts to try to demonstrate how film and popular television operate with some idea of 'national identity', for example. As a major contribution (Hall, in Curran *et al.* 1977) argued, this national identity was maintained by a process classically outlined in Marx's discussion of ideology: the divisions in British society are recognised, but in a strangely evasive manner (social class differences appear as regional or occupational ones, say), and these can then be culturally managed in some media pageant of national unity (Christmas, royal weddings or VE Day celebrations, perhaps).

The same logic is apparent in current affairs programmes too, for Hall and his associates (in Bennett *et al.* 1981). Here, the very structure of the programme lays out a managed division and unity, the former represented by the usual representatives of legitimate different perspectives, the latter by the anchorperson who speaks for the 'common viewer'.

Another approach ('*Screen* theory') drew on different Marxist resources, largely from Althusser and Lacan, and again we have met this work briefly (in Chapter 5) in the particular form of feminist analysis of the 'male gaze' in film. Classically, it will be recalled, gendered 'subject positions' (or 'identities', in our terminology) are constructed as the effect of such a gaze. Pleasure for the viewer was delivered only after submission to the organising gazes of the film.

The main theme for such analyses concerned the organisation of the narrative structure of the film, in other words. The positioning of the viewer arises not so much from his or her identification with the characters, but from a deeper involvement in the story told by the film. The classic work here is the famous article on the realist film by Maccabe (in Bennett *et al.* 1981). Realism is not a matter of authentic content, Maccabe argues, but a matter of narrative organisation. The realist film contains a number of discourses, or perspectives on reality offered by the various characters, but the film's narrative structure operates to arrange them in a hierarchy.

What this means is that the viewer is led to see some discourses as 'correct', others as flawed or limited, and is thus led towards a 'true' perception of the reality of the film. The opening analogy in Maccabe's piece is with a classic novel like *Middlemarch*. The various characters' speech is enclosed within quotation marks, so we know that their perspectives are subjective and attributable. The author's comments surround these speeches, and help us to make sense of them – and these comments are not attributed to anyone subjective, but offer an underlying reality for the viewer. After reading the novel, we emerge with a sense that we have learned something about reality, about the vanity or naiveté of the characters, about the importance of personal lives, and so on.

Films offer similar techniques, argues Maccabe, to guide the viewer's reading. Sometimes there is an all-powerful narrator off-camera (as in documentaries), or perhaps the camera itself shows us the reality which frames the perspectives of the characters, and thus interprets them. To take a scene from a favourite Slovak film (of mine, not Maccabe's): the characters in *The Shop on the High Street* are discussing whether or not the local Nazis are about to round up the Jews, and the camera leaves the discussion to look out of the window, where we see the lorries starting to assemble in the town square. There is no doubt which character has the firmest grasp of reality, and the hero is exposed as a weak optimist trying to deny the consequences of his actions.

This whole analysis is placed in the context of Marxist theories of the subject, for Maccabe. Narrative techniques like these are examples of 'hailing' or the construction of the subject. The viewer is 'positioned' by these techniques, led to a view of reality itself, and allowed to 'discover' it. What seems pleasurable and personal is in fact the result of a structure of 'dominant specularity'. The realist film constructs a sense of reality which is suspiciously manageable and transparent (and, classically, devoid of any Marxist contradictions), but it also constructs a passive viewer, a perfect subject for capitalism. We can generalise away from the Marxist politics of the viewer for a moment and apply this discussion to our focus on identity as such – identities of ourselves, as knowledgeable, insightful individuals with emotions and beliefs, are also the product of narrative techniques like the ones we encounter in realist films.

Maccabe then goes on to discuss techniques which socialists might use to break the hold of this narrative structure, but this need not detain us here. In brief, any attempt merely to bend this narrative structure towards socialist goals (as in 'social realism') is likely to end in an equally passive viewer or a highly conventional reading after all. Properly critical films must break with this hierarchical organisation of discourses altogether, and present much less mediated and organised knowledge to the viewers, to encourage them to think things out for themselves. This leads to a strong support for avant-garde pieces like Godard's *Tout va bien*, of course.

## FROM POSITIONING TO TEXTUALITY

The break-up of the 'positioning' approach we have just outlined has been described already as an acknowledgement that something has happened to the hierarchical narrative structure in popular films. We have described this earlier in terms of a shift from (realist) representation to (nonrealist, hyperrealist) signification. We can trace this conveniently in the work on the Bond film.

The 'Bond phenomenon' has been widely discussed by all the major commentators, including Eco and Barthes as well as Baudrillard, as we have seen. Bennett and Woollacott's work has been cited earlier, but it stands as a clear example of a major development in film studies which reopens the whole question of identity, although actually in a rather abstract '(post)structuralist' manner. In the process, we move away from the ideological straitjacket clamped on the audience in classic 'positioning theory'.

Bennett and Woollacott are so useful here because they began their work with an attempt (in an Open University course unit – Open University 1981) to read James Bond films as ideological in a fairly recognisably feminist and (Gramscian) Marxist manner. A structuralist tinge to the analysis was provided by the early Eco piece (collected in Waites *et al.* 1982) on the structuring 'codes' of the Bond novels, which we have mentioned in Chapter 1.

Bennett and Woollacott began to read Bond films in terms of how their main themes represent some sort of filmic solution to the problems for national identity raised by the latest crisis of British capitalism: Bond serves to embody Britain in a post-imperialist world dominated by the great powers, the Soviet Union (SMERSH), other hostile coalitions (SPECTRE), and the USA (the plentifully resourced but easily outwitted CIA, often represented in the person of the character Felix Leiter).

There were, of course, connected themes of sexuality and patriarchy: Bond operates in a world dominated by the father-figure M, who stands for the law, and Bond uses his own sexuality to dominate women and restore them to their proper political place. The classic example here is the fate of Pussy Galore in the novel *Goldfinger*, who has no strongly heterosexual interests until she is bedded by Bond. She switches sides after her initiation. The result of Bond's intervention is to win her over to his side both politically and sexually, say Bennett and Woollacott. By such means, the hugely popular Bond phenomenon is itself embedded in ideology, via various 'codes', and reproduces it in order to position individuals by delivering a pleasurable experience and a strong conventional political message at the same time.

Later work by the same authors takes a different tack, however (Bennett and Woollacott 1987). The Bond movies develop a momentum of their own, pushed along by the skills and talents of an unusually coherent production team and by the needs of a mass market for Bond, a much wider one than the specific male British readership originally addressed by the novels. The ideological themes become modernised at one end of the scale (for example, *A View to a Kill* centres on a threat to Silicone Valley and refers to a whole technology developed since Fleming's day) and thinned down or replaced altogether at the other end – the strong black female figure of Mayday, in the same film, plays as decisive a role as Bond whose attempt at sexual dominance 'like his Englishness is a damp squib' (Bennett and Woollacott 1987: 352).

The films could still be seen as responding to later versions of dominant ideology – an ironic imperialism, perhaps, or one of those subtle forms of patriarchy where women achieve but have to pay a dreadful price for their transgressions: Mayday is dominant but she still dies at the end in rather public circumstances as we gaze at her, Bennett and Woollacott point out. The films could also still be related to the main themes at a deeper level, as when Solomos and Beck (1994) suggest that various apparently autonomous discourses on racism are related together as metonyms.

Yet some changes seem genuinely inspired by filmic impulses, by the possibilities of signification, to use the terms of our Chapter

2: for example, Bond wins thanks to nicely visual gadgetry rather than the allegedly uniquely English qualities of improvisation, which are far less easy to represent on film. Car chases and special effects are added, borrowing from other successful thrillers, in formulaic spectacular opening and closing scenes.

Above all, however, Bennett and Woollacott chart the increasingly self-referential nature of the Bond movies – the opening scene in *A View to a Kill* recalls and parodies openings in earlier Bond films or, more widely, scenes from Bond movies recall other genres at certain moments, and there are even deliberate, slightly mocking references to other major films – the success of *Jaws*, for example, led directly to the name of one of the more memorable Bond characters, Bennett and Woollacott assure us.

There are theoretical developments to be included in any modern analysis too, and we have already linked Bennett and Woollacott to Barthes's interest in the 'new semiology'. A major shift takes place with the attempt to construe the Bond audience as made up of various 'reading formations', for example. Bennett and Woollacott assign the major function of finding meaning to these reading formations, instead of focusing on the signs manipulated in the film itself. It is not that the audience decodes the film in different ways, they tell us – these different readings constitute the film. 'The film' as a single entity has disappeared, and its ideological meaning can be embedded nowhere else but in audience readings. These might include the imperialist and patriarchal ones we began with – but others are equally possible (although never really developed in the analysis).

Another theoretical departure involves incorporating the work on 'desire' and how this provides a range of unconscious pleasures for the audience. Bennett and Woollacott are suggesting here that unconscious pleasures are much more creative and productive than had been thought (for example, by earlier Mulvey, whose work we have mentioned): men can read the famous scene in *Goldfinger*, where Bond is spread-eagled on a table to be menaced by a laser as an (enjoyable) male rape fantasy as well as the more conventional castration anxiety averted, for example.

In both cases, though, meanings are to be produced in concrete circumstances rather than read off from some general critical theory, with the participants, both the production team and the reading formations in the audience, doing active work rather than just living out some preformed ideological practice. With this sort of analysis, we take a step towards a full recognition of film as signification. The implications of the ways in which films construct identities should also be clear. We have moved away from a 'hailing' model, and, indeed, raised doubts about the whole Marxist attempt to subsume identity under the term 'ideology'.

As became common in cultural studies of the late 1980s, the film audience is allowed a considerable degree of 'resistance', or what Giddens might insist on as 'reflexive monitoring'. Identities are not constructed or reinforced tightly by films any more and we are well on the way to seeing the viewer as a knowledgeable, playful and competent actor, quite prepared to let the film offer a temporary identity, so to speak, but by no means incapable of taking up alternative viewing positions.

Much has been written about the active viewer ever since, and we shall return to the topic later in this chapter. The strands of playful signification at the production end and ironic interpretation at the viewing end are main elements in postmodern interpretations of film, to which we now turn.


## POSTMODERNISM

So far, postmodernism has been discussed in terms of social theory, and we have been involved in discussions of foundationalism, Freudianism and so on (in Chapter 5). Yet postmodernism is also a term used to describe cultural changes, including those often noted in film. There are other areas where the debate has raged, including architecture and photography; Appignanesi (1989) and Docherty (1993) have discussions on these areas too. Although it is not my field, I understand, for example, that architecture has been a major arena for public and critical discussion of postmodernism, especially in the USA, and there are a number of interesting pieces on it.

One debate that strikes a chord immediately with me, however, is Frampton's work (in Appignanesi 1989 and in Docherty 1993). Frampton recaptures nicely the flavour of public scepticism about 'modernist' architecture in Britain, especially those attempts to do social engineering by building colossal rectangular 'streets in the sky', or huge glass and concrete stumps in the City of London in defiance of public taste. Public rejection of these buildings, and of the assumptions that underlay them, led to demands for more local, nostalgic and humanist styles. It is easy to see that the debate also turned on scepticism towards the foundationalist and emancipatory claims of 'modernist' aesthetic theory, and also that, conversely, uneasiness arises with alternatives that embrace mixtures of architectural styles as a kind of self-conscious creation of hyperreality again (Outhwaite and Bottomore 1994 have an excellent short discussion).

## Characteristics of the postmodern film

The debates about social theory can be connected to discussions about postmodernism in film in familiar ways, echoing arguments in the previous chapter. The possibilities include the following points:

- Some critics have noticed changes going on in film and elsewhere, and have generalised from them to suggest some underlying cultural trend or shift going on in society itself, perhaps via some term like *zeitgeist* ('spirit of the times') or perhaps in some other way (appointing individuals to be spokespersons for the whole culture). As with architecture, a local cultural crisis can be taken as a symptom of a much larger one.
- Social theorists, pursuing the implications for culture in the writings on the eclipse of metanarratives, for example, have turned to film theory for specific exemplars to test their theories.
- Various theorists, critics, artists and film-makers have read some social theory and each other and have popularised the term 'postmodernism' to describe what they think is going on. It is not that they rigorously apply social theory and the debates about it (although Hebdige 1988 tells us that 'Hollywood reads *Screen*'), but rather that they apply looser inferences from a received general intellectual debate. (Featherstone 1991 outlines this approach in more detail, and charts the oscillations between critics in Europe and America.) They may well be motivated in doing this as a form of social distinction, as a way of eroding the claims of traditional classes and advancing their own. If this is so, the more flexibly that terms like 'postmodernism' are used, the greater tactical advantage they may yield.

In short, there may be no tightly agreed definition of the term 'postmodernism' in film criticism. There is a debate about stylistic changes in films and TV programmes, and it is possible to connect these loosely to elements in the crisis of social theory we discussed in Chapter 5. Clearly, there will be vagueness and overlap and, as we shall see, a major problem in trying to spot the difference between 'real' or 'serious' postmodernism and its vulgar copies or imitations, simulations even (or between 'spectacular' and 'transgressive' forms in Lash's 1988 account). However, it is customary to list some of the characteristics of film central to the debate:

- scepticism towards metanarratives in social theory might mesh with further departures from narrative in film or TV, the rise of popular non-narrative pieces (including films or programmes as sequences of episodes or spectacles – *Pulp Fiction*, say, or even *Natural Born Killers*). The end of narrative could explain the deliberate absence of tight authorial control, the end of the author in the senses we discussed in Chapter 4;
- anti-foundationalism in social theory might connect with the disinterest in 'depths' in film, in a focus on surfaces and appearances (Almodovar, for example, especially *Pepi, Luci, Bom* . . ., with its 'innocent' and unexplained 'slices of life' approach, and its conspicuous lack of moral commentary on the doings of the characters). Again, there are connections with the end of narrative, and a turn away from realism and representation. We have already discussed Lash's notion of the 'figural' and the 'schizophrenic viewer' in film (in Chapter 2);
- the crisis of representation in social theory might mesh with interests in treating films as signification, as communication, as experiment with the signs of the cinema. This would produce a disinterest in representing the underlying 'truth' and an increase in self-referential ('intertextual' or 'metafictional') elements in film – films would primarily 'be about' other films. This might be done deliberately to 'transgress', alienate viewers and draw attention to film conventions, as in the classic avant-garde, but commercial films would also feature the spectacular or the hyperreal rather than try to confine the meaning of signs tightly to some external reality: Lash mentions *Rambo*, and we could add *Jurassic Park* as examples;
- scepticism about emancipatory claims would extend to 'political cinema' at least, with film-makers like Godard (or Loach or Potter) abandoning their interest in using film to educate the masses, represent universal classes or somehow to 'speak for

humanity'. We might expect even Hollywood to abandon Freudian themes for films (consciously, that is, except as a joke, say in Lynch's *Blue Velvet*), or to stop making 'earnest' films that tell us of the state of the nation ('paranoid cinema' pieces like *The Parallax View* or *JFK*). Irony, playfulness, cultural relativism, parody, pastiche, even plagiarism would all figure instead – as in, say, *Wayne's World 2*;

- the collapse of internal differentiations could help to locate the growth of new or cross-genre pieces, including a number of 'posts' (post-western, post-gangster). More generally, high and low cultures would mix – Bergman would meet Bill and Ted; Beethoven would meet football hooliganism (*A Clockwork Orange*); directors like Ridley Scott would cross between feature film, music video and advertisement, or, like John Landis, direct both horror films and Michael Jackson music video parodies of horror films.

Film criticism would become more playful and decentred, less concerned to point out the sinister operations of ideology (Marxist or feminist) inherent in every film. There would be more interest in the details and processes of signification, perhaps, instead of the main concern with representations: the distinction between the 'reality of the film' and some superior external reality somehow immediately available would be weakened, as critics took seriously the view that it is impossible to get to external reality 'outside (any) text(s)'.

The critic would no longer claim to speak on behalf of Reason, Science, Enlightenment or Humanity as a Whole, but would be much more modest, self-referential and aware of ironies. It would no longer be possible to claim some special insight denied to ordinary people, and the great barriers would disappear between 'critic' and 'fan', or between newspaper reviews and academic criticism. Within critical pieces, we would notice increasingly the phenomenon of the 'slippery pronoun', as critics spoke in the first person (not as some disembodied Voice of Reason), and slid between the identities of 'academic' and 'ordinary viewer'.

## Applying the analysis

Attempts to 'apply' this kind of analysis to actual films reveal some interesting difficulties, however. Denzin's influential piece is one attempt to maintain some kind of critical commentary, interrogating films like *Wall Street* and *When Harry Met Sally* ... or, best known of all, *Blue Velvet*, and finding them still riddled with conservative notions of class, race and gender: 'On the surface benignly playful, [such texts] ... disguise ideology as entertainment ... empty seriality is now the bond which unites the audience, and the electronic image is the only sign of reality that counts' (Denzin 1991: 151). On the other hand, films like *Blade Runner* 'expose the postmodern condition and all its contradictions', and Denzin also admires 'discursive, figural and transgressive postmodern films (*Brazil*), self-reflective cinema (*Speaking Parts*), postmodernist science fiction (*The Fly, Videodrome*), and the morality tales of Woody Allen' (ibid.: 155). As a result, 'the postmodern world ... is too complex, too diverse and too heterogeneous' (ibid.: 157) to be summarised easily – but this also leaves open some radical possibilities.

Denzin's critique can be located without too much difficulty in the 'post-Marxist' tradition, however, an advocate of new articulations, of what we called 'micropolitics' (in Chapter 3), on a rather individualist level this time (involving the creation of 'mystories'), with all the attendant difficulties we discussed above. Reading his trenchant critiques of films like *Blue Velvet* offers an interesting experience for any fans of the film, and will doubtless raise in a concrete way many of the theoretical and methodological issues we have been discussing.

Thus Denzin examines a number of published 'readings' of *Blue Velvet* – 'pornography, parable of sin and redemption, like religious art, a cult film, Gothic, coming-of-age film, trash, mindless junk, *film noir*, murder mystery, small town film, dream film, comedy, surrealism' (ibid.: 74). However, he still insists that these can be grouped into 'two clusters of hegemonic meaning' ('morally conservative' and 'morally liberal'), points out the absence of a crucial reading for him ('the violent treatment of women in the film's text' – ibid.), and then develops his own, showing how the contradictory meanings in the film add up to a 'bad' synthesis, which 'take[s] conservative political stances, while valoriz[ing] and exploit[ing] the radical social margins of society' (ibid.: 79).

Denzin's analysis depends on strong political commitments as well as on skilled resolutions of different readings that preserve them and show their inferiority compared to his own (a technique not far removed from the classic narratives which he admires in 'critical realism'). He knows that other critics disagree: Lash (1988) admires the 'transgressions' of *Blue Velvet* (and, we might add, Lasch 1982 despises Woody Allen films as the very embodiment of the kind of narcissism we discuss in Chapter 7).

This leaves us with the usual dilemmas of trying to establish which of these various readings is 'correct', or, indeed, whether we should bother to try and decide between them at all, and if so, on what grounds. The real problem, for me, is that none of the analyses discusses the essential 'third term' (to borrow a phrase from Dews's critique of Derrida): the concrete reader of the film. Although Denzin urges us to construct our own stories and selves, he is strangely abstract in discussing his own readings: is his analysis his own 'mystory', or is it still some kind of reading that stands for liberated humanity as a whole? We have noticed this problem before – with the notion of a 'reading formation' in Chapter 4, for example.

## Television and video

Analyses of television or video cause similar difficulties. Again, Jameson has been influential here with his essay (collected in Jameson 1992). Briefly, he discusses experimental video as a kind of 'pole case' of television (the 'installation art' of Nam June Paik, and a piece called *AlienNATION*). In his analysis of the latter, he stresses the ceaseless flow of images, the apparently 'senseless' collection of them, which simply defies a normal reading. It is possible occasionally to try and freeze these meanings, to fix them and pin them down as simpler sequences, or to impose themes upon some of the sequences (we gather from the title of the piece that it is about 'alienation', for example), and Jameson says he definitely spots a reference to a particular bizarre murder trial involving 'milk and Twinkie' (ibid.: 93).

Generally, however, the seamless flow of images is what triumphs, endless sequences of signifiers floating free from any referent. This is what Barthesian textuality must be like, suggests Jameson (rather ironically I thought), 'ceaseless renarrativization of already existing narrative elements by each other' (ibid.: 88), the 'pure and random play of signifiers that we call postmodernism . . . metabooks which cannibalize other books' (ibid.: 96). As we might guess from our discussion above, he points out some negative consequences: if all videotexts merely reproduce meaning like this, then 'they all ... turn out to be "the same" in a peculiarly unhelpful way' (ibid.: 95) – and goes on to account for this form in terms of reification rather than of some spontaneous creativity.

This kind of analysis is resisted in the rather humourless and 'generational' special pleading entered by Zurbrugg (1991), who accuses Jameson of having missed the liberating and artistic qualities of experimental video because a 'time wall' prevents him from developing a suitable 'postmodernist sensibility' (that conveniently empty signifier again). However, the themes in the critique have set an agenda for much wider commentary, as Hayward and Kerr's 'Introduction' (1987: 7) to the *Screen* special on postmodernism reveals:

> there is one school of thought which argues that television is in a sense implicitly postmodern since it is comprised almost in its entirety of 'quotations' from non-televisual 'ready-made' texts – stage plays and parliamentary proceedings, novels and public ceremonies, sporting events and cinematic works – and that it then proceeds to cut them up, slow them down, speed them up and generally rearrange and repeat them in whole or in part again and again.

That collection also contains the famous piece by Grossberg which 'identifies "in-difference", "repetitions" and "excess" as essentially postmodern characteristics' (Hayward and Kerr 1987), and focuses on *Miami Vice* as

> nothing but a collection of quotations from our own collective historical debris, a mobile game of Trivia ... the perfect televisual image, minimalist ... yet concrete ... The protagonists spend their lives not so much patrolling Miami as cruising it, only to rediscover the narrative in the last few minutes.
>
> (Grossberg 1987: 29)

## Music videos

The same themes have influenced analysis of perhaps the most often-cited example: music TV or the music video. Here too, for the more experimental ones at least, the initial impression is of seamless flow that defies categorisation or analysis, repetition, excess, quotation to the point of plagiarism, and the refusal of referents. However, there is now a considerable debate about music videos and how to read them.

To summarise some possible interpretations, music videos are very diverse, as you will know probably far better than I do. They can be seen as documentary-like records of performances, as 'extended advertisements', as popular art forms, virtually indistinguishable from prestige experimental shorts (Peter Gabriel videos are often cited, or those produced by experimental filmmakers like the Brothers Quay or Derek Jarman), or as witty, self-referential filmic texts (Madonna videos or *The Making of Thriller*). Amid the complexity, there have been at least two main frameworks developed to read these videos.

The first draws on critical (Marxist and feminist) work on popular music and popular culture. Although the details vary, it is fair to say that this approach sees the music video in terms of the familiar techniques of consumer capitalism, embedded still in a mode of production. A music video can be grasped as an advertisement to promote specific commodities (songs or groups), as a means to involve and manipulate viewers (so as to deliver an audience or to widen and build one). Writers like Jhally (in Angus and Jhally 1989) or Straw (in Frith *et al.* 1993) emphasise these commercial aspects and see music videos as offering a chance to harness some new technology and to exploit new market opportunities.

If the visual components add anything, they are best understood as attempts to domesticate the meaning of music, to win back control over the subversive elements of rock (which usually expressed themselves best in live concert performances). For example, the Hendrix performance of *Electric Stars and Stripes* (the one he delivered at Woodstock, recorded on the film of the same name) could be read as a subversive attempt to redefine American nationhood, to include references to drugs, youth, urban riots and, above all, black hippies like himself. The performance also broke the neat and tidy boundaries of packaged music – it straggled out of a kind of ragged jam session, with references to *Purple Haze*, it went on far longer than the standard three and a half minutes, and it looked as though it was just Hendrix and a few other musicians playing for themselves and their fans, 'authentically'. The visuals that accompany the music are 'alternative', roaming over the emptying fields at the site, depicting the few scruffy rock fans left, some still camping or smoking among piles of rubbish.

On rock videos that feature 'performance clips' as Goodwin calls them (Frith *et al.* 1993), such as Huey Lewis and the News's *The Power of Love*, to take one I have viewed recently, the whole performance is edited, mixed, standardised, sanitised and delivered with a range of cliché shots of the audience looking beautiful, young, sexy and ecstatic, just as the record companies want them: no hints of any subversive drug-taking or youthful rebellion here, and only carefully staged scenes of 'authenticity' (facial grimaces, meaningful looks) in the performers as they play for a select audience, for the camera and, probably, for the fourth or fifth take.

The rock video might also represent another stage in the struggle between commerce and artistic expression, in another variant of the myth of subversion: as Straw points out, you need substantial funds to make a video (far more than the apocryphal bedroom audio demo tape that led to fame and fortune on commercial radio), and record companies can use videos to stress the value of specific songs rather than of groups or individual artists. This limits any autonomy (and the high earnings) that established stars could claim, which was one of the themes in the court case over the contract between George Michael and Sony Corporation.

Those songs can be surrounded by definitely ideological signifiers (especially those centred on young female bodies) or, more recently, the signifiers of 'art', added by 'someone who's read a coffee-table book on Magritte and has probably seen a few film noirs', according to Scarlett-Davis in an interview cited in Berland (in Frith *et al.* 1993). In this way 'music video . . . result[s] in a diminishing of the interpretative liberty of the individual music listener', in Straw's summary of such criticism (ibid.: 3).

As is the way of Marxist analysis, especially its Gramscian variant, a more optimistic reading is also possible, however. Here, to borrow Fiske's particular arguments (Fiske 1987, 1989a, 1989b), music video shares the dilemmas of much modern television output: briefly, in order to be popular such output must avoid too closed a set of meanings. Instead, it must seek to become deliberately open, to leave room for the viewers' own meanings, to become 'producerly' rather than 'writerly'. There is a structured potential for 'recontextualisation', to revert to Straw's commentary for a moment, the ability of the viewer to deny the preferred meanings of a video (in this case) and to add their own.

This is lent strength by the other main theme Fiske borrowed from Barthes, which we discussed earlier – the shift to the audience as the sole producers of meaning. The active audience adds the necessary competencies to the structured possibilities, so to speak. Finally, there is a popular cultural capital too which empowers viewers and enables them to resist bourgeois meanings. Together, these add up to a picture of the audience as able and willing to impose alternative, and even subversive, meanings on the open and playful texts they see and know so well.

Some artists are particularly adept at manipulating the possibilities too, hence the admiration of Fiske (and many others – see Schwichtenburg 1993) for Madonna videos which, a close analysis will reveal, look as if they simply reproduce conventional themes of sexiness or romance, but which really subvert both of these by clever ambiguities, ironies and a skilled playfulness which 'purifies commodities into signifiers' (Fiske 1989a: 192). Young women in the audience have responded, according to Fiske, and have begun to use music videos as raw materials for their own decidedly empowering fantasies and their own daily sexual politics, in a kind of escalation of consciousness begun by the Madonna video.

There are problems with this analysis, as many commentators have pointed out (including me, in Harris 1992). Straw offers two main problems: first, that recontextualisers are going to be limited in their abilities to reinterpret music videos by their own levels of 'ingenuity and connoisseurship' (Frith *et al.* 1993: 19), and secondly, by casting doubt on the escalation scenario. It is more likely, says Straw, that the playful identities on offer will be experienced 'serially' (i.e. one after the other) and pluralistically, that they will be compartmentalised and managed without producing any crisis (as suggested in earlier chapters). In practice, it is going to be very hard to know which types of viewers are going to dominate – the newly radicalised Madonna fans Fiske quotes, or the types depicted in *Beavis and Butthead*.

It is possible to work in another theme here too, by considering the work of 'socially conscious' rock musicians, especially that of Peter Gabriel. Gabriel's videos are often notable for their deployment of avant-garde or experimental techniques. *Sledgehammer*, for example, displayed the work of award-winning makers of experimental shorts like Aardman Animations and the Brothers Quay: the video used a characteristic form of animation involving the use of everyday objects such as vegetables or furniture in a technique clearly borrowed from the Czech surrealist and dissident Jan Svankmajer. Gabriel continued to innovate and experiment, and has recently developed a (rare) multi-media innovation in the form of an interactive CD-i/rock video.

In his collection *Talking about US*, the actual videos are accompanied by some discussion about the processes of making them. In the case of *The Blood of Eden*, for example, Gabriel tells us that the theme is one of unity and separation between men and women, and his hope for a reunion, using as an organising text the biblical story about the Fall. These ideas were amended and developed in discussion with a number of advisers and directors and with his co-performer on the video Sinead O'Connor. Zadok Ben-David's work had also been admired by Gabriel, and he was commissioned to produce some sculptures for the set, symbolising the Garden of Eden. There were other more pragmatic decisions to be taken too: lack of money also helped determine the simplicity of the set, and the directorial team applied their specialist technical knowledge to insist on a black screen technique (rather than a blue one) for the inserts, for example, or to shoot some scenes on miniature sets (involving the special reproduction in miniature of some of Ben-David's sculptures).

Although we have only these short discussions by the participants to guide us, accounts like this seem to be describing the effects of a production team rather like the one identified in the Bennett and Woollacott analysis of Bond movies discussed above. A similar conclusion can be drawn from the detailed discussions of the production of music videos for Wham! (BFI 1989). Do these mixtures of artistic inputs and specialist aesthetics lead to the same conclusions as for Bond movies – that we have here a process of signification, of an emerging cultural practice moving away from any immediate connections with commercialism and thence ideology?

It is clear that Marxist analysis could interpret these apparently autonomous artistic endeavours in terms of the old debates about reproduction and incorporation, as Goodwin (1987) clearly recommends. We have hinted at this debate earlier (for example, in Chapter 1), and much turns on whether the artistic experimental elements are sufficient to escape the controls of the culture industry concerned, whether they can indeed force a moment of shock in the viewer, or whether they will be interpreted simply as titillation or pleasurable scandal. Whatever the case in general, there are good reasons for being pessimistic with music videos specifically, says Goodwin, since the music part of the music video is so conservative, as we shall see.

There are exceptions, of course. Goodwin (1987) refers to the role of rock music in raising consciousness via Live Aid, and there are lively struggles over gender identities for both men and women in music TV (see the pieces by Walser and Lewis, respectively, in Frith *et al.* 1993), which provides a reading based on micropolitics or 'struggle' within the processes of production itself.

The discussion of playful artistic elements also serves to get to the second dominant framework for analysis – postmodernism. Since Kaplan's famous book on MTV (Kaplan 1987), it has been common to cite the music video as a telling example of postmodern style on television (as, for example, does Lash 1988), although Kaplan herself expresses many reservations about this analysis in her book, and is generally critical. If we use the check-list technique discussed in Chapter 5, however, we can find a match between the characteristic styles of postmodernist television and many music videos. Goodwin (in Frith *et al.* 1993: 46) summarises just such a check-list: the collapse of boundaries between high art and popular culture (as we discussed just above); the abandonment of conventionally realist representations and narratives (both in individual videos and in collections of them in MTV slots); a bewildering variety of modes of address to viewers favouring a schizophrenic rather than a stable viewing position; substantial amounts of intertextual references and pastiches of earlier videos and rock styles; a flattening-out of the past into a continuous present; and an abandonment of any kind of political engagement, comment or analysis.

Goodwin and others in the Frith collection proceed to demolish this simple recognition technique, however. To be brief, it all turns on a process of selectively emphasising the visual elements of music videos and ignoring the music altogether. The music is far more conservative, still typically a classic song lasting three and a half minutes, still with the usual tightly structured patterns of verses and chorus, repetitions and standardised scales, still with noticeably standard themes in the lyrics – romance, youthful distress, sentimentality and paranoia, 'big world and little me' (to cite Berland, in Frith *et al.* 1993).

The musical form structures the visual images in ways which cannot be seen very easily if one is coming to the music video from classical film theory, says Goodwin. In the easiest example, the music video confines itself to the limits of the song and becomes a mere little text on a discrete tape, rather than, say, the really experimental forms found in 'installation art' (examples are discussed in Jameson 1992). More subtly, visuals can imitate the conventions of modern rock performances, with characteristic crescendos (explosions, bursts of light) and lighting effects. This helps us to understand the more difficult examples – the emotional strategies of popular music affect the flow of images too, in musical versions of narratives: Walser gives some examples of how chord structures suggest fatalism and closure. The absence of classic film-type narratives has been misinterpreted as an absence of any kind of narrative structure, and the intertextual elements should also be understood musically (there are many types of intertextual reference anyway, Goodwin reminds us in his 1987 piece, including tributes, quotes, homage and, for that matter, still some old-fashioned parody and satire).

In a similar way, MTV cannot be grasped simply as a manifestation of a postmodernist sensibility somehow struggling to express itself, but as a definite development of the music industry. Again, to be brief, 'postmodernism' is best seen in an early phase of MTV, associated with a particular style of music and innovative videos associated with 'New Pop' in the early 1980s. MTV very rapidly diversified and became more conventional under market pressures, leaving 'pomo rock' as a mere sales category (rather like its predecessor 'college radio'), or 'Postmodern MTV' as a conventional attempt to partition the viewing audience (Goodwin 1991). Straw and others (in Frith *et al.* 1993) and other commentators like Laing (1985) offer a detailed materialist analysis of this kind to explain, to their satisfaction at least, the twists and turns of the marketing strategies of the music industry, including its rather extended experiments with film and video before MTV, as embedding many of the apparently autonomous cultural changes visible in music television.

Although writers like Kaplan, Jhally, Goodwin, Frith and Laing disagree about the specifics of these interpretations, what does seem common to them is a view that an 'external' analysis based on either dominant ideologies or subcultural values will not do. But neither will it do to read off the strange styles on view in some music videos as the product of some postmodernist sensibility. Instead, we should shift to complex and concrete analysis of the production conditions of the music video – the precise blend of inputs from the recording companies, the stars, the directors, and the artists, musicians, engineers and technologists (for example, the computer graphics specialists). Both the audience and the viewing conditions remain to be investigated, however.

## RELATIVISM

Several general problems have arisen for me from the discussion of these cases studies. The first concerns the problem of values or worth in these examples we have cited: by concentrating on the forms of postmodernism (repetition, excess and so on), we have already implied that there is something fundamentally similar between 'artistic' experimental video and 'commercial' television like *Miami Vice*. This would follow from the collapse of the distinctions between 'high' and 'low' culture that we mentioned above – but we would have to relinquish all the other ways of distinguishing between the two types and accept a thoroughgoing relativism. Not all commentators are willing to go this far, and, perhaps surprisingly, they include leading postmodernists.

Both Lyotard and Baudrillard, for example, have found it necessary to deny any support for commercially produced pastiche or irony. Mere eclecticism for commercial purposes is how Lyotard describes it (in his Appendix in Lyotard 1986, reprinted as his first piece in Docherty 1993), while Baudrillard is equally doubtful about what he thinks of as a kind of cultural yuppiedom. Both want to argue that there is a real or better postmodernist culture which is more than this, that there would be an important difference between experimental video and a Pet Shop Boys video, for example.

This might seem paradoxical in works which also celebrate the heterogeneous or which deny any 'real' level, and it could be seen as the same sort of problem as the one that confronted post-Marxism – the critique tends to rebound when taken seriously.

However, in Lyotard's Appendix we find a general argument (not specifically related to video) that some kinds of artistic expression are motivated by politics (in a general sense – class interests, for example) and some by commerce. Yet he says it is important to defend other kinds of artistic experiment that genuinely aim at pushing back artistic boundaries purely for aesthetic purposes. This is experiment that heads for the 'unrepresentable', that tries to allude to 'the sublime' – that which releases the recognition that one can conceive of ideas which cannot be represented: 'We can conceive the infinitely great, the infinitely powerful, but every presentation of an object destined to "make visible" this absolute greatness or power appears to us painfully inadequate' (in Docherty 1993: 43). Lyotard thus argues that postmodern aesthetics 'really' continues with the old avant-garde projects, and, further, that it is 'undoubtedly part of the modern' (ibid.: 44), that part of it that celebrates the 'jubilation which results from the invention of new rules of the game' (ibid.: 45).

The aesthetics of the sublime in Lyotard would help us to make a judgement about genuine postmodernist experiment in contrast to commercially inspired eclecticism – if we could be sure of being able to recognise allusions to the unrepresentable, or to distinguish *jouissance* from more mundane forms of jubilation.

In Baudrillard, it seems to be more to do with celebrating aspects like 'seduction' (as opposed to production), the pre-industrial symbolic order, the poetic. These are elusive criteria too, of course, and raise problems we encountered with Barthes (Chapter 4). Can we recognise somehow the sublime or the poetic in ourselves when we look at works of art, or do we need to take into account the intention of the artists again? Is the 'we' who feel the pain and pleasure of the sublime humanity in general, or do we have elites who speak for 'us' in these matters?

## THE AUDIENCE

This is the second general issue which has been implicit in much of what we have discussed. What is the 'normal' audience for TV and video, and in what circumstances do they watch and construct meanings?

In media studies there have been some interesting stages in the ways in which the audience has been conceptualised (Moores 1990), and the stages recapitulate some of the debates we have encountered in this chapter. Thus the earlier work was dominated by 'political' issues arising from the agendas set by radical analysis: was the audience completely 'positioned' by the narrative or 'looks' of the piece, and thus rendered uncritical and vulnerable to the ideological charge of the narrative, or were viewers able to resist these effects in various ways? Forms of resistance, at the centre of work in cultural studies until recently, included an ability to 'recontextualise' the narrative, by drawing upon other cultural resources (other texts, inter-textuality generally) to provide alternative readings, outside of the control of the narrative. This permitted women to pursue ironic, distanced or 'redemptive' readings, even of unpromising material like soap operas, melodramas or music videos, for example (see Geraghty 1991 for a summary).

With a shift to more eclectic, renarrativised or 'indifferent' material, however, the issues change. There is no strong narrative to position viewers or to organise thematic material to be recontextualised. Much more diverse and incomplete meanings are on offer. The viewing subject must be conceived differently too – not as a passive plaything of the narrative, not even as an active resister rooted in oppositional identities, but as a schizophrenic or a nomad: 'We need a vocabulary to describe the shifting and contradictory partial relations of nomadic subjectivity, a subjectivity which is always moving along different vectors and changing its shape, but always having a shape' (Grossberg 1987: 38). The insistence on continued shape arises for Grossberg because he refuses to acknowledge the more extreme formulations of Baudrillard (that the meanings of TV programmes implode altogether, or that 'the masses' have become completely indifferent to it and unaffected).

However, it is possible here to invoke a notion of context again. There are supplementary materials as well as the piece itself, for example: published criticisms, interviews and commentaries on films and TV programmes, as well as fanzines, posters and publicity material provided by the companies themselves ('textual shifters', as Bennett and Woollacott 1987 call them). Even some directors of experimental movies have realised the value of providing commentaries on their films, either in the form of written pieces containing scripts and personal accounts (for example, Greenaway 1988), or interviews with critics, or TV documentaries or discussion which help to explain the films to audiences, which decode some of the 'private languages' and fix some of the puzzling meanings.

Sometimes, as we have seen, films or TV programmes provide

their own forms of inter-textual commentary. As Fiske (1987) points out, 'producerly' pieces (which deliberately leave room for viewers to add in their own meanings) sell, hence the great international success of the notoriously vague and unfinished *Dallas*, which can be inscribed with meaning from within just about any culture. Perhaps TV makes 'indifferent' programmes because the audience has lost interest in strong narratives and social-comment pieces, and has to have its attention grabbed by short sequences of spectacles and multiple appeals (action, clothes, 'stars', sex).

There is also a possibility that TV has a role in creating this sort of inter-textual viewer. Some shows pretend to encourage this sort of viewing. There is a children's show called *Why Don't You Switch Off the Television and Go and Do Something More Interesting Instead?*, a paradoxical appeal if ever there was one. More generally, TV presents playful and ironic pieces like *Moonlighting* or *Soap*, presumably to cater for and 'hook' the ironic viewer, or even thereby reproduces them, as Lasch (1982) implies. *Beavis and Butthead* show you how to watch *MTV*, and in such a crude and heavy-handed manner, you can't help feeling superior. These examples demonstrate recent aspects of the 'struggle' to fix the viewer, as Grossberg calls it, to claim back inter-textuality from the resistance movement, in other words.

Some of the best examples of audience recontextualisation are given in Goffman's (1975) discussion of 'framing' and 'keying', which appeared before there was any interest in media studies. Goffman explores the mechanisms which permit viewers to 'dis-attend', for example, or to manage various 'directional cues' or 'overlayed communication' – the 'stream of signs which is itself excluded from an activity but which serves as a means of regu-lating it' (Goffman 1975: 210).

These mechanisms are used to account for audience involve-ment in a variety of activities including watching the movies. But unlike the major thrust of Gramscian work, Goffman provides examples of ways in which audiences 'normalise' challenging events in films: 'with questions [like]: How has the director managed the effect ...?' (ibid.: 419). Goffman also notes the emergence of experimental film and television in the 1960s – 'the theatre of frames', he calls it, but we could see it as self-referential television – 'much explicit reference to backstage elements ... much joking point made of mistakes ... in fact exactly what would have been normally disattended' (ibid.: 420). He suspects that these effects have become a new convention, a device to 'generate spontaneous involvement': 'One finds, then, frame breaks that come from below but which leave the superordinates – typically performers – in charge' (ibid.: 425).

There are also contexts outside this flux of textuality. Viewers do not always view as isolated individuals, but operate in groups which may be structured by nontextual relations of power. This sort of insight has led to some well-known research in domestic settings, for example, where parents may struggle to control the viewing of each other or of their children (Morley 1991). The research setting itself could provide a context of this kind for viewing too (Buckingham 1991), and no teacher of media studies can fail to be aware that the power relations in teaching can affect the ways in which subjects and meanings are fixed in the classroom.

There has often been a peculiar blindness to this context especially, yet it is probably the most common one in which people are going to be watching experimental pieces (or reading postmodernist analyses for that matter). Featherstone (1991) puts it rather politely by seeing universities as some kind of bulwark against the relativising tendencies of postmodernism (rather nostalgically, perhaps), but it is the practice of assessment and grading which best embodies 'centred reading'. In that context, ambiguity and polysemy can be sources of anxiety, not pleasure. Students' watching of 'transgressive' films in order to be able to 'manage' them might be better understood as a sign of obedience and conformity, not cultural experimentation or resistance to dominant trends.

To pursue this, the behaviour among students when confronted with experimental pieces could be a response to context rather than to the text itself. Hebdige (1988) is not alone in using student reaction as a kind of indicator of the reactions of the young in general. He describes a particular stance towards experimental work (photography in this case) – a kind of nervous, joking, ironic, self-effacing refusal to engage with 'serious' (Gramscian) cultural critique. Hebdige seems to think it arises from some kind of postmodern sensibility which finds affinities with, and explains a stated preference for, the style of *the Face*.

But this stance can also be seen as a reaction to context – it could be just tactical, a way of dealing with a high-powered academic like Hebdige by refusing to come on to his ground. It certainly describes my own behaviour as a student when challenged in seminars by people who knew far more theory than I did. 'Postmodernist sensibility' could really be a kind of pre-modernism, a way of disposing of all that is troublesome in modernism, to borrow Jameson's point; a strategy for those people who have never really begun as yet to tackle Freud, Marx or other proud bearers of the modernist project.

## CONCLUDING THOUGHTS

Film and video are often cited as the best examples of general cultural trends. Marxists and feminists would fasten with particularly fascinated horror upon the deep ideological meanings of westerns or soap operas, and predict dire ideological consequences for the youth of modern societies. As a reaction, postmodernist writers seem to celebrate the endless playfulness and openness of film and video, and cheerfully assume that audiences will follow suit.

As a further problem, much recent commentary, especially that affected by postmodernism, tends to operate at a very abstract level. It is not uncommon for a commentator like Baudrillard to use film, say, as a mere brief illustration of what he means. In discussing 'secondary nudity', for example (Baudrillard 1993: 105), as part of his more general discussion of the body, Baudrillard has this example:

> there is no nudity other than that which is reduplicated in signs . . . The James Bond film *Goldfinger* provides a perfect example . . . In it, a woman is painted in gold, all her orifices are blocked up in a radical make-up, making her body a flawless phallus (that the make-up should be gold only emphasises the homology with political economy), which of course amounts to death. The nude gold-varnished playgirl will die by having incarnated to an absurd extent the phantasm, of the erotic . . .

This is appealing writing in many ways, but a closer examination reveals rather familiar mundane difficulties (no doubt of a kind which Baudrillard could easily dismiss). What sort of example (representative? pole case?) is *Goldfinger*, and how exactly did Baudrillard come to select it as 'perfect'? Are the connections in the film between the gold paint on the 'playgirl' and 'political economy' in Baudrillard's reading or 'really there' in the film? Are there any other episodes which contradict this sinister linkage (does Bond somehow attack 'political economy' when he opposes Goldfinger's evil plan, for example)? Is there a suggestion that everyone would want to read the episode in the film in that way, or would it be possible to see the scene as a typical combination of the self-conscious stereotyping and sensationalism of a film which consolidates the Bond myth, as suggested above in relation to Bennett and Woollacott? How did Eon Productions, who made the film, actually come to depict in it so perfectly the cultural themes that Baudrillard was to analyse?

Similarly, several commentators tend to refer to television as some kind of pure manifestation of postmodernist sensibility too. This rather loose allusion arises from the rejection of the usual social science methodology, as we have seen, and from experiments to abandon the old academic style in favour of a blurring between critic and fan, which we have also mentioned above.

As always, the material itself seems to resist such generalisations and suggests that far more concrete analysis is needed of production teams and audiences. The material I have reviewed in this chapter seems to me to be far more promising and insightful, but readers must judge for themselves.

To be specific, 'postmodernism' seems to refer to far too generalised a set of characteristics to be helpful. It has become a catch-all. The term also seems strangely circular in analysing film or video. As with other 'poetic' readings, postmodernist readings seemed designed to generate the very playfulness and open-endedness that they claim to be able to 'find'. If others are unable to find these marvellously inter-textual references, or to agree they outweigh more conventional depictions, they can be accused of being too old or too lacking in sensibility.

This makes postmodernist criticism look very conventional and conservative after all. Indeed, I am reminded of the state of film criticism (film appreciation really) before the advent of structuralist theory. Critics offered personal readings, often using the film itself as a pretext to deliver some insight into the condition of the world; students were left with little choice but to mimic this style, and those who did so successfully were accepted into the club. Far from opening readings of films and encouraging diversity and pluralism, postmodern critique seems set to return to this poets' closed shop.

# 7

# Personal identities in modernity

In this final chapter, we are going to consider various sorts of discussion about the notion of personal identity. As before, I want to manage two major sorts of discussion, classical sociological work and postmodernist commentary, and to lay out the pros and cons of each approach. Naturally, I shall have to be selective in my examples, and I have tried to focus on central debates in concrete and accessible areas. We can sketch out the main lines of debate before we start on the detail.

Personal identity has been addressed in all the classic sociological perspectives, and there has been a great deal of detailed work. If there is a common strand in this work it is an argument that personal identities must have a social base, that identities are provided (in various ways), supplemented or negotiated, and reinforced in concrete social settings. It is not surprising to find an emphasis on the immediate social contexts provided by families, neighbourhoods and social classes, organisations like workplaces or schools, and less formal but still immediate social groups (dyads often) like those formed in encounters with professionals or with sexual partners. In those face-to-face immediate encounters, powerful social pressures can be brought to bear and significant influence exerted on individuals. As a result, there is an argument that some sort of 'core' identity is established in those social encounters. More generally, the work argues that some sort of face-to-face encounter, some social ritual, is still crucial for fundamental developments in personal identities to take place.

We shall shortly be examining some concrete work which develops these basic points, but it may be possible to see some implications for current discussions of identity which have been at the heart of postmodernist commentary. These latter discussions tend to emphasise the fleeting and playful aspects of identity, and the relatively unconstrained nature of processes involved, like fantasy or the deliberate construction of surface identities. For this sort of approach, classical sociological work seems inappropriate, for a number of reasons.

The fluid nature of identities these days is apparently detectable in a wide range of cultural practices and phenomena, ranging from the changing patterns of nationalism or religious belief (Turner 1991 refers to a religious supermarket where one may pick or choose) to the volatile nature of public tastes in popular music or fashion, and the transient, even imaginary nature of 'community'.

The classic social groups have diminished in influence, it has been argued, for example; this occurs after considerable social change – families are quite different and less stable, occupational identities are no longer fixed and enduring, individuals encounter far more varied and contradictory lifestyles, and there is much more 'reflexive monitoring' (to use Giddens's phrase) of personal identity. Bauman tries to capture this shift as a decline in the influence of social system in favour of agency, a reconceptual-isation of the social context as a (mere) 'habitat' or setting, rather than some deep structure which does 'order-promotion and pattern maintenance . . . legitimation of the state, power, social-isation, culture, ideology etc.' (Bauman 1992a: 190). As a result, the individual is thrown back on his or her competencies, cast adrift from deeper anchorages in a way which really is new. It is clear that the emergence of large-scale consumerism and mass media, with a greatly enhanced range of temporary identities also free of conventional cultural regulation, is another new factor.

This sort of analysis is appealing, and, as we have noted before, it seems to offer a resonance with the lives of many readers – especially students, in my view. The actual analyses are very abstract, however, and lead to the unanswered questions we have noted before – who exactly are the people who develop the new sorts of identities, how typical are they, and in what sort of social circumstances do they arise?

At the very least, the shock of these particular new events is unevenly spread at present, again as most commentators recog-nise, with pockets of the old order remaining intact. Only certain groups have the necessary financial and cultural security needed to operate in the new conditions. A suspicion arises here, and very often elsewhere, that we are hearing about the peculiar plight of the new petit bourgeoisie, especially its politically radical or academic wings, experiencing social insecurity for the first time, and rehearsing its benefits and drawbacks in the characteristic language of social theory: social theory becomes a specialist way of managing the identity politics of this particular group.

As we shall see, there are substantial generalisations involved and a rather ahistorical account of modernity, where it is as if everyone once enjoyed a completely stable identity, but now no one does. Did no one experience any threats to their identities before? Can unstable identities never be restabilised?

There has always been social upheaval, and wars, famines, unemployment, and social and geographical mobility have always offered a challenge to the security of identities. People survive such transitions, perhaps by using a kind of reassertion of biography, a widespread means of fixing their more peripheral identities into a kind of overall narrative – see Goffman (1963), let alone Giddens (1991a). One 'puts things in perspective', as people say, rethinking older identities and even re-inhabiting them by revisiting old haunts and social groups to which one once belonged. One can take 'moral holidays' (Becker's phrase, I think) from the stern demands of the challenging new life, and do 'normal' things again with one's friends.

This last question gets us back to familiar sociological issues again, concerning the underlying social constraints on what looks like a personal or individual matter. As before, we might have established personal freedom in thought, so to speak, but is it quite as easy as that in reality? The areas I have chosen illustrate these dilemmas and difficulties, I believe; as before, I do not have any quick or easy solutions to the problems.

## SOCIALISATION AND REPRODUCTION

Let us begin with a quick sketch of familiar sociological ground, initially using basic functionalist terminology. Every individual enters an existing social system when they are born, and thus receives elements of their identity ready-made. In functionalist sociology, this process is discussed as 'socialisation', and it is usual to see this sort of work of ascribing identities as one of the main functions of the modern family. In families, individuals learn that they are male or female, that they have certain relational statuses in terms of the adults they encounter, they learn basic behaviour and tastes appropriate for children in that society, and so on. Families are very effective at the processes of primary socialisation because, to borrow a Parsonian argument, they operate with peculiarly emotion-laden, specific and personal relationships.

Although participants do not know it themselves, we know families are also affected by wider social forces, because they vary from one society to another, and indeed they have varied over time inside the same societies.

What we might take to be 'natural' behaviour by or towards children, for example, can be shown, fairly convincingly, to be recent and relative. Aries's classic study (see Poster 1978) demonstrates that even the sexual molestation of children by adults was not perceived with the same horror as it is now, for example (although the harm this practice may have caused is quite another matter), and that, more generally, the social history of Europe shows the effects of a number of socially constructed myths of childhood, including the current one which sees children as innocent, naive, asexual, in need of protection to an advanced age, incapable of sophisticated or cynical behaviour, and so on.

Much classic work reviews the status of the nuclear family in the same light, and concludes that the shape of the modern family, the roles, statuses and identities available in it, are affected by social forces of various kinds. There may be a drive to develop a more functional form, concentrated on the 'core functions' (basically, dealing with the emotional and personal), in a society with a developing public sphere, especially an extended education system, which deals more effectively with the other elements (such as preparing for economic and political participation in an impersonal and coolly unemotional society). Or the nuclear family can be seen as the result of a particular combination of economic and sexual dominance. Thus the nuclear family is best grasped as a bourgeois institution which has become widespread as that class dominates society but which originally reflects classic bourgeois concerns for the property rights that men exercise over women and their economic capital when it comes to inheritance: both lead to monogamous patriarchal marriage enshrined as the organising principle for family and kinship.

Sometimes one can add a twist to such Marxist or feminist accounts towards a Freudian interest in the tight moral regulation of women and children (Poster again), perhaps as a kind of early preparation for the discipline of wage-labour or, more generally, for a life on the margins of a labour market specifically, or social life more generally. Defenders of the family see the institution as a vital bulwark against social breakdown, but critics see it as a major site of the reproduction of undesirable constrained or embedded reactionary values. The notion that families constrain identities in the interests of the reproduction of society is thus a widespread one, and one which has been much challenged and debated.

There is a good deal of debate about whether and how families are breaking down, and what statistics on matters like divorce rates (and remarriage rates), or on numbers of children born out of wedlock may mean in this debate. One problem with using such statistics as an index of social cohesion is that those rates are affected by many intervening variables: the proportion of the population marrying in the first place; the relative ease with which couples can get divorced; the extent to which the state is prepared to fund the legal processes involved, and so on.

The notion that identities are shaped in the interests of 'reproduction' has been a major theme in Marxist analysis. Many institutions other than families can be analysed in this light, including the modern education system in Britain and the USA. One early famous analysis suggests a 'correspondence', in essentials, between the levels of the education system and the stratified labour system (and ultimately the class system) of the wider social formation, so that children 'learn their place'. This and subsequent variants have been much discussed (for my own summary, see Harris 1992).

There is another famous variant too, one which picks up on an earlier Durkheimian concern for what might be called the fundamentals of identity, rather than the details or specifics. In a much-debated essay, to which we alluded while discussing Pêcheux in Chapter 3, Althusser (1971) discusses the reproduction thesis in terms of 'ideology in general', the unifying characteristics or general form of specific ideologies. To cut short a long analysis, the notion of oneself as an individual is the main characteristic here, and Althusser draws on psychoanalytic work from Lacan on the processes whereby infants come to recognise themselves as discrete individuals, separate from their parents and from other objects in their worlds – the 'mirror phase' (which we have also discussed earlier, in Chapter 5).

Althusser develops this notion into a broader discussion of how actual social institutions – families, the Church, the media, schools – act as 'ideological state apparatuses', producing this misleading notion of individuality in the people whom they address. Individuals are 'hailed' or 'interpellated' by these institutions (greeted and treated as individuals, recognised only if they accept that they are abstract individuals, very much in the terms the institutions want). Whatever the specifics of the messages that follow, this process of hailing is universal and constant.

What better example could we choose than the paradoxes encountered in the modern university and its assessment system? Success and failure in the assessment scheme can have powerful effects upon your identity, your sense of personal worth and social status, your choice of subsequent career, and the range of fantasies you entertain about yourself and your relations with others. As a student, you have to submit yourself to this system in order to stand a chance of gaining any of the rewards, but to do so also involves you in a serious risk of penalty. To fail is to risk serious mortification and shame. The successful ones may emerge with a heightened sense of themselves as worthy and capable individuals, even though the whole process has involved their subjection to the judgements of others, a deep submission to the authority of those who control the system. Even the most cynical or instrumental students find it hard to deny the system legitimacy: in my experience, instrumentalism rarely escalates into principled dissent.

The system looks individualised: its organising myth is that it measures individual ability and is able to do so with validity, objectivity and a remarkable degree of precision (student work graded on a percentage scale implies one hundred separable degrees of worth in every assignment). There are reasons to doubt all of these claims, however, and there are some compelling analyses of the ways in which assessment schemes can unconsciously reproduce social hierarchies of class, 'race' and gender, or, more generally, reward those with the right amounts and types of 'cultural capital' (Bourdieu 1988 has some limited but telling examples). In examples like this one, Althusserian analysis offers a strong case still, despite the criticisms that the essay has received.

## THE NEGOTIATION OF IDENTITY

General theory, both functionalist and Marxist, tends to over-predict conformity and to operate too readily with general aspects of identity. There are processes sometimes known as 'secondary socialisation' which may contradict the effects of the 'primary' ones or modify them. This happens because social life can offer contradictions (as expectations at work may contradict those of the family for women, for example). Secondary socialisation processes also offer a chance to reflect upon status and identity, as an adult, rather as in Freudian therapy where the therapist works over problems engendered by infantile socialisation, brings them to light, locates them in adult discourses, and subjects them to adult values and rationality. We can also use this topic to link with Giddens's insistence that action always involves a reflexive capacity to monitor one's performance (one reason he objects to Althusser's work as deterministic – see Giddens 1979).

The experience of going to university can offer a major form of secondary socialisation, rather like a religious 'conversion' in adult life (see Berger and Luckmann's 1971 classic for examples and implications). However, conversion experiences may not be entirely typical of this process – it is quite possible simply to add secondary identities to one's existing repertoire, we shall argue. Such possibilities were long ago described in symbolic inter-actionism or even in functionalist 'role theory' (see Collins 1994).

The complexity and relative lack of 'moral density' of adult life can offer a qualitatively different form of socialisation, to use those terms for a little longer. As an adult, you enter areas of social life where you can experience change and discontinuity: changes in work patterns, or in places of domicile; changes in family life as the older generations die off and new ones emerge; an awareness of large-scale social changes as economic cycles bring prosperity and recession; technological change; and the growth or eclipse of the fortunes of your political causes and parties. These changes have 'good' and 'bad' sides, of course: on the one hand, you can achieve identities in new areas and not be saddled just with the old 'ascribed' ones, while, on the other, there is that lurking sense of relativism which grows as the old pre-adult world gets further and further away.

In such complex and low-density cultural areas, there is much more scope for the negotiation of identities, explored best, perhaps, by symbolic interactionist work. The approval and agreement of those 'significant others' we encounter is crucial in the attempt to establish or achieve an identity: others are at minimum the mirrors which reflect back the performances we wish to perfect, and, in the process, the performance itself is modified. This local negotiation is a theme that runs through early studies of the general problems of individuality (as in Mead and Cooley) to the more 'applied' work on the identity problems faced by specific groups like immigrants to the USA (in classic 'Chicago School' concerns), or the fractious world of the modern professional in Hughes or Goffman, where it becomes important, say, for medical personnel to manage their public identities to a very sophisticated level in front of various audiences. Collins (1994) has a good summary of these writers.

Newcomers to student life are in a good position to glimpse such negotiations, as they learn to perform credibly as students. We soon become aware that this requires specific competencies, ranging from a need to seem studious and self-motivated in front of faculty members in seminars, classes or tutorials, to a need to seem diffident, detached, far from committed, more cynical and ironic, much more interested in the social than the academic life of the university in front of peers. Staff too are disposed to divide their lives into 'on-stage' and 'back-stage' zones, as they manage the rival pressures of class- and staff-room, or their public and private lives.

Indeed, it is possible to see this kind of performance as socially necessary, especially in modernity, as when we discussed the problems of 'strategic communication' in Chapter 2. Successful performance requires a certain intention to persuade, to adjust oneself in order to meet the anticipated responses of others, and to defuse any opposition to one's performance as a result. Certainly, it is often easier and more effective for all parties to conform to an expected performance, in order to reduce complexity and uncertainty and to proceed with tasks or purposes. Patients and doctors expect each other to behave in particular ways, for example; and if either breaks out of role, for example during an intimate gynaecological examination, they risk serious local social disorder. Much work seems to go into negotiating and maintaining rather conservative rules for such encounters. We have already discussed whether writers like Goffman wish to read this sort of negotiation simply as a sign of 'inauthenticity' (see Chapter 1).

An excess, or perhaps an increased density, of such performances threatens non-strategic forms of communication, however,
as it 'becomes hard to switch off'. In this way, a kind of cynicism
is likely, as we have already seen. It can appear necessary to relate
to others strategically in most encounters, at least in professional
life. If you realise others are relating to you in the same mode, you
may come to suspect that the whole of social life is an intertwined
nesting of strategic communication. Just as you yourself can pose
as a sincere and open person and permit a few meta-comments
about your roles, the better to perform them convincingly
(Goffman again), then so can others. The social world becomes
disenchanted, to borrow a phrase.

This sort of contagion by strategic communication is not only
endemic in modern political discourses, as we have seen, but it
seems to have affected even the sacred zone of 'love', a classic
location for the most inner and 'core' of our identities. Benhabib's
(1984) discussion of Lyotard, for example, raises this possibility: to
vulgarise, it seems that Lyotard wants to confirm the old saying
that '[love and] marriage is a series of lies which two people agree
to tell each other'. Interestingly, Bauman (1992a) still holds out
'love' as the only worthwhile social relationship, the only one
which still promises to treat others as autonomous individuals –
but his discussion is very abstract and not really grounded on any
actual relationships.

There is also the constant possibility that the other may resist
one's blandishments, or indeed one's attempted rationalisations.
As we shall see below, identities can be fought over as well as
smoothly negotiated and managed, a possibility which can be lost
in classic work. Clearly, some encounters can be imbalanced in
terms of the power of the participants to affect the outcome, and
an abstract focus on some apparently universal capacity to choose
or to negotiate can neglect these constraints.

## MASTER IDENTITIES?

The discussion of power in negotiation opens up the possibility of
a return to classical sociology again. The 'master identities' referred to here reflect the standard sociological working hypothesis
that social class, 'race' and gender are the major determinants of
the individual's chances of successfully negotiating his or her
identities. These three master identities are the primary ones, it is

suggested, the ones that intrude and have a major effect on social relationships, that constrain one's freedom to experiment with playful identities: at the end of the day, when the playing is over, class, 'race' and gender remain as major forms of social division and distinction.

Perhaps the most shocking argument of all for sociologists in postmodernist commentary is that the old master identities of class, race and gender have 'decomposed', and that this seems to be a view shared by radical activists and high-powered analysts of modernity as well as by conservatives and laypersons. As with other debates, we have heard this one before, of course, and there are still grounds for thinking that these major forms of social and cultural division have not really 'disappeared', except in the rather specialist sense we saw in Chapter 4 (that is, that they have been dissolved away primarily, perhaps exclusively, in the new theory).

There are certainly older attempts to rescue social class as a master identity, despite surface fragmentations in, say, Poulantzas (1975), where the apparent 'decompositions', the noticeable splits and fractures among groups who have only their labour to sell, can be grasped as the product of many complex and concrete determinations at different economic, political and ideological/ cultural 'levels', all of which still emanate from the basic structure of a capitalist society. Marxists have always pursued this sort of strategy, as we have seen: what is on the surface needs to be explained by some deeper structure.

Accounts such as that of Poulantzas do look like special pleading, however, where all is going to be safely gathered back under the heading of class in the end. We might well suspect the presence of foundationalism, dogmatism and incoherence in such argument. The same problem can arise for more conventional sociological studies that try to fix social class or 'race' as master identities by demonstrating empirical patterns and regularities based on these variables.

There has been a flurry of recent contributions to debates on these matters, accessed most conveniently, perhaps, in some short articles in the journal *Sociology*. Goldthorpe and Marshall (1992), for example, continue a long discussion with a variety of critics about the continued stability of socio-economic positions over generations (which is what 'social class' usually refers to in such work), even when set against perceived changes in social mobility, education and voting behaviour. Although anxious to disconnect themselves from a general Marxist class theory, Goldthorpe and Marshall insist that social class analysis still has a future, still offers fruitful areas of research, and has a lot more empirical grounding than the new groupings which everyone seems keen to talk about, including those based on consumption or the kinds of temporary identities that we shall be discussing.

The critics raise some familiar problems, including some about the standing of such empirical findings, especially if any organising theory is no longer asserted (the main theme in replies such as Pahl 1993 and Holton and Turner 1994). If these patterns are merely empirical ones, they are open to the usual objections: for example, it could just be that traditional sociology always looks for class as a variable but never seeks others, or that empirical patterns could be reinterpreted if data were to be grouped differently. The groupings used in Goldthorpe's schema are far from 'value-free', Holton and Turner insist. The theoretical implications need to be drawn out if we are to avoid parochialism and mere data-collection.

In my view, two major implications follow. First, all contributors seem to be convinced of the redundancy of the 'strong' (Marxist) theory of social class as the key variable to explain the major aspects of community life and identity (in our terms here). However, secondly, the other options seem equally flawed. Holton and Turner, for example, have no time for 'industrial society' alternatives, while Goldthorpe and Marshall challenge those who believe in the social significance of groupings such as those based on consumption patterns to put them to some empirical test: the categories of some more recent nonclass analyses are also far from value-free.

We have mentioned something of the dilemmas for the old 'strong' theories of 'race' and gender, but they are still lively issues too. The political and analytic pros and cons of seeing 'race' or ethnicity as a master concept outside of all social constructions are well discussed in interchanges between Solomos and Beck (1994), on the one hand, and Mason (1994), on the other. It is still obvious that skin colour has always been an important and immediately recognisable sign in a system of ethnic ranking and it can serve as a means of representing (stereotyping in some cases) people's identity in everyday life; but studies of ethnicity have encountered greater complexities, including something like the 'splintering' we discussed above, as 'blackness', say, gets combined with other identities like localism, social class, gender, age, immigrant versus resident statuses and so on. The last one is an important difference in legal and political terms in modern Britain, reminding us that these identities are not all generated 'spontaneously' by the people concerned.

At the cultural level, a greater diversity is apparent. Julien and Mercer (1988) introduced what promised to be *Screen's* last 'special issue' on 'race' with this theme. After periods of absence from cinema, black people first appeared in roles which were strongly 'ideological' in the classic sense, reflecting dominant conceptions of black people as slaves, aliens, animals, natural comics or whatever, as we have seen. But we might be witnessing an 'end of representation' again, with black people as much as with women or proletarians (see also Aronowitz, in Giroux *et al.* 1989), perhaps in the form of 'colour blindness', or in a more playful rendition of black identities. Examples so far are thin on the ground, perhaps, and one can think of far more conventional if liberal depictions (the 'critical realist' pieces like *Boyz 'n' the Hood*, or for that matter *Schindler's List*): but it is worth considering television soap operas where the characters just 'happen' to be black people, or TV comedy shows such as *Desmond's* or *Chef*.

## Condensation or articulation?

In Britain, as McRobbie notes, the debate has ensued in a particular context in the politics of popular culture, for example. Briefly, the activist politics of the 1970s and 1980s in Britain had also turned upon the potential of the three 'major condensations' of political identity – social class, 'race' and gender – and their apparent decomposition. There were theoretical challenges to the assumption that these were privileged or 'foundational' condensations too, which reawakens the debates in Chapter 5. Politically, the decomposition revealed itself in the emergence of separatist activist groups (especially black women), or the less activist defection of members (especially working-class persons) from the general 'new left' coalitions of the 1970s.

One response, 'overdetermined' as always by a combination of theoretical, political and academic interests, was to turn towards a general theory of 'articulation', it could be suggested. The political advantage of this turn lies in the possible solution it offers to the clash between, on the one hand, the requirements of activist politics to retain some notion of the old active subject, a political need for some grounded faiths or sacred values, and, on the other, the unanswerable critiques of these very notions and groundings by postmodernism. As we have had occasion to do before, we can only pity the poor radical intellectual, torn as ever between faith and commitment and academic critique and rigour.

We have mentioned articulation and post-Marxism already in Chapter 5, but it is important to recapitulate a little here. For a time, it seemed possible to square the circle with 'articulation', a process of uniting individuals into politicised groups, via a special political discourse rather than by waiting for the social system to restabilise and recondense identities. Once more, intellectuals had a role, too, to perform this articulation; or, since the moment seemed to be endlessly deferred in practice, at least to deconstruct the articulations of political rivals. Consciousness could be raised by demonstrating the lack of any social or natural constraints on what women or black people could do and achieve politically, by demonstrating that the only fixed reference points were provided by discourses.

Thus, although the programmes are still sketchy, the splintering of feminisms could be analysed and explained, rather than just regretted, with an attempt to deconstruct existing conservative discourses which explain the splits in terms of natural differences between, say, black and white people. Having disarticulated and preserved differences, new rearticulations could be attempted, not on the basis of a simple unity between women, but on some more complex recognition of explicit alliance. For me, the whole debate is still reminiscent of earlier (failed) socialist attempts to build 'popular fronts' based on alliances between all those groups united (in political discourse at least) by their exclusion from 'state monopoly capitalism' (see Jessop 1982). We have also discussed the problems. 'Articulation' gives too much freedom in a way, in that any identity can be articulated with any other, and in that commercial and professional articulators are indistinguishable from radical or emancipatory ones.

As before, then, no easy answers can be offered to the problem of the apparent decomposition of master identities. Inequalities have not gone away just because there might be a theoretical crisis in sociology or cultural studies, and of course there is a strong sense in which political groups assume a shared identity (as women or as black people) in and through political action. Yet there are grounds for questioning some of the fundamental practices and working assumptions of sociology and cultural studies that work with 'master identities'. The debate is far from over, however.

## THE MICROPOLITICS OF IDENTITY

Identities are fixed by political processes, although not at the grand level of social systems, perhaps. It would be especially misleading to assume that the possible crisis of the theme of master identities means that no political processes or forces remain: this leads to rather loose discussion of identity as an aspect of general theorising about postculture, consumerism, the decline of Marxism and empirical sociology, and the rest. To take one obvious example of what has been overlooked, we shall all face the deep indifference accorded the old, and find ourselves treated as if our age were the master identity which cancels out all those achieved in the past.

How is it possible to assert confidently that representation has been replaced universally with signification, for example, when so many people experience the crudest attempts to represent them, to refuse to acknowledge their own signifying practices in the sorts of stereotyping or institutional labelling they experience, or to argue that identities are now dedifferentiated, when so much time is spent in everyday life, and above all in micropolitical activity, in constructing and applying differentiations? It is a bad mistake to assume that only old theorists want to fix meanings, or that the decline of the major social divisions of the past has now produced completely autonomous, text-like identities which are accepted by other participants. To borrow a quotation from Collins, cited in a recent piece of research on careers: 'it is not only . . . sociological theorists that may contribute to reifying the world, . . . [it is also] . . . the practice of people in everyday conversations' (Evetts 1992: 1).

Academics with solid and secure backgrounds and particularly sheltered lives may have escaped these kinds of struggles over identity, and also failed to grasp, perhaps, the ways in which participants manage them. They must have been extremely remote from their own organisations to have stayed so aloof, though, since once more universities offer excellent examples of the negotiation and processing of identity. Grading is a classic example of an institutional attempt to reassert a master identity in the face of initial diversity going on at the local level, another example of re-representation with an official denial of interest in the signification practices which produce the judgement and grade, another detailed differentiation process.

The effects on people's identities have been discussed already, and are among the most far-reaching, I would suggest. The fit between my experience as a pedagogue and the general account of organisational effects on identity in the classic work like Goffman's *Stigma* (1963) is still striking. Educational organisations in particular produce personal identities; for example, with detailed records of individuals, their personal details, their demographic backgrounds, their individual grades, aspirations, out-of-class interests, personal tutors' reports and filed references for employers.

Like the doctor, in Goffman's example, able to detect syphilis, university faculties claim to be able to detect special aspects of people's identities unknown to the general public and, indeed, only recently apparent to the clients themselves – their ability to do higher education. Stupidity in higher education institutions is an 'acquired stigma', lurking there unknown in all the freshmen who appear at the start of the year, waiting to be diagnosed by our special techniques and assessment devices: the first few assignments launch them on a 'moral career'. Goffman suggests that acquired stigmata are particularly difficult to bear because they are invested with the value judgements of people who always thought they were normal until specialists (in this case) dragged out their inner flaws.

Of course, students try to 'pass' and 'cover' their flaws in much the same ways as the stigmatised more generally. They try to conceal poor grades, or try to bluff and evade in seminars, perhaps even by masking their real inability to succeed by various more acceptable 'lacks' – they pose as forgetful persons, or as ill-organised or vague ones, often in a rather charmingly eccentric manner in Britain, rather than admit they could not grasp the main points of a difficult piece of Marxist theory, or they hide their poor spelling behind illegible handwriting. Some display that peculiar alertness to and perceptiveness of 'normal' society characteristic of the would-be passer in Goffman, and reproduce a kind of cleverly detailed academic style to gloss over the gaps in their scholarship: as a tutor, I can often recognise elements of my own bluffing or evasion in these excellent performances. Often, students co-operate to pull off such performances collectively, and will assist each other with helpful staged questions in discussions (especially if they are formally graded), with much support and sympathetic nodding, feigned surprise, interest, insight and enthusiasm, or with the covert circulation of notes, reviews or old essays, and even with occasional collective authorship.

Pedagogues produce detailed and individualised grades as part of a complex intersection of 'external' and 'internal' requirements – our external validators and paymasters expect us to produce them, and we also claim to be able to operate them as part of our professional expertise and judgements. Grading is in some ways merely part of our duties to diagnose the learning difficulties of our students. As Bourdieu has argued so persuasively, however, our professional judgements mesh seamlessly with the whole structure of judgements and taste adopted from, or lived as second nature by, the urban, male bourgeoisie. This apparent harmony between the demands of the external social system and the quite autonomous requirements of a more local professional code of conduct is characteristic of many other cultural institutions and organisations, including the media and the leisure industry (see Berking and Neckel 1993 on the organisation of the urban marathon, for example).

Several important organisations exist specifically to offer personal identities to clients, then, but those who work in more general ones can find they are being offered identities too. In some cases, these are expected to become master identities, to take over their lives, for their occupants to become 'organisation men and women'. In other cases, something about the organisation of the workplace carries over into wider social identities. For example, hard manual work was once a source of pride in oneself as a 'proper man', and this affected the whole issue of gender relations (Willis 1977), and had a wider impact on dealings with 'soft' institutions like schools. Conversely, conventional gender relations in families are reinforced and extended for women by a conventionally feminised workplace, such as the junior school (Steedman, in Lawn and Grace 1987).

More broadly, the structure of work can come to symbolise or allegorise the political structures of the wider society and one's personal place in it. The classic studies here were often inspired by an interest in voting behaviour (the concern for the 'working-class conservative'), and, to be brief, the local power arrangements of the workplace were seen as very important. Was the boss a remote figure high above the mass of workers on a noisy, machine-regulated shop floor or was he or she in frequent personal contact in a more egalitarian manner? Were the work conditions, including the type of payment and entitlements of various kinds, polarising or communitarian? Different combinations and possibilities could produce different symbolic models of the class system more generally, ranging from polarised 'them and us' views to 'ladder' or 'money' models of individuals usually separated by small gradations of salary.

As the momentum of this kind of work developed, more and more complicating factors were examined: friendship and leisure patterns outside work; 'distributive groupings' such as housing patterns; and longer-term 'structuration factors' such as social mobility chances. Bulmer's (1975) collection of work on 'images' of society retains the interest in politics and preserves the complexity, but also stands as an example of the continuing role of occupation as a kind of concrete manifestation of broader 'social class' factors in identity.

More locally, the occupational worlds of various groups have been examined, including those of the professional, as they undergo what used to be called 'occupational socialisation' – acquiring the values, roles and public identities suitable to their status. Work on the school teacher as a professional (Ozga 1988, for example) tends to stress the demands made on individuals by the institution, including an increasing pressure to conform, to acquire an open-ended commitment, to work long additional hours, to live the role as it encroaches further and further.

It is clear that this kind of commitment itself emerges after an unsettling period of negotiation, strategic operations and manipulations. Ball and Goodson (1985) offer a collection which contains much interesting analysis of the processes at work on teachers as they enter their occupational world and have to negotiate with the constraints on their practice that they find there. These constraints often centre upon the pupils, who can so affect the self-esteem of the new entrant that he or she ceases to think of themselves as a competent social actor at all, and is forced to leave the profession (see Riseborough's chapter for a detailed account of some of the tactics employed by pupil 'teacher mincers').

Successfully managing hostile pupils is often a 'critical incident' in the decision to 'invest' one's efforts, to make sacrifices in order to achieve some sort of satisfactory occupational identity. Equally important, however, are the staff and the management, who can pose serious difficulties for the would-be professional as they introduce new regimes, new career-structures, new pressures, arrange for mergers with other institutions, or whatever.

Some entrants have clearly 'burnt out' under the strain of the massive organisational pressures, while others have probably coped by pursuing some of the instrumental 'careerist' strategies described in Ball's book (1987) on the micropolitics of the school – strategies such as 'GASing' (gaining the attention of superiors by high-profile activities of various kinds), or forming various alliances, sometimes around educational ideologies, sometimes via witch-hunts or exclusions.

An echo of this work appears in modern management techniques too, especially those intending to create organisational cultures to overcome the alienation of rationally controlled work on the shop floor (see, for example, Starkey and McKinlay 1994 on the new approaches at the Ford Motor Company).

Management has as its disposal a range of techniques to control the workforce, from increased supervision and electronic surveillance systems (see, for example, Jenkins 1994) to a variety of techniques and manipulations of the workplace, such as 'quality circles', flexible working, workforce counselling, job enrichment and periodic management 'retreats' to places as various as luxury hotels or survival training courses (see the list in Crook *et al.* 1992). There are some interesting debates about whether this kind of work practice is going to be effective in actually creating new organisational cultures, and whether they are ultimately benevolent or oppressive, whether the new arrangements are growing inevitably as the economic order changes, or whether only a core multi-skilled and nomadic workforce is likely to benefit – and so on. What seems clear is that there is a continuing recognition of the importance of occupational identities.

This work has been particularly neglected in postmodernist commentary, perhaps on the grounds that occupational constraints are less influential than the more free-floating and playful 'cultural' activities taking place in nonwork time. It is one-sided to ignore work; it is quite possible, for example, to see the increased interest in play or escape as explicable by the increased levels of commitment and control required at work in the first place. Of course, there are other motives and reasons for leisure too (see Moorhouse, in Rojek 1989).

## Sexual identities

This topic demonstrates some of the possibilities of constructions of identity in a particularly clear manner, and it is an area of universal interest. The sociology of sexual identity offers the usual range of possibilities and methodologies, as Brake's (1982) useful collection makes clear. We are all aware that gender is a social construct, and that ideas about right and proper conduct for men and women (both heterosexual and homosexual) have changed considerably over the last few years; but there is also an argument that sexual identity and sexual conduct itself involves far more than just biology and is instead saturated with social aspects and struggles. Even the most unpromising early survey-based analyses (reported in Brake 1982) reveal that social class had a strong effect on sexual preferences and sexual behaviours, for example, and it would be interesting to see if this is still the case.

More interactionist material, especially the classic work by Plummer (in Brake 1982), introduces much more flexibility into the area of sexual identity. To be brief, Plummer argues that sexual fantasies are crucial in the formation of sexual identity, for example, and that, more generally, sexual interest, arousal and successful sexual contacts have to be negotiated as actors stumble towards making sexual sense of themselves and of others. Cultural competencies are crucial here as we try to grasp the differences between, say, paid sex, rape and a willing fantasy of forced sex, or between the nudity encountered in the shower room or medical examination and the nudity that might be a prelude to sex. The whole area is one where Goffman's metaphors of social life as dramaturgy are particularly apt: in one of his most forceful statements, Plummer insists that sexuality is best understood as a self-monitored script. Cultural competency can make sexual any activity (playing football, for example, while fantasising about having sex with the players), and it can also desexualise any activity (such as men fingering naked women as they lie on couches in the course of a medical examination).

This seems like a rather interesting preview of much of the more recent material on fantasy and culture as a text, and it is possible to detect in Plummer's work (the chapter in Brake 1982 is the reference I have in mind throughout) a kind of early advocacy of nomadic identities. Since human sexuality is so flexible and so cultural, it is hardly surprising to find so many variations of it emerging as signifying activity in its own right.

We are much more open about all this than we used to be, and many of us are far less ready to condemn homosexuality, sado-masochism, transvestism or whatever as 'perversions' or 'fetishes'. Although empirical evidence is very difficult to obtain here, for obvious reasons, these practices and preferences might well be far more widespread these days.

Indeed, as a recent article in the *Guardian* newspaper about pornography revealed, there has been an explosion of interest and sales in 'what the trade calls euphemistically "specialist" [magazines] – bondage, rubber worship, whipping, tattooing, old women, fat women, black women, fat black women, shaved women' (I am merely quoting the terms used in this discussion). The implication here is, obviously, that it is men who buy such magazines, but even here, there could be social patterning. A correspondent to the debate, writing from prison and call-ing himself a 'professional pornographer', seemed to endorse Plummer's view that the middle classes are more likely to indulge in this kind of activity (since they have the cultural capital to operate with heavily symbolised sexuality): the majority of other people apparently bought straight heterosexual videos.

Yet Plummer is also well aware that although these sexual identities may be infinitely extendible or polymorphous in pri-vate, among consenting adults or in fantasy, they still become the subject of struggles and attempts to constrain them in the public domain. In other words, there is still a micropolitics of sexuality to attempt to fix the endless permutations and variations.

This is a clear theme in the classic accounts of Freud, where there is a clear division of sexual identities into normal, healthy, socially approved ones, and the perversions, fetishes or neurosis-inducing ones. Freud shares with some structural anthropologists (espe-cially Lévi-Strauss) a focus on the incest taboo as the root of more general social and political orders, for example. More broadly, social critics, including some Marxist ones, have seen the social controls on sexuality as closely linked to capitalist institutions such as private property (via the reproductive role of the mon-ogamous marriage, as we explained above), and have sometimes even seemed to appeal to sexual energy as the force most likely to oppose regimes which attempt to control pleasure in the interests of political stability (see Reich and Marcuse, in Brake 1982).

The obvious and open controls on sexuality may have disappeared in our society (illegitimacy is no longer such a stigma, homosexuality is no longer criminalised, pornography is more available, sex education videos are best sellers), but there are still constraints. In private, there may be new norms, perhaps. Shere Hite's rather notorious work (Hite 1981) shows a continuing high level of anxiety about sexual performance, feelings of guilt and 'duty', and a strong interest in delivering female orgasms through intercourse, especially among young males, and this could clearly be interpreted as yet another case of private and subjective behaviour unknowingly reproducing 'work-like' system requirements, much as has been suggested for health and fitness crazes or other displays of disciplined bodies.

Morris's review of Foucault on sexuality (in Brake 1982) offers perhaps the broadest commentary of all on the more public politics of sexuality. It is necessary as usual to be brief, but the first point to notice is the ways in which sexual identities have been fixed, classified, commented upon in a number of special disciplines – Freudianism, Catholicism, the law, sociology, and so on. These discourses operate in a special way for Foucault, as we have seen (in Chapter 3), both to control sexuality and police pleasure, and, more positively, to multiply and extend knowledge about it (one of the reasons there is so much discussion about sex in our lives). Thus sex can be made to appear as the great secret, as the expression of your real self, as some natural and healthy 'authentic' behaviour. Because of the productive power of discourse and the convenient centrality of sex, discussions about sexuality can be joined in dominant discourses to other areas of social life, and become a part of 'disciplinary regimes' embracing population control, 'sexual hygiene', the necessary discipline and control of women or children (the 'four strategic ensembles . . . the hysterical female, the masturbating child, the Malthusian couple, and the perverse adult', in Morris's summary).

Much of this connection between sexuality and power is familiar to us as a result of the emergence of gender politics, especially feminisms and various 'gay rights' movements. Just about every area of social life has been seen to be involved in the policing of sexual identities or genders (the relation between these two concepts is still a matter of debate). Families can produce subordinate identities for women, for example, as can schools, jobs, the housing market, the mass media, leisure provision, religion, the law and criminal justice system, and nearly everything else. These forms of subordination run from conscious discrimination to more subtle ways of defining activities to privilege males (the notions of a 'proper career', 'girls' subjects' at school, a 'suitable home-owner', a 'properly brought-up child', 'real' leisure that is separate from home life, the 'dominant look' of mainstream films – and so on).

As the most detailed and relevant example of the ambiguities, we can think of the issues surrounding sexual harassment and codes of conduct at various universities. A number of recent cases in Britain which have come to public attention involve attempts by the universities concerned to regulate sexual activity among students (and between students and staff). What is of interest to us here, without taking sides on the political issues, is the detailed attempt to list proscribed activities in those codes and regulations – including 'comments about the way a woman looks' or 'lewd remarks or glances' (according to another *Guardian* article), as well as the more obvious 'requests for sexual favours' and 'intimate physical contact'. A recent draft code relating to college lecturers like me strongly advised against inviting students to lunch or discussing sexual matters in front of them, presumably in any circumstances. The code at Antioch College in the USA, reports the *Guardian*, says that 'each stage of petting and intercourse must be accompanied by the unequivocal consent of the woman'.

These codes seem to recognise Plummer's point that any activity can indeed be a sexual one, but then try to fix the possibilities to a short list in a rather arbitrary way, and certainly a far more detailed way than has been the case. Actual cases where students have been charged with offences under such codes have shown something rather interesting (to be abstract for a moment again) about the sexual mores of students. On the one hand, there is sexual experimentation and a range of sexual activities, while on the other, there are increasing attempts to demand for students protection from sexual harassment. At the very least, then, there is a difficult social situation to be negotiated in order for certain kinds of common sexual activity to take place without risk of legal or organisational penalty, and, for good or ill, we are far from free and unconstrained 'postcultural' exploration.

## PLAY AND FANTASY

The discussion of sexual identity did introduce the topic of fantasy into sociological analysis, however, and in areas where it becomes possible to escape the immediate social constraints, fantasy is clearly important. It is not surprising to find that much research on leisure and tourism becomes increasingly interested in fantasy, or, to put it in less psychological terms, in cultural embellishment or signification.

One way of coping with the cynicism, confusion and despair of the cultural disenchantment summarised above is to seek relief in temporary escapes from the stale old culs-de-sac of identity and performance, and there has been much recent work on what might be called adventures of identity, including fantasies enjoyed by youth when they dance or play (see the huge range of examples offered in Rojek 1993, for example). Although there are spectacular electronic adventures available to the modern explorer, conventional cultural activity has always offered escape and temporary residence of this kind, not least in the form of those ecstatic religious rituals we discussed in Chapter 1. What is new about modernity, arguably, is the much-enlarged range of options, the skill with which they are constructed, and their deep connections with commercial operations.

Video games provide enough novelty, unpredictability and excitement to permit wide choices, variations and a strong illusion of individualism or of 'authorship' of one's personal game, as Fiske (1989a) describes it. Certainly in the games I have played, the illusion is fostered that only your own skill, strength of character, determination not to give up, your flexibility and cunning will lead to success against the enemy: the games are usually abstract and stylised enough to calm respectable fears about personal violence, and sufficiently easy to permit reasonable success.

To take another example, much popular music has always managed to provide easy access for a wide range of people to the identities at the centre of the songs. As Chambers (1985) notes, somehow the classic love ballad always blends itself unerringly into youthful fans' own personal circumstances of having just had an exciting new encounter, tragic break-up, betrayal and loss, sexual experience, or whatever. Other forms offer space for techno-fantasy or sexual ambiguity, or engage deep longings for a romantic life in the countryside, or living as a rock group on the margins of society. The British author Dennis Potter was not the first playwright (or film-maker or advertiser) to notice the tremendous power of popular songs to act as biographical markers, to encapsulate vivid memories or to deliver an 'emotional realism': the songs in his pieces recreate the moods of postwar Britain as effectively as the careful costuming or set design.

Frith's account of amateur musicians (in Grossberg *et al.* 1992) also emphasises the widespread fantastic or actual attempts among the audience to become popular musicians themselves, however temporarily. He also points to some of the hidden structures of such fantasy. When white males decide to 'have fun', for example, they tend to associate black music with 'fun' and spontaneity in a way which is not far from the kind of 'structural' racism of which Hall complains (in Bridges and Brunt 1981).

Tourism too has been analysed in terms of 'escape'; Urry (1990) offers a widely read account of how the tourist company can attempt to locate the customer in a temporary identity via various types of organised 'gaze'. If you visit a British holiday camp, for example, you will find identities available to you for the duration – a 'family' identity, perhaps, where the kids play sport while you relax with your partner over a meal offering just the right level of novelty, sophistication and cost; or youthful and playful identities on offer to those who want to dance or nightclub again. There are also some more 'showbiz' fantasy identities provided in the organised 'serious' competitions (such as the Butlin's Pentathlon), ballroom dancing or talent shows.

For those with less populist tastes, there are 'real' holidays, travel rather than vulgar tourism, politically aware 'responsible tourism'. As we have suggested in the Introduction, however, you will often need a tour company to arrange a really authentic escape from tourism. The paradoxes of tour companies offering 'tourist-free zones' for their clients or organising visits to 'unspoiled' places are nicely analysed in Munt (1994).

It is not only popular culture that offers these possibilities. Classical music or 'serious' novels and plays can profoundly affect the people who consume them and can also serve as more general commentaries to mark moments of personal significance. I know little about opera, but I have seen extracts from *The Magic Flute*, for example, reduce people to tears, and most members of the (rather respectably bourgeois) audience seemed to have little trouble suspending disbelief and entering fictional worlds at a recent performance of *Richard III* I attended: I even heard them cheerfully discussing the characters as if they were real people in the theatre bar afterwards.

People from different social backgrounds seem equally involved in sporting events and as prone to find some personal or symbolic national significance in the fortunes of the national rugby or football team or in the fate of British athletes. It is very easy to succumb to that 'irresistible urge to allegorise the sports contest', as Guttmann (1986) puts it. There are problems with a still-common view that the capacity to manage fantasy and role play is limited, or that somehow it is all a recent phenomenon.

There is also a gender politics of fantasy: if (young working-class) male sexuality is regarded as a rather brutal, direct and self-centred activity, it is easy to claim fantasy as somehow characteristic of women and girls, and as morally and politically preferable, rather as McRobbie and Nava (1984) do in their account of disco dancing.

This view is perhaps less common these days. Research on male fantasies tended to be dominated by discussions like Thewelheit's (1987) of the appalling visions of members of the pre-Nazi *Freikorps* and their obsessions with blood, sex and racial purity. Accounts of male homosexuality restored the role of more creative or playful male fantasies, perhaps (for example, Dyer on gay disco, in Bridges and Brunt 1981). General studies of sexuality like those above provide more detail about, and less immediate condemnation of, the range of heterosexual males' fantasies. After the shift of focus away from the spectacular public youth subcultures of the 1970s, and after more attention to 'quiet', 'normal', 'suburban' male youths, analysts discovered the equally important 'bedroom culture' for those groups too (Frith, in Grossberg *et al.* 1992).

If fantasy is so prevalent, what does this imply for analysis? It is easy to see fantasy as an escape from the old determinations of social groups, which implies all the free-floating 'postcultural' qualities of daily life as in much postmodernist commentary. Yet already there are reservations, perhaps. The very term 'fantasy' implies an opposite, less-unconstrained 'reality' which awaits, and we have implied already that that reality is increasingly controlled and dominated by the world and the logic of work. Worse still, most analysts have argued that fantasies themselves are also exploited and manipulated by commercial organisations, that the field of fantasy is far from empty, that it is already saturated with signs and signifying processes. Baudrillard himself argues this with his concept of hyperreality, as we have seen already, but in many ways the arguments are best displayed in the work on consumerism, to which we now turn.

## CONSUMERISM

Critics and analysts have always been divided over the emergence of a mass market for consumer goods and the patterns of behaviour that this produces among consumers. Our own experiences as consumers reveal the ambiguities. For some, the pessimists, consumerism represents the most insidious face of capitalism: it encourages people to choose to buy goods that only serve to corrupt them, sap their independence, and bind them tighter to the key institutions of private property, the wage labour system, economic growth as a universal goal, and so on. Who has not felt this pull towards dependency and exploitation, especially as a smoker, say?

This pessimistic view dominated early writing on the topic, as Tomlinson's introduction (in Tomlinson 1990) shows, especially in Britain. Consumerism was going to have a number of effects for the early critics, some of which may seem rather comic today, including effects on the 'moral economy' of ordinary people who would be encouraged to spend beyond their means, acquire goods beyond their income range, and, not far beneath the surface, try to rise above their station. American readers may be interested to know that US goods were particularly suspect in Britain in the 1950s, as Hebdige (1988) points out: American styling connoted an easy and rather corrupt life, a subversion of central British values, and its impact was thought to be particularly harmful for the young.

We have already suggested, in the Introduction, that this attitude of appalled fascination with America affected a whole later generation too, such as Eco and Baudrillard. We have little space to discuss this further, but the issues are nicely focused for me in the work on the Disney theme park. Briefly, Eco (1987) describes Disneyland as the home of hyperreality, with its several levels of illusion (displays include dummies as well as real people in costume, reconstructed shops are real shops as well, fake pavilions include real imported trees, and so on). This permits

Disneyland to partake in a 'fetishism of art' and to engage in 'disguised merchandising'. Finally, although the park is a place of leisure, visitors are processed with legendary Disney efficiency, and 'must agree to act like robots'.

We have discussed Baudrillard's brief account already (Chapter 5). He, like Eco, draws upon a very solemn structuralist analysis of Disneyland offered by Marin (1977) which sees the whole point of the site as offering a phoney version of the contradictions of American society, only to reintegrate them all smoothly in the organising narrative of Main Street. As with Eco and Baudrillard, Marin offers little detail of the background context of the Disney enterprise, especially its economics, and refrains from actually asking any visitors what they think of it – criticisms to which we return.

## A culture industry?

Although such pessimism was associated with conservative or liberal analysts in Britain, or with maverick intellectuals in Italy or France, the usual example, much cited in most accounts, derives from the work of the 'Frankfurt School' (the 'critical theorists', as they preferred to call themselves), a group of exiled German scholars which included Marcuse, Horkheimer and Adorno. I have complained before (Harris 1992) about the rather strange and selective way this work has been received, especially by the more optimistic 'British activists', of whom more below, and fortunately there are some good, thorough studies of the work of this group (such as Held 1980, Bernstein's excellent Introduction in Adorno 1991, and Crook's Introduction in Adorno 1994).

Clearly, it is necessary to select quite drastically, but for me the most important theme in critical theory on this topic is not the famous concept of 'false needs' associated with Marcuse's best-seller (Marcuse 1964). Critics who cite this work can easily gloss Marcuse's contribution as a variant of more popular critiques of the manipulative power of advertising and its use of Freudian theory to try to appeal to unconscious desires. What seems more interesting is another theme: the emergence of a 'culture industry', and its capacity to offer an expanded, hugely diverse and seemingly 'individualised' range of products, to incorporate rival systems of cultural provision, great individualists and 'art'. In this expanded sense, the system reproduces itself, not simply, as in some fantasy of 'brainwashed' consumers, but much more dynamically, complete with an acknowledgement of individual taste, choice, personal fulfilment and artistic autonomy. The system covers all the options and therefore manages to 'flatten out contradictions', to use a Marcusean phrase.

It is not enough, therefore, simply to indicate areas of relative autonomy and freedom, relative personal choice, areas of consumer resistance or whatever without asking about the overall political and social significance of this sort of activity in the long term: does resistance to a particular product threaten the system or merely help it adjust, for example? As Bernstein (Adorno 1991: 23) puts it:

> Adorno's theory and analyses continually call attention to the difference between pseudo-individuality and individuality, pleasure and happiness, consensus and freedom, pseudo-activity and activity, illusory otherness and non-identical otherness ... If the surface logic of the culture industry is significantly different from the time of Adorno's writing, its effects are uncannily the same.

However, a more recent commentary has received more attention, especially in the USA. Lasch (1982) has written a close analysis of modern society which bears a strong resemblance to early work by the critical theorists on the 'authoritarian personality'. This time, however, it is the narcissistic personality which is at the heart of the work. As in Adorno earlier, Lasch finds deep connections between this personality disorder and the social changes in work, mass culture and family life that have occurred. The whole work offers a trenchant critique of all the main features of modern culture, including precisely those which have been celebrated in postmodernist commentary.

Thus, for Lasch it is the tragically weak ego structures of narcissism that explain so much of the immediacy and refusal of depth and involvement that commentators have noticed: the narcissist refuses 'deep' engagements because he or she fears the intrusion of the real world into the carefully contrived and rationalised inner subjective world. This fear accounts for the charm and the ironic 'nervous, self-deprecating humour' of modern culture, expressed best in the Woody Allen film. Such a stance helps to deflect criticism and disclaim responsibility, and prevents viewers from judging the truth of the performance:

participants are led to deny the importance of the inner life by the sheer banality of the 'personal reflections' of such a style.

This kind of false self-awareness is fostered in 'progressive' educational ideologies, and is also on offer in the therapy movement. These are enhanced by the culture of bureaucratic organisations, which encourage classic narcissistic mixtures of abstractness, detachment and grandiose egos, and the same themes dominate mass culture. What all these trends have in common is that they fill the void left by the collapse of forms of social solidarity, discipline and restraint which fostered genuine forms of social encounter (Lasch is close to Durkheim here). On offer instead is a limited instrumental calculation designed by various professionals and experts as a solution to the dreadful 'disorder and anarchy' of private life. All this is dressed in the language of personal liberation and freedom from constraint, but this 'freedom' operates only via the warped personality structure of the narcissist with its need for social approval, its fear of dependence, its 'inner emptiness' and rage, and its 'pseudo self-insight' (Lasch 1982: 33). In all these examples, but developed best perhaps in the chapter on education, Lasch argues that apparent permissiveness conceals social controls: the decline of parental authority is replaced by the advice of the expert psychologist; the cult of 'participation' preserves hierarchical forms of organisation; and the eclipse of authority leaves a cynical 'gamesmanship' as the only recourse for the underdogs.

The whole effect of the detailed arguments in the book is to seize back the initiative from optimistic postmodernist commentary, rather as Jameson does, but with far less flexible theoretical resources than Lasch has at his disposal. Thus Lasch echoes Baudrillard on occasion, with his discussion of the ways in which people live via electronic images, and how we behave as if 'we were being recorded and transmitted too' (ibid.: 47), or when he notes the collapse of the distinction between illusion and reality fostered by 'over exposure to manufactured illusions' (ibid.: 87). But this is an unalloyed social pathology for Lasch, explicable in fairly conventional modernist terms of the decline of social solidarity and the rationalisation of public life, even in the need for classical class analysis. Lasch ends by urging us to adopt a radical political stance, to end the whole system and its need to create new demands and anxieties, to control production and to re-establish 'communities of competence'.

Lasch over-generalises, and his work, like that of critical theory before him, has been seen as pessimistic in one characteristic sense – he has not discussed resistance to the system.

## Consumerism as a way of life?

As we have hinted in the last few sentences, fashion, at least among left-wing commentators, switched in Britain to a more optimistic and activist reading of modern consumerism some-where around the mid-1980s. McGuigan (1992) argues that the switch was of a type which is rather badly thought-out, between opposing terms, in the manner of an inversion, and there are the usual combinations of theoretical, political and academic factors involved. In the mid-1980s, there was also a mild economic boom in Britain, and the relatively well-off were enjoying their first experiences of guilt-free consumerism: doubtless something of this atmosphere affected even academics too.

These factors combine in the image of the modern consumer as an active (usually female) reader of, or player with, the crafty messages attached to consumer goods by advertisers and other manipulators. Thus shoppers are able to enjoy trying out the goods without actually buying them (Fiske 1989b), or are even able to bring pressure to bear by boycotting goods that are ecologically or politically distasteful. Nava (1991) has an inter-esting list of successful consumer boycotts and is sufficiently enthusiastic about them to argue that they are far more effective a form of politics than conventional strikes or campaigns. More generally, consumerism became fun, playful, creative, a triumph for rebellious subjectivity; the latest embodiment, in other words, of a long-popular belief in the human spirit and hope.

Even when a purchase has taken place, the goods in question can be brought into a new circuit of culture and meaning by the purchaser. Purchasers can lend cultural significance to the goods they buy, and in their own ways, and studies of youth culture provide many of the best examples. Hebdige points to the genuine creativity with which punks in the 1970s constructed a whole subversive style around everyday objects (such as safety pins, leggings and plastic garbage bin-liners) as well as some rather specialised ones (rubber bondage gear). Willis's several explora-tions of popular culture pursue the same themes, as British bikers struggle with the British motor cycle industry over the style, look and market for bikes (Willis 1978); or later, as the young un-employed successfully develop aesthetic projects with the cheap or second-hand goods they can afford (Willis 1990). Fiske has also done much to popularise this view of the real creativity of the young consumer, with essays such as the ones we have discussed on the video games player as author, or on the Madonna fan as successfully emulating the playfulness of the star herself and breaking gender stereotypes as she uses Madonna videos for personal projects.

For most writers on postmodernity, consumerism has become central to modern identity itself, as a kind of generalisation from the examples above, as Featherstone's (1991) comprehensive and sceptical account reveals. As the old social groups decline and identity is liberated from their influence, it is argued, personal identity becomes tied more and more closely to consuming behaviour. We fix our identities in the goods we purchase, or we use goods we have purchased as signs of our identity in the processes of differentiation and solidarity ('life politics', in Giddens 1991b) that we all engage in. As the consumer market is flexible and more dynamic than the older ways of regulating identities, much more fluidity is apparent: people can change their identities more frequently, experiment with them, select more options from a cultural supermarket, with far less commitment than before. The usual social effects of modernity are therefore displayed acutely in consumer behaviour, in particular, the collapse of internal differentiations, as 'consuming' becomes emblematic of freedom and choice as one shops around for a religion or a politics. Some consumers also experience the anxiety and anomie, arising from an excess of choice and a lack of guide-lines, however, and various consumer pathologies may result (like 'style fascism' among the young, permanent feelings of unfulfilled desire or the inability to act without a shoppers' guide of some kind).

It is possible to discuss these approaches critically in several ways. The core of the critique, for me, is the tendency for a number of general commentaries to gloss over important specific differences. The 'culture industry', for example, is probably far too general a term to encompass the important differences within and between the products and processes involved. Some products are clearly more closed off and ideologically permeated than others, for example; or, to put it in a more conventional way, the culture industry makes available a wide range of meanings, some of which are going to be quite critical of capitalism even if only in the sense of offering some hint of an alternative way of life. The range of control thus varies from tight censorship, through a more tolerant market system, to an indifference towards the content of the cultural product, to a vague encouragement to resist.

The specifics of production can also have an effect which is hard to capture by the simple use of a term like 'culture industry'. As we saw in the last chapter, the production teams in activities like making Bond films seem to have carved out for themselves, at least temporarily, some area of relative autonomy from immediate financial or technical control. The music business also seems to offer examples of complex cycles of autonomy and reasserted control, a kind of permanent tension between the 'artistic' and the financial or industrial elements within the industry itself. We are on familiar ground here, since various classic studies of the micropolitics of organisations have long noted the relative autonomy of sections of bureaucracies, broadcasting organisations, political parties and even educational organisations (on such 'loose coupling', see Weick, in Westoby 1988).

The real point at issue, for many critics of the old pessimism, is that such meanings, signs, texts can be received in circumstances which are not tightly controlled by the culture industry, despite all its infernal arts and perverted psychological theory. However, once again, the audience this time has often been generalised in a way which closes off some possibilities. It is clear, for example, that the consumer enters a rather complex and variable relationship with the product and its producers. Some products will be saturated in advertising and other discourses, dominated by brands and other devices, while others will be left relatively untouched, uncontaminated by established texts, so to speak. Some products may be at the heart of contesting campaigns, of course, and come complete with opposing texts attached (for example, Coca-Cola or McDonald's). Some products are 'necessities' (food) while others can be taken or left (charity screensavers), consumers are brand loyal in some areas and not in others – and so on.

The circumstances in which those products are produced may be little known or understood, or widely discussed, often following the activities of various consumer groups. (While everyone knows about tuna and dolphins, the mystery of the source of interest remains as deep as it was in Marx's day, we have already argued.)

Consumers will vary according to their knowledge and their competencies. There are 'connoisseur consumers' (Tomlinson 1990), who are knowledgeable and highly competent, often having been informed by various specialist publications (including novels in the 'shopping and fornication' genre, perhaps, as well as specialist guides), or via their membership of informal networks of like-minded persons. This sort of consuming probably produces much of its pleasure by being heavily invested with symbolic, allegorical or more general cultural significance, rather as some sexual activities are, as we saw above. By its very nature, this kind of consuming is confined to a minority.

At the other end of the range are various pathological consumers, as we have suggested already. These people suffer anxiety and insecurity and face deep shame as they struggle desperately to buy the right goods at the right price, and then to display them to best effect. These consumers risk mortification of the self if they fail the constant tests which life appears to offer them. This kind of behaviour can affect one's deepest sense of self, and the marks can appear on the very body (as the results of constant dieting, for example – Giddens 1991b). Here we seem to have a pathological oversymbolising, where the mere activity of wearing a particular type of jacket takes on huge significance as a sign of the entire person and their worth. Consumers who are unable to resist such shaming activities seem exactly like the victims of a fashion or culture industry, experiencing the classic paradoxes of the subject, finding themselves only by submitting to a judgemental process over which they have no control.

In the middle is a range of other types of consumer, who can exercise some degree of control and resistance. Here we encounter the window-shoppers and proletarian shoppers mentioned in Fiske's (1989a, 1989b) accounts, for example, those who are able to resist the hard sell by refusing to get involved in actual purchase. Then there are those who purchase the goods but refuse the meanings bolted on to them by the producers, and are able to reintroduce quite different meanings when they gain control of the commodity and take it home.

My own current interest concerns interviewing visitors to Disney sites, to find out how they managed the experience.

Although we are still at an early stage of the project, it is already clear that some (British) visitors were rather sceptical about the world of Disney, reluctant to visit at first, put off by their anticipation of sentimentality, and persuaded only by junior members of the family. Some seemed quite capable of being critical while visiting – one woman was reminded of the sinister open prison village of *The Prisoner* while visiting EPCOT, while others thought of the low wages or poor work conditions of the Disney personnel.

Others seemed quite happy to enter the 'deep frozen infantile world', in Baudrillard's phrase, although none of them so far seems to have been minded to speculate about reality or ideology. Of course, neither Eco nor Baudrillard ever questioned any actual visitors before arriving at their particular conclusions, and they do not seem even to have noticed any obvious tourists getting between them and the landscaped vistas. This abstractness is best illustrated in Marin's formative piece, however, which tends to turn largely upon the map of Disneyland as the text for analysis, not even the actual site, let alone the actual site on a hot day in August when the tourists swarm.

Zukin (1990) exposes the layers of economic and political policy 'behind' the development of the Disney empire to rectify this overemphasis on the cultural aspects of the operation. We have no space to develop this point, but much the same sort of abstraction characterises the work on normal cities and the tourist experience, as we have suggested already. Davis's (1992) excellent commentary reveals the inside story of the intense political struggles shaping the landscape of Los Angeles, which have been simply passed over by visiting *flâneurs*, exiled critical theorists and visiting European postmodernists alike.

## Giddens: modernity and self-identity

Giddens's work has been mentioned before, and has recently been the subject of some critical analysis (for example, by Warde 1994), so it is convenient to focus upon it here as a demonstration of the prospects and difficulties in moving to a more concrete debate.

We have previously met Giddens's work in terms of the methodological issues he raises. Here we turn to the more substantive topics, and again we find considerable innovation expressed in a pair of books on modernity (Giddens 1991a and

1991b). The first of these argues that we are undergoing a period of social change best described as radical modernism rather than postmodernism, and Giddens sets out the differences in a table (1991a: 102). For our purposes here, the main point is to assert the complexity of social life under radical modernism, the dialectical links between the forces of abstraction and fragmentation in social life, and above all, perhaps, the role of an active reflexive social self instead of the gloomy notions of the self being dissolved or dismembered into endless 'nomadic subjectivities'. This is very much in the spirit of what I have been attempting here, with my insistence on the constraints and freedoms of personal identity; indeed, Giddens makes much of the work of Goffman for more or less the same purposes as I do above.

The book also emphasises two additional themes in Giddens's sociology. There is the importance of the military in social affairs, but above all the need to think of new ways to consider the organisation of social life across time and space. Giddens suggests that social life is no longer bounded by 'societies' in the shape of nation states, and that globalisation has penetrated everyday life. In this sense, social life needs to be co-ordinated across vastly enlarged spaces. Time too has to be reorganised, the past systematised and the present regularised into standard timetables. The effect of these reorganisations is to change social ordering, and this is the key for Giddens to the transformation from traditional to modern societies. There is no space here to discuss it, but this is why we have to modify standard sociological concepts designed to grasp these transformations – including the notions of differentiation and dedifferentiation which lie at the heart of several major accounts of modernity (including Lash 1988 and Crook et al. 1992).

Instead, Giddens proposes that we think in terms of the disembedding and re-embedding of everyday social activity. Disembedding arises when actions are lifted out of their immediate local contexts and organised instead in more extensive and abstract systems of co-ordination. Examples of this could include familiar experiences such as working in large multinational companies which are co-ordinated globally. Here, money is the major mechanism of control. Giddens also emphasises the role of 'expert systems' which disembed our daily actions and organise our lives more abstractly – as in the way we travel as part of a gigantic system of expert co-ordination of air traffic, the design and maintenance of aircraft, and so on.

In such systems, new forms of trust are needed, and Giddens spends a good deal of time explaining what he means by trust. In essence, we can no longer rely on the mechanisms which gave us confidence in the adequacy of our social knowledge (and these include the traditional 'social bonds' of kinship, community and religious belief). Giddens says the whole of our modern social life is founded on a deep ignorance of the ways in which things work, and a rather abstract trust in the experts and their systems.

This rather frightening picture need not lead to insecurity or to a feeling of having been colonised (Habermas's phrase) by expert systems – we learn to trust in normal infancy, and to acquire 'ontological security' thereby. We do acquire some awareness of expert knowledge for ourselves, and we also have the opportunity to re-embed our activity by encountering actual experts, learning from them, and checking our trust in them face to face. Giddens (1991b) also places a lot of significance on 'lifestyle guides'.

This all depends on a reflexive, monitoring self. Thus the empty pragmatism of Lasch's work is but one stance for individuals to take in modernity: others include 'sustained optimism' (based on some enduring personal faith), 'radical engagement' (such as follows membership of a new social movement), and 'cynical pessimism' (where one copes with risks with black humour, or a wry celebration of anachronism) (Giddens 1991a: 135–6).

Giddens clearly favours strong, organised selves rather than the disorganised and anomic consumers who feature in Bauman's work (according to Warde), or the empty narcissists of Lasch's account. Giddens wants to acknowledge that the 'existential questions' (life, death and so on) have always generated anxiety and reflexive adjustments, and he draws upon some general psychology and some classic sociology to demonstrate this. But he also wants to argue that 'modernity' offers distinctive and specific forms of challenge to the old adjustment mechanisms, and describes the complex combinations of globalisation and the development of specialised 'abstract systems' that have transformed social life and made a considerable impact on the personal and intimate spheres. As we have seen with Barthes and others, this is an important step in suggesting that there really are major changes that mean we must adopt new terms, which Giddens proceeds to develop against postmodernist writers and, less explicitly, against conventional sociology too. Across this land-scape roam all the types of consumer we have discussed, the connoisseur and the pathological (the latter include those who have been psychologically damaged by early disruptions to the normal processes of developing trust, and thereby develop path-ologies in managing anxiety and risk).

Giddens tells us that his analysis consists of an attempt to develop some ideal types, and to discuss symptoms of more general trends and processes (Giddens 1991b: 2). This reopens a nagging problem in reading the arguments, however: after a while, the main question for me becomes rather a quantitative one: how widespread exactly are the different types – such as the consumers who engage in 'life politics', the ones who consult various guides and introductions to counselling as part of their continual 'reflexive monitoring' of themselves and their pursuit of their life-plans?

This question is an important one if we are interested in pinning down the specifics of modernity (and, secondarily, in driving off postmodernism and reclaiming the ground for Giddens's soci-ology). To put this rather too bluntly, if there are still only a few new lifestyle consumers, it is hard to see anything particularly specific about modernity, and the old pre-Giddens sociology can cope. If, on the other hand, there are overwhelming numbers of new lifestyle consumers, perhaps too much ground will have to be given to the postmodernists who want to argue for a complete radical transformation of social life, one which renders all soci-ology redundant, and, incidentally, which runs the risk of predict-ing far more social change than we can observe at present.

Giddens also wants to explain the persistence of social order amidst change. I do not want to suggest that the issue is entirely one of numbers, but a soft form of quantification does seem integral to Giddens's argument, especially when he relies on a version of an escalation scenario (which we have met before) – that the pluralisation of lifestyles has now reached a level at which the old coping mechanisms to stabilise identity are overwhelmed. How far up the escalator are these processes nowadays, though?

Hard data and hard evidence of a conventionally sociological kind are clearly inappropriate for Giddens in this argument, and we should expect nothing less than a very broad interdisciplinary analysis. We find a very wide variety of theoretical resources – psychology offering apparently universal models of socialisation and charting pathological cases (mostly via the work of Laing); classic sociological work like Goffman's; philosophical analysis based on Husserl or Wittgenstein; and the construction of a new interlocking set of terms ('trust', 'commitment', 'sequestration of experience' and so on). The overall effect is to produce a dazzling *tour de force*, although there is still room for some sceptical questions.

For me, these arise as usual whenever I try to get beneath the overall effect and ask more detailed questions about what is actually being claimed. The discussion on 'commitment' (Giddens 1991b: ch. 3) crystallises the problem here: it is clear that Giddens intends the terms to refer to a special kind of chosen relationship which replaces the old 'external' ties that used to bind us to each other. Yet when he argues that 'A person only becomes committed to another . . . when he or she decides to be so' (ibid.: 95), it is hard to see whether he is describing a relationship that is now increasingly common (calling these actually observed new kinds of chosen relationships 'committed' ones), or merely defining his terms clearly (reserving the term 'commitment' to mean 'chosen relationships').

Only the first interpretation would count as an argument in the old sense, as some kind of evidence for modernity and modern identities. If we are discussing new terms, however, we might still need to offer some sort of evidence for their empirical applicability before we could claim them as ideal types. It would certainly be helpful to go beyond some of the very rudimentary ideal types outlined at times – to progress, for example, beyond the rather abstract 'black woman heading a single-parent household . . . [who] . . . is virtually obliged to explore novel modes of activity' (ibid.: 86), to actual case studies at least.

Among other examples of a similar nature, the discussion on the applicability of the concept of the 'self as a project' is also problematic. Are we to infer that there is or is likely to be universal interest in the use of texts like the one Giddens cites on counselling and self-therapy? Is the use of life-plans universal or about to become so? If such behaviour is not common, perhaps we have an interesting exploration of a marginal case, like the ones cited by Goffman, Garfinkel or Laing, which are to be read as telling us something about normality itself, but which are not seen themselves as typical. What is less acceptable, however, is a variant of the essentialist approach we discussed in relation to the work of

Hindess and Hirst earlier – that 'therapy ... [just] expresses ... [social] change' (ibid.: 80) – which opens up that whole debate about how it does this and through what agency (see Chapter 4).

Apart from these problems, this essentialism also seems to render Giddens's analysis chronically incapable of any critique, even a sociological one, of the apparent turn towards therapy, the careerism and self-centredness of the life-planners, the obvious limits of the pursuit of 'pure relationships' and 'quality' in the desired responses of others. It is the function of these aspects of connoisseur consumerism that interests Giddens here, the way they act as symptoms of social changes. The questions of validity, of the possible ideological work done by these notions, are to be 'bracketed' (ibid.: 80).

There are also some debatable slippages between what philosophers do and what ordinary people do when they question reality: 'The integral relation between modernity and radical doubt is an issue which, once exposed to view, is not only disturbing to philosophers but is *existentially troubling* for ordinary individuals' (ibid.: 21 – original emphasis). I suppose that much turns on the phrase 'once exposed to view', and here philosophers and ordinary individuals are quite different in terms of how they seek out this 'integral relation' and pursue radical doubt. To be brief, as Giddens knows well, philosophers do it from theoretical and professional commitments, from a disinterested stand-point, wanting to follow arguments wherever they lead and so on, while participants have doubts thrust upon them and usually want to overcome them as quickly and economically as possible. Much of Giddens's analysis goes on to describe how 'ordinary individuals' are in practice 'relatively protected from issues which might otherwise pose themselves as disturbing questions' (ibid.: 185), principally via the mechanisms of trust and commitment that are required whenever a 'leap' into action is necessary.

The usual reservations about inequality and divisions among groups of consumers are found, but there are also confident assertions that lifestyle choice and life-planning, or rather their influence, is 'more or less universal' (ibid.: 85). In this spirit, the differences between the lifestyle choices of affluent consumers and those of the poor are fundamentally similar since there is always a choice of lifestyle, even 'under conditions of severe material constraint' (ibid.: 6). We have seen, and criticised, this sort of

argument before, and the main problem with it is that all specificity is lost in favour of a substantial generalisation geared to a
theoretical project: to a participant it must seem absurd to equate
the choice one has as a 'poor' person between paying either the
rent or the gas bill, and the choice one has as an affluent academic
deciding whether to holiday in Florida or the Algarve. This
specificity is lost in statements like 'life political issues . . . centre
on questions of how we should live our lives . . .' (ibid.: 24).

## CONCLUDING THOUGHTS

There is much more to discuss on the topic of identity than is
currently on offer in 'postmodernist' writing, or even in the more
sociological material on modernity, that can often seem to be
agreeing on the social consequences even while quibbling about
the theoretical frameworks. That work tends to offer a simple
escalation model of the growing autonomy of identities from
traditional social constraints, such as traditional work patterns or
families, or, more generally, away from social necessities of
various kinds. This kind of autonomy leads to an explosion of
differentiation, we are told, as people use their new-found freedom to roam unfettered into and out of different temporary
identities. Eventually, the sheer variety, plausibility yet incompat-
ibility of these identities lead to an ironic dedifferentiation: people
simply cannot separate out 'core' and 'peripheral' identities for
themselves or for others, and lead the rest of their lives as nomads
or game-players.

This model has been applied as a kind of backdrop to analyses
of consumerism, popular culture, tourism and politics, as we have
seen, but the specifics of identity have served more as a token or
emblem of these wider interests. It seems to me that much
conventional work has been overlooked in the drive towards
discussing the general models of (post)modernity and its origins.

By contrast, I have tried to suggest here that this older discredited or unfashionable work still offers a fruitful legacy to
understand the problems of identity as participants are likely to
experience them, a focus I have defended earlier as an important
one still. Participants may well have experienced the kinds of
social dislocations described in the 'loss of the social' accounts,
although even here this is likely to have been unevenly experienced. But this is hardly new, and the recent experiences

charted in popular culture are quite likely to look puny compared to the dislocations produced by the wars, famines, migrations, divorces, bereavements or serious illness and disfigurements, which are part of the reality of many lives, past and present.

Then and now, participants manage these challenges to their identity in some of the ways we have suggested here: they contextualise them, separate and manage them as part of their biographies, narratives and discourses. They prioritise them, they respond pragmatically and, above all, they struggle concretely, not at all as philosophers do. The concrete level of institutional struggles cannot be overlooked by participants – place of work, encounters with state bureaucracies and authorities and, above all perhaps, educational experiences are likely to involve serious attempts to manage identities as urgent priorities against powerful interests trying to represent the complexity in manageable and loaded terms.

Supported by this sort of experience, it is possible to suggest that many participants will find the playful challenges of cultural diversity encountered on TV or while window-shopping fairly easy to manage – and these are supposed to be the crucial elements of modernity. This is not to deny that some experiences provided by what I have called 'temporary identities' can have powerful effects, but it seems unwise to place the emphasis on these activities as the most important constraints on identity for everyone. I can get lost in a video game, and I do like to 'allegorise' my performance, but my world is not going to collapse if I fail: losing my job or my family or discovering I have an incurable illness is quite another matter.

For some people, video games are far more serious. There are the 'addicts' identified in some journalistic accounts who do spend their lives in the arcades, apparently, and who steal to keep playing. But probably more important still are the cultural commentators who want to see video games as representing social trends, moral decline, threats to the young – or, for that matter, signs of postmodernity. As I have argued before, such commentators do take culture very seriously, far more seriously than many participants. They report their contacts with the diversity and bewildering complexity of it all, using terms such as 'schizophrenia', 'delirium' or 'vertigo'. Popular culture and its diversity clearly offer some sort of challenge to their identities as people and as analysts, but there is little evidence as yet, even in the work of the finest commentators, for the view that this sort of concern is more widely spread. From a participant's perspective, much of the concern seems self-induced, a theoretical artefact: not so much real schizophrenia, perhaps, as a kind of hypochondria?

# Conclusion

Only limited conclusions are appropriate here, I believe. I have tried to outline a series of debates about how best to understand social and cultural change, and I have said on several occasions that no simple answers are available. Each of the powerful general theories we have been examining (and their corresponding 'root metaphors') – whether from Barthes and Baudrillard, Foucault or Habermas and Giddens – are plausible but also obviously limited. Some overpredict cultural autonomy and playfulness, others underpredict these qualities, while Giddens operates with a dialectical relation between them which I tend to find both admirably sophisticated and strangely abstract and evasive.

At the general level, Habermas's work still appeals. The tradition from which it arises has always been very open and self-critical about its origins in the spirit of the best of 'reflexive modernity'. There is certainly no naive foundationalism in critical theory. Habermas has developed his own insights in a series of encounters with philosophy and sociology that have pursued the same openness. As a result, Dews is able to argue very plausibly for Habermas's turn to the ideal speech situation as the triumph of the old goal of developing an 'empirically falsifiable philosophy of history with practical intent' (Dews 1992: 8), and to dismiss postmodernist (and poststructuralist) options as failing on each of those terms.

If there are particular themes which appeal to me, one is the insistence that rational enquiry is the only way to proceed, instead of the 'excessively' subjective and poetic manoeuvres of postmodernism. I have singled out in the previous chapters the problems of the metaphor of 'social life as a text' in this methodological sense, and I find it simply evasive to have recourse to poetic

219

writing or to 'postmodernist sensibility' at crucial moments. I am a sociologist by training, so it is not surprising, perhaps, to find that questions arise for me in the assumptions about readership and typicality involved in these procedures.

Another appealing theme is the acknowledgement that solutions to the problems we have been discussing will not be found in philosophy, and that we have to move off the abstract 'epistemological' level. Instead, philosophy, like science, needs to come back under the control of interaction, to use Habermas's terms, to be challenged, in principle at least, by demands that it be not only logical and valid but sincere and socially appropriate.

The problem is that Habermas himself remains fairly abstract at this point (with the possible exception of his forays into the political sphere). The notion of the ideal speech situation is an excellent critical tool and can be used to expose the limits of distorted or strategic communication (as in the classic project to defend the 'lifeworld' against 'colonisation' from the economic and political levels), but even Dews finds Habermas's attempts to develop a positive model of unrestrained communication 'ambiguous'. Indeed, Habermas's own interviews and comments in the rest of the Dews (1992) collection look rather tactical at times, as he modifies his own approach largely to try to take care (briefly) of criticism like Lyotard's (for example, in ch. 6).

In order to overcome some of these abstractions, I find myself drawn to concrete critical analyses such as those undertaken by Foucault (or, to allow Habermas his point, Adorno). There seems to be universal approval for work on the micropolitical level too (for example, Goffman on the politics of identity). There is one type of concrete analysis which has been strangely omitted, however, and I have been trying to force it on to the agenda throughout: we would benefit from an insider's reflexive account of the workings of the university in modernity.

University life and its effects on the production of knowledge (or culture) have been implicit in a number of the discussions we have had. Implications have been drawn for the fate of the university in Lyotard and Baudrillard, for example. Both Barthes and Foucault, I have suggested, are fully aware of the micropolitics of the production of knowledge and the pressures to move on or to consolidate a research programme. More generally, the whole debate about postmodernism is a debate which is connected to interests, not only the interests of classes in Bourdieu's sense, but more specifically the interests of the academic sub-section of those classes, it could be suggested. How those interests connect would be of great concern in any insider account.

To take an obvious example, pedagogues have to manage competing claims of pluralistic tolerance in classroom debate and rather authoritarian assessment schemes outside it. The classroom itself would be a wonderful site to explore some of the more abstract issues about the norms of discourse and the risks of intervention in Habermas, say. The more general context of university work would offer a rich case study to ground many of the abstract discussions about the politics of identity or con-sumerism found in Lasch or Giddens: what better location to study the interactions between 'expert systems' and face-to-face 're-embeddings'?

University intellectuals have been strangely unreflexive in these respects, although the contexts in which they work have had influences like those we noted above for Barthes or Foucault (or those on the Gramscians that I explore in Harris 1992). I think the context has influenced many students too: going to university can deliver experiences that are characteristic of an acute form of the cultural dislocation of modernity.

In my own case, I went to university from a provincial grammar school, and entered a cosmopolitan and culturally diverse faculty, situated in the very centre of London. In such circumstances, it might be expected that newcomers experience a kind of culture shock as it soon becomes apparent that their values are simply not as universal or compelling as had been imagined. The 'good' side of the shock could be that a tremendous number of new pos-sibilities and choices open up, a variety of ways of life, ranging from a chance to experiment with personal appearance, cultural tastes and diet, to a more introspective review of political beliefs.

The academic regime of large universities also encourages this encounter with variety and with relativism. To parody (and embellish) slightly, one memorable seminar session deliberately set out to encourage individuals to express as clearly as possible what it was they wanted to argue about a particular topic, and then the rest of the group were invited to criticise as effectively and as radically as they could. I learned a set of effective critical techniques and the need to acknowledge them in my arguments, but the experience also included a sense of anxiety, initial outrage at hearing things you believed in doubted so effortlessly and so casually, and a sense of vertigo as it suddenly became obvious that none of the usual options offered any safer ground than a score of others which had not been even considered.

The experience can eventually prise people away from their cultural roots in substantial ways. University life can differ in both the quantity and the quality of the challenges it offers, compared to secondary school, say, and coping strategies can come under strain. An instrumental stance towards the university can help to keep some of the challenges at a distance, especially when supplemented by a few of those distancing and ironic conversational techniques (like learning to play the philosophical game – see Lévi-Strauss's memoir discussed by Bourdieu 1986). There is something about academic argument, especially in social science, however, that threatens to transcend the merely instrumental, that makes it meaningful in and for itself. Enough of the claim to have a universal address, regardless of class origins or connections, can persist. This can weaken from within defensive attempts to reduce it all to mere bourgeois style.

The retreat to the private no longer suffices either. Philosophy and social sciences intrude uninvited into 'private' beliefs and practices. Nor is the private sphere necessarily a place of continuity, stability and certainty any more, away from home and familiar surroundings and relatively adrift in a large city. One can return periodically to those familiar surroundings, but they are now located differently in time and space – in the past and increasingly towards the margins of the social life of the university.

To paraphrase and vulgarise the much more elegant formulations of the experience in writers like Benjamin (cited in Clifford 1988), students can find themselves overwhelmed by cultural diversity and strangeness, embarked on a one-way cultural voyage, facing backwards, unable to see the future and yet powerless to stop a strong current propelling them there. It is likely that such people will never return fully to their past lives. They will still have identities, or elements of identity, derived from that past, but such travellers soon become aware that they cannot make a future of those old identities, as Clifford (1988) puts it.

Reflecting on this sort of direct experience focuses and grounds many of the abstract discussions we have been pursuing in this book. There is some sort of affinity between postmodernist commentary and student experience, I believe, and for a while it is possible to see oneself as a student living a textualised life in a society of signs. As usual, the real challenge is to resist easy homologies, and to become more critical. Only then can one see the context which constrains the signs.

# Bibliography

Abercrombie, N., Hill, S. and Turner, B. (1980) *The Dominant Ideology Thesis*, London: Allen & Unwin.

Adlam, D. (1979) 'The case against capitalist patriarchy', *m/f* 3.

Adorno T. (1991) *The Culture Industry*, edited and with an Introduction by J.M. Bernstein, London: Routledge.

—— (1994) *'The Stars Come Down to Earth' and Other Essays on the Irrational in Culture*, edited and with an Introduction by S. Crook, London: Routledge.

Alexander, J. (ed.) (1990) *Durkheimian Sociology: Cultural studies*, Cambridge: Cambridge University Press.

Althusser, L. (1971) *'Lenin and Philosophy' and Other Essays*, London: New Left Books.

Angus, I. and Jhally, S. (eds) (1989) *Cultural Politics in Contemporary America*, New York: Routledge.

Appignanesi, L. (ed.) (1989) *Postmodernism ICA Documents*, London: Free Association Books.

Atkinson, P. (1985) *Language, Structure and Reproduction: An introduction to the sociology of Basil Bernstein*, London: Methuen.

Austin-Broos, D. (ed.) (1987) *Creating Culture: Profiles in the study of culture*, Sydney and London: Allen & Unwin.

Ball, S. (1987) *The Micro-politics of the School*, London: Methuen.

Ball, S. and Goodson, I. (eds) (1985) *Teachers' Lives and Careers*, London: Falmer Press.

Barthes, R. (1973) *Mythologies*, London: Paladin.

—— (1975) *S/Z*, London: Jonathan Cape.

—— (1977) *Image–Music–Text*, London: Fontana/Collins.

Baudrillard, J. (1983) *Simulations*, New York: Semiotext(e).

—— (1993) *Symbolic Exchange and Death*, London: Sage.

—— and Lotringer, S. (1987) *Forget Foucault and Forget Baudrillard*, New York: Semiotext(e).

Bauman, Z. (1987) *Legislators and Interpreters: On modernity, postmodernity and intellectuals*, Cambridge: Polity Press.

—— (1992a) *Intimations of Postmodernity*, London: Routledge.

—— (1992b) *Mortality, Immortality and Other Life Strategies*, Oxford: Polity Press in association with Basil Blackwell.

224

Becker, H. (1973) *Outsiders: Studies in the sociology of deviance*, New York: Free Press of Glencoe.

Benhabib, S. (1984) 'Epistemologies of postmodernism: a rejoinder to Jean-François Lyotard', *New German Critique* 33: 103–26.

Bennett, T. (1990) *Outside Literature*, London: Routledge.

Bennett, T. and Woollacott, J. (1987) *Bond and Beyond: The political career of a popular hero*, London: Macmillan Education.

Bennett, T., Boyd-Bowman, S., Mercer, C. and Wollacott, J. (eds) (1981) *Popular Television and Film*, London: BFI Publications.

Berger, P. and Luckmann, T. (1971) *The Social Construction of Reality*, Harmondsworth, Middx: Penguin.

Berking, H. and Neckel, S. (1993) 'Urban marathon: the staging of individuality as an urban event', *Theory, Culture and Society* 10, 4: 63–78.

Bernstein, R. (ed.) (1985) *Habermas and Modernity*, Oxford: Polity Press.

BFI (1989) *Wham! Wrapping: Teaching the media*, London: BFI Publications.

Bocock, R. and Thompson, K. (eds) (1992) *Social and Cultural Forms of Modernity*, Cambridge: Polity Press, in association with the Open University Press.

Bourdieu, P. (1986) *Distinction*, London: Routledge.

—— (1988) *Homo Academicus*, trans. P. Collier, London: Polity Press.

Bovone, L. (1993) 'Ethics as etiquette: the emblematic contribution of Erving Goffman', *Theory, Culture and Society* 10, 4: 25–39.

Brake, M. (ed.) (1982) *Human Sexual Relations: A reader*, Harmondsworth, Middx: Penguin.

Bridges, G. and Brunt, R. (eds) (1981) *Silver Linings: Some strategies for the eighties*, London: Lawrence & Wishart.

Bryant, C. and Jary, D. (eds) (1991) *Giddens' Theory of Structuration: A critical appreciation*, London: Routledge.

Buckingham, D. (1991) 'What are words worth? Interpreting children's talk about television', *Cultural Studies* 5, 2: 228–44.

Bulmer, M. (ed.) (1975) *Working-class Images of Society*, London: Routledge & Kegan Paul.

Callinicos, A. (1985) 'Postmodernism, post-structuralism and post-Marxism?', *Theory, Culture and Society* 2, 3: 85–102.

Cashmore, E. (1987) *The Logic of Racism*, London: Allen & Unwin.

Chambers, I. (1985) *Urban Rhythms: Popular music and popular culture*, London: Macmillan.

Clarke, J. and Critcher, C. (1985) *The Devil Makes Work: Leisure in capitalist Britain*, London: Macmillan.

Clifford, J. (1988) *The Predicament of Culture: Twentieth century ethnography, literature and art*, London: Harvard University Press.

Clough, P. (1992) *The End(s) of Ethnography: From realism to social criticism*, London: Sage.

Collins, R. (1994) *Four Sociological Traditions*, New York: Oxford University Press.

Cook, P. (ed.) (1985) *The Cinema Book*, London; BFI Publications.

Cooke, P. (1988) 'Modernity, postmodernity and the city', *Theory, Culture and Society* 5, 2–3: 475–93.

Coward, R. (1977) 'Class, culture and the social formation', *Screen* 18, 1: 75–105.

Craib, I. (1992a) *Anthony Giddens*, London: Routledge.

—— (1992b) *Modern Social Theory*, 2nd edn, London: Harvester Wheatsheaf.

Crook, S. (1991) *Modernist Radicalism and its Aftermath*, London: Routledge.

Crook, S., Pakulski, J. and Waters, M. (1992) *Postmodernization: Change in advanced society*, London: Sage.

Culler, J. (1976a) *Saussure*, London: Fontana/Collins.

—— (1976b) *Structuralist Poetics*, London: Routledge & Kegan Paul.

Curran, J., Gurevitch, M. and Wollacott, J. (eds) (1977) *Mass Communication and Society*, London: Edward Arnold, in association with the Open University Press.

Davis, M. (1992) *City of Quartz: Excavating the future in Los Angeles*, London: Vintage.

Denzin, N. (1991) *Images of Postmodern Society: Social theory and contemporary cinema*, London: Sage.

Dews, P. (1987) *Logics of Disintegration*, London: Verso.

—— (ed.) (1992) *Autonomy and Solidarity: Interviews with Jurgen Habermas*, London: Verso.

Docherty, T. (ed.) (1993) *Postmodernism: A reader*, Cambridge: Harvester Wheatsheaf.

Donald, J. and Rattansi, A. (eds) (1992) *'Race', Culture and Difference*, London: Sage.

Downes, D. and Rock, P. (1988) *Understanding Deviance*, Oxford: Clarendon Press.

Dunning, E., Murphy, P. and Williams, J. (1986) 'Spectator violence at football matches: towards a sociological explanation', *British Journal of Sociology* XXXVII, 2: 221–44.

Durkheim, E. (1956) *Education and Sociology*, London: Collier-Macmillan.

Eco, U. (1979) *The Role of the Reader: Explorations in the semiotics of texts*, London: Hutchinson.

—— (1987) *Travels in Hyperreality*, London: Picador.

Evetts, J. (1992) 'Dimensions of career: avoiding reification in the analysis of change', *Sociology* 26, 1: 1–21.

Featherstone, M. (1991) *Consumer Culture and Postmodernism*, London: Sage.

Fiske, J. (1987) *Television Culture*, London: Routledge.

—— (1989a) *Reading the Popular*, London: Unwin Hyman.

—— (1989b) *Understanding Popular Culture*, London: Unwin Hyman.

Foucault, M. (1979) *The History of Sexuality*, vol. 1, London: Allen Lane.

—— (1980) *Power/Knowledge: Selected interviews and other writings, 1972–1977*, Brighton: Harvester Press.

Fowler, R., Hodge, B., Kress, G. and Trew, T. (1979) *Language and Control*, London: Routledge & Kegan Paul.

Fraser, N. (1984) 'The French Derrideans: politicizing deconstruction and deconstructing the political', *New German Critique* 33: 127–54.

Freud, S. (1974a) *Introductory Lectures on Psychoanalysis*, Harmondsworth, Middx: Penguin.

—— (1974b) *New Introductory Lectures on Psychoanalysis*, Harmondsworth, Middx: Penguin.

Freund, E. (1987) *The Return of the Reader: Reader-response criticism*, London: Methuen.

Frisby, D. (1984) *Georg Simmel*, London: Tavistock Publications.

Frith, S., Goodwin, A. and Grossberg, L. (eds) (1993) *Sound and Vision: The music video reader*, London: Routledge.

Frow, J. (1990) 'M. de Certeau and the practice of representation', *Cultural Studies* 5, 1: 52–60.

Gane, M. (1983) 'Anthony Giddens and the crisis of social theory', *Economy and Society* 12, 3: 368–98.

—— (1990) *Baudrillard – Critical and Fatal Theory*, London: Routledge.

Gellner, E. (1992) *Postmodernism, Reason and Religion*, London: Routledge.

Geraghty, C. (1991) *Women and Soap Operas*, Cambridge: Polity Press.

Geras, N. (1987) 'Post Marxism?', *New Left Review* 163: 40–82.

—— (1988) 'Ex-Marxism without substance', *New Left Review* 169: 34–62.

Giddens, A. (1976) *New Rules of Sociological Method*, London: Hutchinson.

—— (1979) *Central Problems in Social Theory: Action structure and contradiction in social analysis*, London: Macmillan.

—— (1981) *A Contemporary Critique of Historical Materialism*, London: Macmillan.

—— (1982) *Profiles and Critiques in Social Theory*, London: Macmillan.

—— (1991a) *The Consequences of Modernity*, Oxford: Polity Press, in association with Basil Blackwell.

—— (1991b) *Modernity and Self-identity*, Oxford: Polity Press, in association with Basil Blackwell.

Giroux, H. and Simon, R. and contributors (1989) *Popular Culture, Schooling and Everyday Life*, Granby, Mass.: Begin & Garvey.

Goffman, E. (1963) *Stigma*, Harmondsworth, Middx: Penguin.

—— (1975) *Frame Analysis*, Harmondsworth, Middx: Penguin.

Golby, M., Greenwald, J. and West, R. (eds) (1975) *Curriculum Design*, London: Croom Helm.

Goldman, R. and Papson, S. (1994) 'Advertising in the age of hypersignification', *Theory, Culture and Society* 11, 3: 23–54.

Goldthorpe, J. and Marshall, G. (1992) 'The promising future of class analysis: a response to recent critiques', *Sociology* 26, 3: 381–400.

Goldthorpe, J., Lockwood, D., Bechhofer, F. and Platt, J. (1969) *The Affluent Worker in the Class Structure*, Cambridge: Cambridge University Press.

Goodwin, A. (1987) 'Music video in the (post)modern world', *Screen* 28, 3: 36–55.

—— (1991) 'Popular music and post-modern theory', *Cultural Studies* 5, 2: 174–203.

Greenaway, P. (1988) *Fear of Drowning by Numbers/Règles de jeu*, Paris: Dis Voir.

Grossberg, L. (ed.) (1986) 'Postmodernism and articulation: an interview with Stuart Hall', *Journal of Communication Inquiry* 10, 2: 45–61

—— (1987) 'The in-difference of television', *Screen* 28, 2: 28–46.

——, Nelson, C. and Treichler, P. (eds) (1992) *Cultural Studies*, New York: Routledge.

Guttmann, A. (1986) *Sports Spectators*, New York: Columbia Press.

Habermas, J. (1972) *Knowledge and Human Interests*, London: Heinemann Educational Books.

—— (1974) *Theory and Practice*, London: Heinemann Educational Books.

—— (1976) *Legitimation Crisis*, London: Heinemann.

—— (1984) 'The French path to postmodernity: Bataille between eroticism and general economy', *New German Critique* 33: 79–102.

—— (1987) *The Theory of Communicative Action*, vol. 2 *The Critique of Functionalist Reason*, Cambridge: Polity Press, in association with Basil Blackwell.

Hall, S. (1988) *The Hard Road to Renewal: Thatcherism and the crisis of the Left*, London: Verso.

—— (1993) 'Identity', *Ten.8* 2, 3: 24–31.

—— and Jefferson, T. (eds) (1976) *Resistance Through Rituals*, London: Hutchinson.

—— Critcher, C., Jefferson, T., Clarke, J. and Roberts, B. (1978) *Policing the Crisis: Mugging, the state and law and order*, London: Hutchinson.

——, Hobson, D., Lowe, A. and Willis, P. (eds) (1980) *Culture, Media and Language*, London: Hutchinson.

Hammersley, M. (ed.) (1989) *Controversies in Classroom Research*, 2nd edn, Buckingham: Open University Press.

Hammersley, M. and Woods, P. (eds) (1976) *The Process of Schooling: A sociological reader*, London: Routledge & Kegan Paul, in association with the Open University Press.

Hargreaves, J. (1986) *Sport, Power and Culture*, Cambridge: Polity Press.

Harris, D. (1987a) *Openness and Closure in Distance Education*, Brighton: Falmer Press.

—— (1987b) 'Educational technology and the "colonisation" of academic work', unpublished paper presented at the British Sociological Association Annual Conference, Leeds.

—— (1992) *From Class Struggle to the Politics of Pleasure*, London: Routledge.

Hayward, P. and Kerr, P. (1987) 'Introduction', *Screen* 28, 2: 2–10.

Hebdige, D. (1979) *Subcultures: The meaning of style*, London: Methuen.

—— (1988) *Hiding in the Light*, London: Comedia/Routledge.

Held, D. (1980) *An Introduction to Critical Theory: Horkheimer to Habermas*, London: Hutchinson.

Heritage, J. (1984) *Garfinkel and Ethnomethodology*, Cambridge: Polity Press.

Hindess, B. (1977) *Philosophy and Methodology in the Social Sciences*, Hassocks, Sussex: Harvester Press.

Hite, S. (1981) *The Hite Report on Male Sexuality*, London: Macdonald.

Holton, R. and Turner, B. (1994) 'Debate and pseudo-debate in class analysis: some unpromising aspects of Goldthorpe and Marshall's defence', *Sociology* 28, 3: 799–803.

Honneth, A. (1985) 'An aversion against the universal: a commentary on Lyotard's *Postmodern Condition*', *Theory, Culture and Society* 2, 3: 147–57.

Jameson, F. (1992) *Postmodernism, or The cultural logic of late capitalism*, London: Verso.

Jenkins, A. (1994) '"Just-in-time regimes" and reductionism', *Sociology* 28, 1: 21–30.

Jessop, B. (1982) *The Capitalist State*, Oxford: Martin Robertson.

Julien, I. and Mercer, K. (1988) 'De margin and de centre', *Screen* 29, 4: 2–11.

Kamuf, P. (ed.) (1991) *A Derrida Reader Between the Blinds*, London: Harvester Wheatsheaf.

Kaplan, E.-A. (1987) *Rocking Around the Clock*, London: Methuen.

Kingdom, E. (1980) 'Women in law', *m/f* 4.

Kroker, A. (1985) 'Baudrillard's Marx', *Theory, Culture and Society* 2, 3: 69–85.

Kuhn, A. and Wolpe, A.-M. (eds) (1978) *Feminism and Materialism*, London: Routledge & Kegan Paul.

Kuhn, T. (1970) *The Structure of Scientific Revolutions*, 2nd edn, Chicago: University of Chicago Press.

Laclau, E. and Mouffe, C. (1987) 'Post-Marxism without apologies', *New Left Review* 166: 79–106.

Laing, D. (1985) 'Music video – industrial product, cultural form', *Screen* 26, 2: 78–84.

Lane, D. (1985) *State and Politics in the USSR*, Oxford: Basil Blackwell.

Lasch, C. (1982) *The Culture of Narcissism*, London: Sphere.

Lash, S. (1988) 'Discourse or figure? Postmodernism as a "regime of signification"', *Theory, Culture and Society* 5, 2–3: 311–36.

Lawn, M. and Grace, G. (eds) (1987) *Teachers: The culture and politics of work*, London: Falmer Press.

Leach, E. (1970) *Lévi-Strauss*, London: Fontana/Collins.

Lechte, J (1994) *Fifty Key Contemporary Thinkers*, London: Routledge.

Lévi-Strauss, C. (1977) *Structural Anthropology*, London: Peregrine Books.

Lukes, S. (1975) *Emile Durkheim: His life and work. A historical and critical study*, Harmondsworth, Middx: Penguin.

Lyotard, J.-F. (1986) *The Postmodern Condition: A report on knowledge*, Manchester: Manchester University Press.

Maccabe, C. (ed.) (1981) *Talking Cure: Essays in psychoanalysis and language*, London: Macmillan.

Macdonell, D. (1986) *Theories of Discourse: An introduction*, Oxford: Basil Blackwell.

Mannheim, K. (1972) *Ideology and Utopia*, London: Routledge & Kegan Paul.

Marcuse, H. (1964) *One-dimensional Man*, London: Sphere Books.

Marin, L. (1977) 'Disneyland: a degenerative Utopia', *Glyph* 1, 1: 50–66.

Marx, K. (1956) *The Poverty of Philosophy*, London: Lawrence & Wishart.

—— (1973) *Grundrisse*, Harmondsworth, Middx: Penguin.

—— (1977) *Capital*, vol. 1, London: Lawrence & Wishart.

—— and Engels, F. (1956) *Selected Works*, 2 vols, London: Lawrence & Wishart.

Mason D. (1994) 'On the dangers of disconnecting race and racism', *Sociology* 28, 4: 845–57.

McCarthy, T. (1984) *The Critical Theory of Jurgen Habermas*, Cambridge: Polity Press.

McGuigan, J. (1992) *Cultural Populism*, London: Routledge.

McLennan, G. (1988) 'Structuration theory and post-empiricist philosophy: a rejoinder', *Theory, Culture and Society* 5, 1: 101–9.

McRobbie, A. (1991) 'New times in cultural studies', *New Formations* 13: 1–19.

—— (1994) *Postmodernism and Popular Culture*, London: Routledge.

—— and Nava, M. (eds) (1984) *Gender and Generation*, London: Macmillan.

Mennell, S. (1985) *All Manners of Food*, Oxford: Basil Blackwell.

—— (1992) *Norbet Elias: An introduction*, Oxford: Basil Blackwell.

Mepham, J. and Ruben, D.-H. (eds) (1979) *Issues in Marxist Philosophy*, vol. 3, Brighton: Harvester Press.

Merck, M. (1987) 'Difference and its discontents', *Screen* 28, 1: 2–10.

Merton, R. (1968) *Social Theory and Social Structure*, New York: Free Press.

Moi, T. (ed.) (1986) *The Kristeva Reader*, Oxford: Basil Blackwell.

Moores, S. (1990) 'Texts, readers and contexts of reading: developments in the study of media audiences', *Media, Culture and Society* 12: 9–30.

Morley, D. (1991) 'Where the global meets the local: notes from the sitting room', *Screen* 32, 1: 1–15.

Morris, M. (1988) 'Banality in cultural studies' *Discourse* 10: 3–29.

Munt, I. (1994) 'The "other" postmodern tourism: culture, travel and the new middle classes', *Theory, Culture and Society* 11, 3: 101–24.

Nava, M. (1991) 'Consumerism reconsidered: buying and power', *Cultural Studies* 5, 2: 157–74.

Norris, C. (1992) *Uncritical Theory: Postmodernism, intellectuals and the Gulf War*, London: Lawrence & Wishart.

Open University (1981) *Popular Culture (U203)*, Milton Keynes: Open University Press.

Outhwaite, W. and Bottomore, T. (eds) (1994) *The Blackwell Dictionary of Twentieth Century Social Thought*, Oxford: Basil Blackwell.

Ozga, J. (ed.) (1988) *Schoolwork Approaches to the Labour Process of Teaching*, Milton Keynes: Open University Press.

Pahl, J. (1990) 'Household spending, personal spending and the control of money in marriage', *Sociology* 24, 1: 119–38.

Pahl, R. (1993) 'Does class analysis without class theory have a future? A reply to Goldthorpe and Marshall', *Sociology* 27, 2: 253–8.

Palmer, R. (1969) *Hermeneutics*, Evanston, Ill.: Northwestern University Press.

Pêcheux, M. (1982) *Language, Semantics and Ideology*, London: Macmillan.

Perec, G. (1992) *53 Days*, London: Harvill.

Plant, S. (1992) *The Most Radical Gesture: The situationist international in a postmodern age*, London: Routledge.

Polya, G. (1990) *How to Solve It*, Harmondsworth, Middx: Penguin.

Poster, M. (1978) *Critical Theory of the Family*, London: Pluto Press.

—— (1984) *Foucault, Marxism and History: Mode of production versus mode of information*, Cambridge: Polity Press.

—— (ed.) (1988) *Jean Baudrillard: Selected writings*, Cambridge: Polity Press.

Poulantzas, N. (1975) *Classes in Contemporary Capitalism*, London: New Left Books.

Ree, J. (1984) 'Metaphor and metaphysics: the end of philosophy and Derrida', *Radical Philosophy* 38: 29–33.

Ricoeur, P. (1971) 'The model of the text: meaningful action considered as a text', *Social Research* 38, 3: 529–62.

Ritzer, G. (1993) *The McDonaldization of Society: An investigation into the changing character of contemporary social life*, Thousand Oaks: Pine Forge Press.

Rojek, C. (ed.) (1989) *Leisure for Leisure*, London: Macmillan.

—— (1993) *Ways of Escape: Modern transformations in leisure and travel*, London: Macmillan.

—— and Turner, B. (eds) (1993) *Forget Baudrillard?*, London: Routledge.

Savage, M., Watt, P. and Arber, S. (1990) 'The consumption sector debate and housing mobility', *Sociology* 24, 1: 97–117.

Sayer, D. (1991) *Capitalism and Modernity: An excursus on Marx and Weber*, London: Routledge.

Schroeder, R. (1992) *Max Weber and the Sociology of Culture*, London: Sage.

Schutz, A. (1971a) *Collected Papers I*, The Hague: Martinus Nijhoff.

—— (1971b) *Collected Papers II*, The Hague: Martinus Nijhoff.

—— (1972) *The Phenomenology of the Social World*, London: Heinemann Educational Books.

Schwichtenberg, C. (ed.) (1993) *The Madonna Connection: Representational politics, subcultural identities and cultural theory*, Boulder, Col.: Westview Press.

*Screen* (ed.) (1993) *Screen Reader on Sexuality*, London: BFI Publications.

Sewell, G. and Wilkinson, B. (1992) '"Someone to watch over me": surveillance, discipline and the just-in-time labour process', *Sociology* 26, 2: 271–90.

Sivanandan, A. (1990) *Communities of Resistance: Writings on black struggles for socialism*, London: Verso.

Sloterdijk, P. (1984) 'Cynicism: the twilight of false consciousness', *New German Critique* 33: 190–206.

Smart, B. (1990) 'On the disorder of things: sociology, postmodernity and the "end of the social"', *Sociology* 24, 3: 397–416.

—— (1993) *Postmodernity*, London: Routledge.

Sofia, Z. (1992) 'Hegemonic irrationalities and psychoanalytic cultural criticism', *Cultural Studies* 6, 3: 376–94.

Solomos, J. and Beck, L. (1994) 'Conceptualising racisms: social theory, politics and research', *Sociology* 28, 1: 143–61.

Starkey, K. and McKinlay, A. (1994) 'Managing for Ford', *Sociology* 28, 4: 975–91.

Sturrock, J. (ed.) (1979) *Structuralism and Since: From Lévi-Strauss to Derrida*, Oxford: Oxford University Press.

Stzompka, P. (1986) *Robert K. Merton: An intellectual profile*, London: Macmillan Education.

Taylor, I., Walton, P. and Young, J. (eds) (1973) *The New Criminology*, London: Routledge & Kegan Paul.

Thewelheit, K. (1987) *Male Fantasies*, Oxford: Polity Press.

Thompson, J. (1983) *Critical Hermeneutics: A study in the thought of Paul Ricoeur and Jurgen Habermas*, Cambridge: Cambridge University Press.
—— (1984) *Studies in the Theory of Ideology,* Cambridge: Polity Press.
Tomlinson, A. (ed.) (1990) *Consumption, Identity and Style*, London: Comedia and Routledge.
Truzzi, M. (ed.) (1968) *Sociology and Everyday Life*, London: Prentice-Hall International.
Tseëlon, E. (1992) 'Is the presented self sincere? Goffman, impression management and the postmodern self', *Theory, Culture and Society,* 9, 2: 115–28.
Turner, B. (1981) *For Weber: Essays in the sociology of fate*, London: Routledge & Kegan Paul.
—— (1991) *Religion and Social Theory,* London: Sage.
Turner, R. (ed.) (1975) *Ethnomethodology,* Harmondsworth, Middx: Penguin.
Urry, J. (1990) *The Tourist Gaze: Leisure and travel in contemporary societies*, London: Sage.
Vattimo, G. (1992) *The Transparent Society,* Cambridge: Polity Press.
Waites, B., Bennett, T. and Martin, G. (eds) (1982) *Popular Culture Past and Present*, London: Croom Helm/Open University Press.
Walker, P. (ed.) (1979) *Between Labour and Capital*, Brighton: Harvester Press.
Warde, A. (1994) 'Consumption, identity-formation and uncertainty', *Sociology* 28, 4: 877–98.
Westoby, A. (ed.) (1988) *Culture and Power in Educational Organizations*, Milton Keynes: Open University Press.
Whannel, G. (1986) 'The unholy alliance: notes on TV and the re-making of British sport, 1965–85', *Leisure Studies* 5: 129–46.
Williamson, J. (1978) *Decoding Advertisements: Ideology and meaning in advertising*, London: Marion Boyars.
Willis, P. (1977) *Learning to Labour: How working class kids get working class jobs*, London: Saxon House.
—— (1978) *Profane Cultures*, London: Routledge & Kegan Paul.
—— (1990) *Common Cultures*, Milton Keynes: Open University Press.
Wolff, J. (1985) 'The invisible flâneuse: women and the literature of modernity', *Theory, Culture and Society* 2, 3: 37–49.
Wollheim, R. (1971) *Freud*, London: Fontana.
Women's Study Group (1978) *Women Take Issue*, London: Hutchinson.
Woods, P. and Hammersley, M. (eds) (1993) *Gender and Ethnicity in Schools: Ethnographic accounts*, London: Routledge.
Woolfson, C. (1976) 'The semiotics of working class speech', in CCCS (eds), *Cultural Studies* 9, Birmingham University.
Young, R. (ed.) (1981) *Untying the Text: A post-structuralist reader*, Boston, Mass.: Routledge & Kegan Paul.
Zukin, S. (1990) 'Socio-spatial prototypes of a new organisation of consumption: the role of real cultural capital', *Sociology* 24, 1: 35–56.
Zurbrugg, N. (1991) 'Jameson's complaint: video art and the intertextual "time wall"', *Screen* 32, 1: 16–34.

# INDEX

* classical marxism's
debt to the enlightenment
was so great that it
was left to Romanticism &
explore the everyday lives
of 'the people' and the signature
of emotions and the invested
in the realm of the

   popular.

---

① Marxism + the demise of
      the popular

② Post-marxism and the Politics
   → of ~~Reality~~ ~~Post modern~~ Truth

③ ~~Postmodern Political Economy~~

③ ~~Post~~ ~~no~~ Re Reality the Sway of
           the Spectacle

④ Play, Feeling and Spectacle

⑤ The Spectacular world of Flexible
        Accumulation